Singing at the Top of Our Lungs

Singing at the Top of Our Lungs

WOMEN, LOVE, AND CREATIVITY

Claudia Bepko and Jo-Ann Krestan

HarperPerennial
A Division of HarperCollinsPublishers

A hardcover edition of this book was published in 1993 by HarperCollins Publishers.

SINGING AT THE TOP OF OUR LUNGS. Copyright © 1993 by Claudia Bepko and Jo-Ann Krestan. All rights reserved. Printed in the United States of America. No part of this book may be used or reproduced in any manner whatsoever without written permission except in the case of brief quotations embodied in critical articles and reviews. For information address HarperCollins Publishers, Inc., 10 East 53rd Street, New York, NY 10022.

HarperCollins books may be purchased for educational, business, or sales promotional use. For information please write: Special Markets Department, HarperCollins Publishers, Inc., 10 East 53rd Street, New York, NY 10022.

First HarperPerennial edition published 1994.

Designed by George J. McKeon

The Library of Congress has catalogued the hardcover edition as follows:

Bepko, Claudia.
    Singing at the top of our lungs : women, love, and creativity /
  Claudia Bepko and Jo-Ann Krestan. — 1st ed.
     p.   cm.
  Includes bibliographical references and index.
   ISBN 0-06-016805-6 (cloth)
   1. Women—Psychology. 2. Love. 3. Creative ability. 4. Self-esteem in women. 5. Interpersonal relations. I. Krestan, Jo-Ann.
  II. Title.
HQ1206.B363   1993
155.6'423—dc20   92-54738

ISBN 0-06-092499-3 (pbk.)
94 95 96 97 98 AC/RRD 10 9 8 7 6 5 4 3 2 1

When one does not love too much, one does not love enough.
PASCAL

Contents

Acknowledgments

We BEGAN THE READING AND THINKING for this book in earnest in January 1990 on an out island in the Bahamas where we had gone to relax after our last project. We had written on addiction in *The Responsibility Trap*, and on women's socialization in *Too Good for Her Own Good*, and freely acknowledged to ourselves that we indeed wrote what we needed to read, and taught what we needed to learn. The next thing we needed to explore apparently was joy, because our first working title for the new project was *Vital Passions* and we were in love with the project from the beginning.

Early on, sociologist and author Ruth Sidel, family therapy researcher and author Froma Walsh, and psychologist and author Rita Freedman generously talked with us at length about qualitative research, methodology, and project design, and we thank them for their encouragement and sharing of ideas.

Dorothy Bradley, Jo-Ann's aunt, was the first to read the early section of the manuscript, and said to us the first precious words of encouragement about the book: "This is your best one yet." Jenny Hanson read the manuscript in many incarnations, and participated in invaluable and interminable discussions with us about the conceptualization. She also inspired us by concurrently working to redesign the form of her own life to fit her passions, shifting a major portion of her energies to becoming an interpretive naturalist in mid-life.

Lois Braverman and Joan Ellis read the completed manuscript on short notice and gave us indispensable suggestions. Virginia Rutter also read the completed manuscript and her respectful reading of our ideas and clear-minded incisive queries about our stance on various issues forced us to a clarity that we might have evaded. Thanks also to Harriet Goldhor Lerner and Rachel Hare-Mustin for reading specific chapters, and always being willing to discuss ideas. Lois Braverman and Harriet Lerner also deserve our gratitude for their personal friendship over the years. And thanks to Joan Laird and Ann Hartman for taking our self-serving suggestion and buying a camp on Golden Pond where we spent with them what precious few days of relaxation we managed to snatch this past summer. Thanks to Alan Scult for his conversations with us about time and being. And thanks to producer Kate Wenner for her example of "trusting the process" during a five-month film project. Thanks also to Cobie Smith, Sandy Bishop, Betsey Alden, Barb Schnurr, Ann Brayman, Kidder Smith, and the women's community in Brunswick, Maine, for their interest in this project and their personal support during its completion. And of course, we thank Marsha and Jeff Ellias-Frankel, Dotty Smith, Madeline and Dick Muise, Walt Marz, and Helen and Rudy Krestan for being tolerant and loving. Also thanks to Ellen Fox and all the women who so generously helped us collect data.

Joy Harris, our agent, was behind this project from the start, and has been there for us with her enthusiasm and her wise perspective on the publishing business. Janet Goldstein, our editor, was brilliant, hard-working, and enthusiastic as always. We particularly thank her, this time, for believing in us enough to let us follow our own passions and write the book we ultimately wrote, although it may have strayed considerably from our original proposal.

Rosemary Tuck transcribed hours of interviews, and handled administrative details too myriad to recall. Her husband, Mike Tuck, tried to get us quickly computer literate. Carol Fritzson joined us for the last year and completed many of the lengthy interviews we needed typed in a rush. Irene Favreau typed yet another installment of what seemed never-ending transcripts. Without the help of these professional and knowledgeable people, this book could not have been produced.

And then there were the "kids," a nickname they tolerated from us. Lynn Maloney, Sara Waldrop, and Becky Austin, all recent college graduates in their early twenties, kept us honest, grounded in the nineties, challenged on our feminism, and feeling young and humble. Lynn was an extraordinary interviewer and did those interviews, as well as much other work, we could not handle ourselves. Sara interviewed also and did much of the initial literature search. Their network around the country helped us gather data. Lynn and Sara both helped us design the research questionnaires. As Lynn was leaving for Thailand and Sara for Washington, D.C., Lynn put Becky in touch with us to see the project through to completion. She worked for hours on the methodology and on everything from data analysis, to footnotes, to literary detective work, to analysis of parts of the text, to letting our dog out.

All of them tolerated unreasonable hours, terrible pay, Claudia's worrying about them (Becky co-led a seven-week wilderness trip of adolescent males largely in terrible weather and Lynn trekked through the Himalayas for months with orders to send periodic postcards), Jo-Ann's opinions on how they should live their lives (from romance to career to family issues), and interruptions from phones, cats, dogs, visitors, and Federal Express. They were absolutely essential to this project. We cannot thank them enough.

We also want to acknowledge our collaboration and celebrate our partnership. These past two years have been incredibly complex. Through the joy and the tragedy that have marked them, this book has provided the narrative thread to keep us focused on love and creativity in our own lives, even while we have paused to honor the verities of death and sorrow. We sadly marked even the unexpected death of one of our interviewees, Nancy West. We salute each other for managing to sing at the top of our lungs, and for being able to embrace the whole truth of our lives. And we thank (belatedly) Norman Levy and more currently Dick Chasin for their support in helping us through that process.

Finally the women themselves. As Holly Near wrote, "There's something about the women." There *was* something about the women, three hundred of them, who participated in the survey, the questionnaire, and the interviews that transformed our view of women's lives. We are indebted to them, to our seminar participants across the country, to our clients, and to the many men we also talked with. If we have any regret about this project, it's focused on all that we've had to leave out of this book—women's words, their wisdom, their energy, their stories. There was so much more all of us might have said. We thank all these women for their generosity of spirit and their time.

When women's concerts first incorporated signing for the hearing impaired into their performances, Holly Near wrote:

> *One woman weaves a message*
> *singing the sounds of silence*
> *another wheels her chair to the center of the stage*
> *changing minds and attitudes*
> *with eyes that hear, and hands that see*
> *these women, working, living . . . independently*

and I look to you
I look to you
for courage in my life.

All women are, in a sense, differently abled, not by biology but by socially constructed mythologies from which they have had to liberate themselves. We do indeed look to them for courage in our lives.

Preface

MANY IMAGES WILL RESONATE as you read through the ideas and stories in this book. But two are inescapably bound to jar you—the one is of a woman smiling, the other is of women singing. If, as we suggest, smiling is the problem, then singing is the solution.

Images and metaphors come to our minds through strange and circuitous routes. The image of the woman smiling was visual at first, we saw her standing at her front door, issuing signs of greeting and welcome to family, friends. The more sinister side of the smile was that it seemed somehow scripted, as if the woman behind it had no choice, as if she were playing out some preordained role of the perfect woman, feminine, loving, attractive. The smile was directed outward, the woman behind it obscured, the smile's authenticity as a statement always questionable.

Images of singing have been more dominant but have less clear roots in the evolution of this book. Besides the fact that many of the women we talked to sing or speak of singing or wish they could sing, somehow singing became a metaphor for some deep energy, the absence of which could lead to empty smiles.

Perhaps it was the summer retreat one of us attended where the Institute's campus rang with refrains hummed, whistled, sung. Other people on retreat that week came to learn about the spiritual dimension of song and so, like wandering minstrels, what they did was to sing constantly, singly, in groups, and it came to seem natural and wondrous that this habit of people singing at the tops of their lungs should punctuate the rhythms of the daily routine. When the retreat was over, it was sad that this singing wouldn't be more a part of life in the real world. On the last day, we all gathered as a group and sang in Latin, "Donna Nobice Pacem," as a round, Give Us Peace. There was the sense that peace *could* perhaps be bought—for the price of beauty, community, and a song.

Or perhaps it was the image, retrieved by one daughter from an old box in the cellar after her mother's funeral, of that mother standing proudly, expressively, at a microphone at a high school minstrel show many years before, singing. And remembering that just before she died, the mother had pondered why she had allowed her life to be taken over by "other people's priorities," and to have become so empty. She had told her daughter then, wistfully, "I used to sing, you know."

Or it may have been the client who in therapy one day asked shyly if it would be appropriate to sing a song. Out of the pain of a broken relationship, and grief that came from some very dark place in her heart, she wrote a song, "Rainbow Path." It was a song of healing and affirmation and seemed one of the surest signs that she was recovering from her long depression and marking progress in her long process of change.

Once singing came to mind as an image, quite simply, we began to see it everywhere as a symbol for the act of expressing most directly and purely what is deepest in our hearts. We learned that there are many different forms of singing, many ways of being in tune with ourselves and the larger whole of the world. So while we use many terms to talk about the shapes of women's lives and energies in this book, it is really a story about singing, as Holly Near might say it, the kind of song in which we're "singing for our lives."

In most cases, the men and women whose stories appear in this book have all given their permission to be quoted and identified directly. To protect the identities of other respondents at their request, the following pseudonyms have been used and other identifying data has been changed:

Samantha, Mike, Jill, chapter two

Carol Smith, chapter three

Sarah Richman, William, Penny Mather, Alison, and Jonathan Black, chapter five

Barbara, Elena, and Pat Taylor, chapter ten

Sarah and Luis, chapter twelve

Mary Casey, Lilli Cohen, and David, chapter thirteen

LOVE STORY

CHAPTER ONE

A Passion of Her Own

ANN SEBRELL EHRINGHAUS WAS TWENTY-TWO when she and her new husband climbed the deck of the Cedar Island Ferry as it glided into Silver Lake Harbor at Ocracoke Island, North Carolina. The year was 1971.

Eyes squinting into a strong and constant wind that smelled of salt and fig blossom, Ann took in the perfect circle of the natural harbor. There were a few fishing trawlers and some oyster draggers riding their moorings, bows pointed northwest into the prevailing wind. She was on the forward deck of the *Morehead City* which had brought her from the town of the same name, twenty-odd miles to the southwest. She watched from offshore as the whitewashed lighthouse came into focus above a cedar grove. Then the village itself emerged, holding the harbor in a casual embrace. There were forty or fifty houses and a couple of two-story gray-shingled buildings, the fish house, and a sign she could just make out from the ferry, "Community Store." There were lines of boat slips with short slanted docks, clustered mostly at ten and three o'clock, if you saw things that way.

The way Ann saw things, she was home. With the clarity of perception that has characterized all of her life choices, she knew that she had found a place where she "fit." In an hour and a half she and Michael were hired to be two of the five teachers for Ocracoke's thirty-one children. Contracts signed, house rented, they got back on the ferry and left to get their belongings.

"A friend in Chapel Hill had said, 'Some island off the coast wants two teachers, preferably a married couple.' That's all the data I had. So I went home and I got out maps and I studied and I decided Ocracoke had to be the island. From the minute we turned into the harbor on the ferry, I knew this place was for me."

It was as if a recognition that had always been there on the edge of consciousness burst through.

Low and curved like a weathered seahorse with its head and neck outstretched, its eye the village, between Pamlico Sound and the North Atlantic, Ocracoke Island extends for sixteen miles into the sea. Her shoreline is one continuous, wind-sculptured, cedar-clad dune and wilderness beach. Directly beyond Silver Lake at the southern end of the island lies "Teach's Hole," the salt tomb of the legendary Blackbeard. The winter population in 1971 when Ann arrived was 690. There were two general stores and no pharmacy.

Such isolation would not be for everyone. But Ann wanted to be in a place where she could see the line of the horizon. She wanted freedom. Ocracoke is a place that sets no limitations on imagination save the bounds of commitment to community, being part of the fabric of village life, population now 660 in the winter. The place demands constant choice, renewal of decision. The weather dominates. Northeasters howl in and the power is out during summer thunderstorms that come in off the gulf stream. Here the soul has room to grow.

What kind of a life could a woman build here? It seems a life of adventure grounded in relationship. Ann's life has included marriage, divorce, then a lover, then solitude surrounded by deep friendships and community. She has gone from being a teacher to photographer to owner of a bed-and-breakfast. Still active as a photographer, she has now had several one woman shows of her work; she is part of the protest group against offshore oil drilling; she goes "off island" to teach art in the rural mountains of North Carolina, and recently has traveled to California to study the ancient Chinese art of *Feng Shui*. After a three-year struggle to lease an abandoned house on a now uninhabited island just beyond Ocracoke, she is beginning work on her second book of documentary photography. Is she rich? She thinks so, though not economically.

We are talking in the living room of Ann's bed-and-breakfast, Oscar's House. Ann is sitting on a low bamboo couch. Opposite her, on the wainscoted wall behind the potbelly stove, are two photographs. One is of a woman, standing, looking at a portrait of herself on a wall. The portrait the woman looks at contains within it yet another portrait of herself as a young girl. Next to it is an Edward Curtis photograph of an Indian, bought from a lady in Atlanta. "I picked it because some days I think this person looks like a man and some days I think it looks like a woman, and I really like that about it. And I like how simple the person is. Not much for ornamentation, just a shell and a feather."

Beyond the living room's heavy glass doors we can just glimpse a pinball machine and a life-size cardboard cutout of a Gerber baby. Out back behind the kitchen is a deck that has been built around a salvaged stage set of the Von Trapp family dining room from a production of *The Sound of Music*. As is true for most islanders, much of Ann's house is salvage, aesthetic salvage, used artfully, deliberately.

The woman is as interesting as the setting. Creative energy seems to have coursed through her life sculpting its shape. The current has also carried the added energy of love for a man, and always there has been energy for friendship and spiritual questioning.

Ann blends life and art. Six months a year she does photography, writes, thinks. The other six she runs Oscar's House, her own bed-and-breakfast. She has carved a shape, created a form that fits her energies, few rough edges rubbing up against her spirit, those that do, part of the process.

"I have always followed my own inclinations," she says. "And I have done that whether I am in a relationship or not. I feel like I've lived my own life."

Relationship and self-expression complement each other for Ann. Her life-style is a realization of the vision that must have taken shape as she stood on the deck of the *Morehead City* twenty years ago. It has developed in the same way that photographic images develop under her skillful, intuitive hands in her darkroom. In the summer, she runs Oscar's House and in winter, she focuses on her photography. She sees the two activities as coherent parts of the pattern of her life. Running the bed and breakfast is simply another phase of a process. "I just see it as kind of my information-gathering period. I'm finding out things from people all over the universe and bouncing back to them things that I've been reading or studying. Then the other six months is much more of an inward, quieter, let's take this and turn it into art, photography." All experience gets translated into her work. This seems clear when Ann talks about the ways she spends her time: "My political involvement is greater than ever, my business is busier than ever, and I'm doing more photography than ever." All of them are passions. All of them form the foundation of her spiritual life.

Every moment seems lived fully as if in a burst of light. Sharing what makes her feel alive, Ann says, "All kinds of things. Swimming in the ocean, laughing. One of my favorite moments is at the house when six or seven strangers sit down to breakfast, and by the end they're laughing and talking and discovering how interested they are in each other. That just makes me feel great. And frequently I haven't said that much, but I've helped to create an atmosphere and encouraged people to express themselves. I tell them that all the time when they're checking in. I say, you know, if you feel like just bursting into song, sing. Tell us a joke. Write a poem. Do anything. I think people see my life as being a creative expression of who I am and that encourages them to also think about that in their own life."

In her book, *Ocracoke Portrait*, Ann is even more eloquent as she talks about the interplay of life and art. "Through the years, Ocracoke has shown me both what it means to be part of a community and how important it is to be self-sufficient. It has taught me the value of finding a balance within the environment as well as within myself. These photographs were made as part of *living* at Ocracoke. They were not considered a separate activity; they were neither posed nor prearranged. While walking, riding, or boating, there would suddenly be a moment when all the pieces fit together, when something would ring out. This moment became a photograph . . . Ocracoke—a place where there are many moments that ring true."[1]

LIVING THE PASSIONATE LIFE

Ann Ehringhaus was one of over three hundred women who participated in the research for this book. In many ways she is unique. Her life is not typical of that of the vast majority of us who fit the more conventional patterns that society judges reasonable for a woman. Ann is a person who prizes freedom, a person who has shaped her life carefully, deliberately, in a way that makes the best use of her strengths, resources, and needs.

From an outsider's perspective, Ann is passionately and deeply engaged both with herself and with the lives of the people around her. She has found a shape and structure for her life that fits. She owns, operates, and manages her life, and the price of ownership is that daily she faces new choices that require a vigilant responsibility for the ongoing expression of her own vision. Ann's life follows a path that integrates relationship with a passion for self-expression. Creative energy dominates. More than most of us, Ann knows what moves her, what is deeply meaningful, and her outer life has evolved into a coherent expression of her inner sense of self.

We open with this profile of Ann Ehringhaus because she is a woman who lives outside the cultural "love story" that shapes most women's lives. Her choices fly in the face of all that we're taught to believe about what makes a woman happy: children, a man, a primary relationship, domestic life, a career in the corporate or academic or business world, preferably all of the above at the same time. The outcome of Ann's choice is that her sense of herself isn't a divided one—the energies of caring and doing are woven together into one integrated flow and she feels whole and alive.

For most of us, love and creative energy feel like the split ends of our psychic and emotional lives. When we focus on relationship, we feel uncomfortable about not accomplishing more. When we focus on our more self-expressive impulses, we feel guilt that we're not relating more. What gets lost in the struggle is our sense of passion—the awareness of what moves us. We end up feeling like divided selves who try frantically to balance obligation with need, responsibility with satisfaction. Not knowing how to shape our lives to meet our conflicting desires, we may find it easier to simply conform to the social conventions of the day.

In the nineties, confusion about our roles is couched in the language of conflict between our own psychological well-being and family needs. But somehow these definitions of the problem only reinforce a sense of our dividedness, our emptiness, our disconnection from ourselves.

The real problem is an absence of passion and what seems a narrow range of choice for expressing and accessing it. In the process of conforming rather than choosing, of thinking that love and creative energy are separate and distinct, we lose touch with aliveness and joy, we fail to be wholehearted about our own lives. We lose interest, excitement, appreciation. We become heartsick. Particularly in this time of contradictory and confusing social values, it's often difficult for us to know what we care about deeply. Not only do we suffer but the community around us suffers as well, because it loses the benefits of our energy, dedication, and spirit.

When we misread ourselves, when we live solely by the conventions of the day or the dictates of an oppressive social structure, we risk becoming addicted, obsessed, trapped. When we don't express ourselves coherently, we become depressed. We forget what moves us, and our deepest needs and passions are obscured.

As therapists, we have worked for many years with women who struggle to recover from addiction and to redefine their sense of themselves. But, as we discussed in our earlier book, *Too Good for Her Own Good*, once we recover from addiction, many of us still fight to free ourselves from the bonds of female socialization. Once liberated from our physical and emotional addictions, liberated from antiquated notions of female goodness, where do we move next?

Our work in this book was motivated by our curiosity about larger themes in women's lives. Instead of focusing on problems, we felt it was important to understand women's strengths. At the end of *Too Good for Her Own Good*, we talked about moving toward wholeness. We describe it as a process of reclaiming one's creativity and one's power to choose. In this book, we wanted to explore what women feel passionately about and how they come to embrace their own creativity. We were acutely aware as we examined these themes that our socialization still often limits women's access to their inner lives.

Part of our task here is to understand how certain ideas we learn about the ways women love and the ways women create confine us and rob us of our passion. The other is to explore the ways that women shape their lives to overcome a sense of being split by these two seemingly conflicting energies—the power to love and the power to create.

ABOUT OUR RESEARCH

In talking to the women who participated in the study that is the basis of this book, we wanted to know what was important to women today. How moved were they either to engage intensely in relationship or intensely in self-expression. Was it true that women today knew themselves only in relationship or had the world changed? How did they balance, integrate, or choose between caring and doing, self and other? What choices made their lives most meaningful, made them feel most alive, most centered, most passionate themselves? We also wanted to understand what happens when a woman is blocked from the knowledge of what moves her, or what happens when she knows it but fears expressing it.

We were clear that by love, we meant, "that which one cares deeply about," whatever touches the heart. And we were clear that by creativity we meant "the act of expressing, constructing, generating something new, putting one's own stamp on one's life, creating a bridge from one's inner world to the outer world." We make a distinction between what is creative and what is *artistic*—by creative we mean a type of energy and authenticity, not the forms of artistic creation that may be specific expressions of it. Passion was the word that best suggested the power of both love and creativity as we understood them. To be passionate means to be authentic, to put the energy that is uniquely one's own into the world. To be passionate means to be connected with the soul and spirit of the self.

Sensing that love and creative energy are the core elements that determine the course of a woman's life, we wanted to understand the possibilities women have found for shaping their lives and how they create forms that become the external "medium" for their feelings. How do we choose and how important are the forms of our relationships, gay, straight, married, single, the forms of physical space we occupy, the way we shape our time, our routines, the way we choose partners, environments, careers? How do we find the courage to change when a form doesn't fit?

As one would turn a glass prism, collecting and reflecting light differently, or listen acutely to the sounds of a night forest, we have watched and listened, pursued with our questions, talked with women in doctors' offices, in cities, on islands, on boats, in campgrounds, in planes. We have turned to women in therapy with us, to our friends and colleagues, trying to trace patterns, if any, seeking common themes, hoping to learn from the arrangements of women's lives.

We questioned women in many different formats. About forty filled out open-ended written questionnaires, a sample of which appears on pages 265–268. From their responses we developed a multiple choice survey that was given to some two hundred twenty more. We chose forty-five additional women to provide us with in-depth personal interviews. These women were exceptional in that they seemed to us to model passionate engagement with their own lives.

From our surveys and interviews, we learned about the tremendous diversity of women's lives, about the pains of their conflict, about the joy and exuberance of their solutions to it.

Our data surprised us by demonstrating that a high percentage of women still believe that relationship is more important than self-expression and are confined by the belief that they are good at love but not at being creative. It's clear that it's easy to get distracted and alienated from what moves us and that we don't often know how to reclaim our passions and shape our lives to suit us better. Not surprisingly, we found that the female rules of "goodness" are still a major block. Fears of being too selfish, the tendency to give time to everyone but oneself, feeling "ugly," assuming one had too little talent, or feeling guilty about taking oneself seriously were all common patterns expressed in the data.

But our discussions with women also revealed the high degree of creativity most of us express in our very solutions to these conflicts. We have met with women from all kinds of diverse backgrounds and their stories are rich with the energy of struggle and of success at shaping lives full of their own unique passions. We rarely left an interview or finished reading a questionnaire being less than inspired by the degree of women's energy and vitality. This was true whether we spoke to an accomplished artist or to a woman struggling as a single mother to support her child on welfare while she waited for the time when she could take a poetry workshop. It was true of the sixty-year-old woman who had lived the first twenty years of her adult life raising five children within a traditional marriage and then had chosen a lesbian life-style, and it was true of the twenty-two-year-old who puts romance second to her intense passion to live her own life exactly on her own timetable and is off to Alaska to lead wilderness trips for women. And it is true of our encounter with the corporate executive, who, having met her career goals at thirty-five, then turned down a promotion and chose to be a full-time mother.

THE SHAPE OF THIS BOOK

Part One of this book explores the larger cultural "story" of women's experiences and the ways that our ideas about love and creativity have been constructed and maintained by the pressures of political and economic life.

Part Two draws on our survey data and our interviews to outline the dominant patterns that emerge in women's lives. We use four basic terms to describe women who most embrace those patterns: Lovers, Artists, Leaders, and Innovators. Each category captures a woman's clearest sense of herself on a continuum of energy for relationship versus energy for self-expression. We describe these shapes and the profiles of the women who adopt them in depth.

Finally in Part Three we talk about passion and form, the qualities critical to embracing a passionate life and the choices that can lead us to see and think differently, weave the tapestry of caring and doing more artfully into our lives.

This is not a book of self-help, although we hope it is helpful. We didn't want to set up fixed categories and dichotomies that would do violence to the fluidity of women's lives. Our attempt is to describe patterns of energy, to discern the patterns of meaning that evolve in the ways women think about their experience, feel it, know it, try to express it. Each of us lives a story on a blank page of time. Our task was to capture the aliveness and complexity of women's lives while trying, at the same time, to discern what factors shape them.

This is not a book about problems, it's a book about questions. We think of ourselves too often in labels and in terms of pathology and we often forget that it is the forms we choose for our lives, the labels that are imposed, rather than our inner spirits themselves, that create the confinement and conflict we experience as "problems." Our hope is to leave you with questions for yourself. Does the form you've chosen for your life fit, is it meaningful, does it provide the structure for an authentic expression of who you are? Do you feel free to change what doesn't satisfy?

We open with Ann Ehringhaus and women like her whose sense of the shape of their lives is clear, women who paid attention to their own vision. They serve as models for the kind of blending of energies that we can all ultimately strive for. We chose women who had the courage to access their passions and the maturity to embrace a radical change in order to find forms that fit those passions. Their lives are not the lives that most of us might choose to lead, but they are, in the words of writer Eleanor Munro, "templates for action"—women whose choices mirror themes we can all recognize in our own attempts to live more authentic lives.[2]

For Ann Ehringhaus, environment, choice of livelihood, and freedom from a primary relationship were all critical to the form that expressed her dominant energies. Her friend and fellow islander, Mary Nolan, chose the same environment, Ocracoke Island, but her life took on a much different form. If Ann's energies are primarily creative ones, Mary's are primarily relational. While her life is no less creative than Ann's, what moves Mary most is her passion for connection. Mary's is a story of particular courage and a story of radical change.

THERE IS NOTHING RATIONAL ABOUT LOVE

When we first met, Mary Nolan had just come from walking a piece of the wide, remote, and windswept beach that covers twelve miles along the north shore of the island. Mary wore faded jeans and a comfortable old chamois cloth shirt that was robin's egg blue. Her glasses hung on a cord around her neck, her short brown hair was barely disturbed by the wind. She carried a bag full of garbage with her—debris she had picked up from the beach. Like Ann and all the islanders, she is deeply concerned with protecting the beaches. Mary wants passionately to help sustain the pristine beauty of the island. "This is a healing place," she says. "We can't let them destroy it with their damned oil wells like they've destroyed every place else."

Mary is seventy-five years old. She moved to Ocracoke fifteen years ago with her lover, Pat. Her friends like to describe her as a woman who's lived "many lives." Mary was married, had two children, recovered from alcoholism at age forty, left her husband at forty-five. She went back to school to become a psychiatric nurse, and at age fifty met her female lover, Pat, with whom she lived for twenty years until Pat's death four years ago. About a year and a half after Pat's death, Mary became involved in a new relationship that she finds loving, supportive, and "fun." Fun and play are important to her, essential to her happiness. The beaches of Ocracoke are her playground, her "backyard," as she calls it. In her "new life" as a part-time counselor on the island, she has been known to do therapy on the beach. What, she thinks, could be more therapeutic?

Unlike Ann, who always knew what moved her, Mary embraced passion more slowly. Now her life is dominated by a deep contentment and wholeness lived in the shadow of grief. Her love for Pat was the central force in her life.

Mary tells us that Pat was never less than a central force in the lives of anyone who knew her. Pat believed that "living well is the best revenge." When friends arrived on Ocracoke to visit, often she would charter a fishing boat captained by her ninety-year-old native islander friend, Thurston, to take them all out on Pamlico Sound. They would watch the sunset, eat iced clams on the half-shell, drink champagne and mineral water. Pat always said it was important to "blow the city out of you." Then there would be lively conversation late into the night.

Pat and Mary shared a love of the beauty of the island, a love for fishing, for "messing around with boats," and a deep intellectual companionship that was sustaining.

As we sit in the fading light of an Ocracoke day watching the moonflowers begin to open in her front yard, Mary talks about the quality of her companionship with Pat.

"There was one morning that's a beautiful picture in my mind . . . it's one of those visual images that you carry that are so special, I have several of them, but this particular morning we were going sea trout fishing. The water was very calm and we went out in the little boat, there wasn't a ripple, and you could not distinguish the horizon. There was a softness, a color like lavender blues, very pale pastel colors, and the horizon between the ocean and the sky, it was indistinguishable. It was like drifting through a Maxfield Parrish painting. Gentle . . . the sun was just rising. We just sat there in the boat and watched this and felt it and shared this experience and she was as full of this beauty as I was. It was just lovely."

Mary thought of Pat as "the love of her life." When Pat died, she felt literally that it "ripped a hole, like something was torn out of me.

"And that's passion," Mary tells us. "That's passion.

"It was an investment, an involvement, it was an intertwining of ourselves in each other's lives . . . it was touching, holding, caressing, listening, being there for each other . . . closeness, knowing that you can depend on someone, knowing that person will understand and support and accept, even though you fight and disagree. God, I did love her. But I can even now see her face right up close to me with her eyes slanted like this (Mary demonstrates a hard, horrible face) and her little face in front of mine just livid with rage at times with me. You don't get that angry at people you don't love. The opposite of love is indifference."

When we ask Mary if she thinks love is rational or irrational, she laughs. "What the hell has it got to do with reason?" She thinks love may become more reasoned as it matures, but it rarely begins that way.

Since Pat's death, Mary has embraced her "new life" by viewing her pain at Pat's loss as an opportunity to grow and learn more of what life has to teach her.

"This has been the most rewarding part of my life, these last few years I've been doing counseling on the island here. I enjoy watching people come alive when they come in and talk to me about their sadness and I listen and I offer them choices. It's fantastic to see people change, to see people begin to blossom and open up. One of the most important things about my getting sober was getting my choice back."

In the past three years, Mary has also returned to what was a childhood love of writing. She writes of her time with Pat, she writes of the process of her own change. She writes poetry. She attends a creative writing class off island once a week.

As she becomes more inward, she also reaches out to others. She is a member of the county Board of Health. Once a month she makes the long round-trip journey by ferry to the mainland and back to attend meetings. She feels intense concern for the health of the islanders and the quality of the health center there. She still commits two nights a week to helping other alcoholics, after thirty-five years of her own sobriety. She says, "It was January of 1957. I finally capped the bottle after four years of trying."

And she pays slow, deliberate attention to life's detail: She feeds seventeen stray island cats, numerous birds, goes to the beach in her jeep most evenings to watch the sunset, and creates intricate collections of shells and flowers that adorn her windowsills. She lives simply on a small pension in a trailer that sits nestled in pine scrub on a high spot in the middle of the island. Material things mean little to her, she thinks she has more than enough. She attends a "Sunday School" group called the Seekers. Mary watches for signs of the sacred—she finds them daily in the beauty of the island.

Recently someone commented to her that people who move to islands are just trying to escape reality. She was perplexed and then thought, "But this *is* reality. Why does one want all the other distractions we have created that we tell ourselves are important. Money, cars, houses, stress, striving, competing, crowds, violence. There's something fascinating about this island. I know it as a healing place, as a loving place, a supportive place, a community. This is more real to me than any of that other." She thinks of the beauty of the island, of the world, as a kind of classroom in which her task is to continually learn and absorb.

We see Ann and Mary moved by an energy that is, right now, mellifluous, flowing, integrated. There are no sharp twists and turns. Both women have found structures for their lives that go far beyond the conventional but that uniquely address their particular styles of caring for others as well as caring for themselves. Their decisions took courage and the willingness to take risks, the willingness to change when the flow of energy was blocked. To shape their lives as they do requires presence of mind enough to question external expectations and to decide what "love" and what "passion" look like from their individual vantage points in the world.

Most women intuitively know whether the "shape" of their lives fits their dominant energies. When it does, one experiences a sense of harmony, wholeness, "rightness" with self and with others. One feels alive, engaged, "flowing." There are few questions asked, only awareness and involvement, a continual moving forward. Such a woman may appear intense or deep and boundless. However her energy appears, one is inescapably caught and inspired by its presence. When those energies are blocked, a woman has a feeling that she's living somebody else's life instead of her own. She senses that there's some secret that she's hiding from herself, that there's somewhere she wants to go but she can't quite get there. In most cases what she knows is that she's living her life with herself left out, that caring for others has blocked her caring for and expressing of herself.

THE WORK IS SACROSANCT ON EVERY LEVEL

Passion also flows in cities. Lucy Lippard, an art writer and activist, author of sixteen books, is a woman whose intellectual energy dominates her life. Looking at her work, one would say she has a passion for mixture.

Lucy lives in New York City. Most urban dwellers tell themselves periodically that the pace of city life is too stressful. In their fantasies they are always moving to the suburbs or to the country to find a "simpler life." Most also say that they would feel starved without the stimulation of the city. This conflict of needs remains an ongoing refrain amidst the daily frustrations of city life.

Lucy, more than most, has resolved the conflict. She spends five months of the year in a cabin in the foothills of the Rockies, and presents occasional seminars for the University of Colorado at Boulder. Summers she spends at her family's camp on the Maine coast. But her loft in SoHo is the place she identifies as home. She has owned it for twenty-four years.

The themes of a city life echo in Lucy's work—the intellectual, political, and cultural diversity, the noisy intensity, the vast range of personalities and life-styles, the aesthetic stimulation that can reach a fever pitch, the ambition, the frantic race to succeed. And yet there is the sense of being at a center of energy, the heart of all that's new, innovative, sophisticated, chic.

Contradictions abound in Lucy's life. She is privileged and proletariat, urban and country. She lives a private life but has a clear public voice. In New York she is cofounder of a number of activist and feminist artists' groups.

Lucy's life is like her aesthetic vision. Perhaps because her sense of pattern blends diverse forms and images into a new whole, her life is a mixture, a collage with one dominant theme, one intense inner imperative which is her commitment to self and to work.

We ask her what connects all of the things she likes to do. Her response: "Contradictions, again. I like activities that I do alone. I like writing, hiking, and sailing. The older I get the more important nature is. I now have lived enough of my life that I can look back and see some patterns and that certainly is one. On the other hand, I really like people and I always make communities around me. I like meetings and I like to have people in my house and I like to feed people, and at the same time I like to spend most of my time alone, preferably outdoors. I've always lived for the idea of everything connecting to everything."

Relationship is important, particularly with her twenty-seven-year-old son, but relationship does not divert her from her writing. Lucy has had no one major love relationship in the past ten years. There were several important men before that.

"I have been with various men almost all or virtually all of whom are good friends now . . . and they all have been very different people and they have all been involved with the arts on one level or another. It wasn't like any relationship broke up over work per se because I got into all of them as who I was and I don't think there was ever any question that the work was important and that I earned my own living. Certainly my overwhelming passion has always been my work, so all my friends and lovers know that.

"Every man I have been with has opened a whole territory that has been extremely interesting and I am really grateful to them for that. But I have always had a pretty short attention span for relationships, which is part of my collage aesthetics I think. I live my life in a very spontaneous way and feel trapped when I can't live that way."

Speaking about other women whose work had to be fit in around their relationships she says, "I think a lot of women, that is the average woman artist of my age anyway, wanted it all and tended to be married and tended to have children or wanted to, or was involved with some-body and was trying to juggle a lot of things. So was I."

Lucy follows where her energy leads, pursuing her inner dialogue with herself. But in no sense does her energy feel scattered when one is in her presence. At fifty-five, she is a small, wiry, intense woman whose concentration of intellectual and verbal power has the tautness of a coiled spring. With her intelligence go humor, a certain detached perspective on herself, and a deep laugh. No dark glasses hide the eyes. She seems to integrate both great concentration of energy and the spaciousness of a sky wide enough to hold it.

Lucy's interests are wide-ranging and include not only feminism and art, but the Vietnam War and archaeology. She is a socialist fascinated by the struggles of women and artists of color. She is also a published novelist.[3]

How does Lucy see her own life? "I think I've had a very lucky life as much as anything. Although one person told me, 'Well, you have been through a lot of bad stuff, haven't you?' And I said, 'No, I have had a really terrific, lucky life,' and she laughed and she said, 'Yes, that's just how you handle it.' I was stunned. It had never really occurred to me that I had had a difficult life."

So relationships are important to Lucy, but her soul and her spirit are in her work. Her passions for creative expression and relationship differ and diverge, with the work representing more the sense of aliveness that defines her. Her creative expression is a natural out-growth of her own deep curiosity and interest in the world around her—it represents her need to make new connections on intellectual and aesthetic levels.

Perhaps it doesn't occur to Lucy that she's had a difficult life because the shape of her life fits her passions and her needs. Rough spots and turbulence are tolerated with more resilience when there is some essential coherence and self-acceptance in one's life.

Lucy loves and works in the balance that is right for her. She lives in the places for the periods of time that make internal sense. She is not fearful that, being a woman, she is too intellectual, too selfish, not relationally involved enough. She is concerned with what concerns her. She does what she loves to do.

THE COURAGE TO SHAPE A LIFE

We present these three portraits of uniquely different women to throw into sharper relief our vision, as authors and as therapists, of the power a woman has to shape a life that fits when she accesses her passionate self, when she has achieved the capacity to be the subject of her own life story.

Looking at extremes makes the subtle complexities of our lives more clear. Most of us are more free to be shapers than some of the women who will speak in this book, but we are also less free than Ann, Mary, or Lucy. All of us struggle with critical questions about love and creativity. How do we balance and nurture our connections to others while maintaining connection to ourselves, to our own work? Is there a fit between our inner and outer lives? If not, what are the constraints? If not, how can we change?

In the postmodern world that we live in where no particular form is in fashion and where all styles, motifs, and stories seem to have equal relevance or irrelevance and equal weight, we live in a chronic state of confusion about what is meaningful. What is love, who feels it and what happens to it? In an age where AIDS has made all of us fearful of sexual expression, where Communism dies and long-cherished enemies are suddenly friends, where there is no longer a traditional family form and where the definitions of what is male and what is female are being radically revised and in some cases discarded altogether, how do we trust what we feel, or for that matter, how do we even know what we feel? The culture in general has few models or images to guide it, no solid lessons from history to mentor us through the confusion of modern times. But women in particular must struggle for new stories and new models of love because ours more than any have been constructed by others in ways that have denied us our rightful agency in the world.

We see the passionate woman as one who is subject, one who has the courage to tap into her most vital energies and who actively shapes them to create a life that fits for her. She is a woman who is wholehearted, mature, who understands the demands of transforming herself, a woman who has the courage to change. She may be highly relational, highly creative, or both. The key is that she takes charge, she, not others, defines the form of her life. She has a strong inner voice and she lets it lead. She makes choices, she makes commitments, she makes mistakes. But she pursues a passion of her own. She sings at the top of her lungs.

These words of Holly Near, political activist, singer, and songwriter, most capture the energy of a passionate woman:

My creativity and my political work are linked. I don't go out and do this work out of guilt or out of responsibility, though I used to. Now I do it because it makes for the life I want to have. It creates the memories I want to look back on. It creates the substance. It creates the passion with which I make love. It promotes the tones that get into the music. If I didn't think and feel the way I think and feel, I couldn't sing the way I sing. You can't just leave out one part. The bread won't rise if the yeast isn't there. I *like* this life. I like it when it's hard, I like it better when it's not, but I know you don't get the sweet part without the bitter.[4]

CHAPTER TWO

The Object of His Affection

IT IS LATE IN THE FALL of 1991. At the hangar of the Naval Air Station that houses four squadrons of our North Atlantic defense fleet, six men are taking a break from evening duty. Every two and a half minutes, the deep whine of a P3 overhead shudders the corrugated tin walls of the hangar. P3s are large propeller planes; they loom in the skies like leftover footage from a World War II film. They are gradually being phased out. The men are sitting around the interior of the hangar; some are squatting on their heels, others on folding chairs, sitting on batteries, on unopened shipments of plane parts.

One of the men, a young blond wearing a crew cut and a leather flight jacket, says to the others, "Hey, what do you call a Jewish American Princess making love on a waterbed?" In response to the silence, he answers himself. "Lake Placid." The others laugh.

Mike sits a little to the side of the others. He is conspicuously silent in the laughter that follows the sexist, ethnic joking that goes on almost like a ritual among them. Mike eats the peanut butter sandwich he has packed for himself. He and Samantha had an argument this morning. She refused to give up her evening to bring him dinner tonight. When the men in the squadron have overtime duty, their wives typically pack a hot meal for them and deliver it to the hangar. The women sit on the fringes and watch the men eat until it's time to take the dirty dinner pails home. The other wives are there now, just out of earshot of the jokes.

It is not just the P3s that look like leftover World War II footage. The context within which Samantha is a "Navy wife" might be a forties or fifties film starring Jimmy Stewart. The women's movement has come and gone here leaving barely a trace.

But Samantha has begun to make changes, she has begun to question the form of her marriage and things are tense at home. In one recent conversation with another "Navy wife" who called to ask Mike about one of the men's projects, Samantha says, "Mike can't come to the phone right now, he's doing dishes." The other wife says, "How on earth did you get him to do that?" When Mike tells her, "I'm out of razor blades, you should have remembered to buy them," she tells him, "Did you write that on the shopping list?"

When Samantha met Mike they were nineteen years old, sophomores at a Montana college. Samantha's mother had committed suicide when she was four. Her biological father, an alcoholic, died soon afterward. Mike's mother raised five children, with a combination of food stamps and grit after her alcoholic husband deserted the family when Mike was born. Mike grew up among four sisters and a determined mother, his only male role models his father's brawling, Irish, alcoholic brothers.

Mike and Samantha shared a set of common old-fashioned values when they met. They were going to create a different family from those they had known as children, a family that ate supper together and went to the park on Sundays. "I always thought we were gonna be 'Family Ties,' I really really did. When the baby was born we almost named her Mallory."

Samantha was going to be a teacher. Mike had always dreamed of flying. Neither knew what his joining the Navy would mean: six moves in eight years; deployment cycles; six months of his being away and then a year at home. Some of the Navy wives made videotapes of their husbands months before a deployment so that, after their husbands left, they could stick the tape in the machine while the children ate breakfast. The video created an illusion of Daddy's presence that often conveyed more than his physically being there. Navy as first family was the accepted rule of thumb.

Mike loved flying. And at first Samantha kept teaching, resuming her career with each move, adjusting to each new group of friends, each new locale, happy that Mike was happy. Resilient, she was able to follow the thread of her own work from place to place.

She would not have described herself as creative, not particularly, although she had a passion for nature, for the aesthetic. She loved the Montana mountains where she and Mike met and she was described by peers as a creative teacher. She longed to have children of her own and Mike wanted a child too.

Then Jill was born.

"I had my whole life mapped out. I was going to go back to work. I had planned the bulletin boards for my class. Then when she was born, the birth, what I went through, I felt like somebody took a stick and beat me down into the ground and I couldn't get up. It was a traumatic event in my life and no one would believe me because birth is supposed to be wonderful. I sat and cried every day for weeks and months. It was more than postpartum. I remember sitting at the table. It was dawn; I was all alone. I washed the bottle, I fed the baby, I did the diapers, I cleaned the sink, I made the breakfast. Then the baby would cry again and I'd sit and cry with her."

ABANDONED PASSIONS:
THE RELATIVE ABSENCE OF LOVE

When a year had passed, Samantha began to feel that she had lost some part of herself. Our interviewer met with her and several of her friends, other Navy wives, to conduct a group interview for this book. Samantha herself was curious to know if any of her friends also felt they had lost themselves in marriage, and she asked what parts of them they felt they had put away. Each of them had abandoned some early creative interest. Later she said that these friends whom she thought she knew well came alive to her in a different way during this meeting. She discovered parts of them she hadn't known before. One had seriously played the flute. Another had been an art major in college. They had never talked before about their creative interests until this interview. They had talked little about many of the things that were most important to them.

"Everyone had something they put aside to live the life they're living now, they put stuff on a shelf, like the woman who played the flute," she said. She was struck by the one exception. "There was only one of us who seemed to keep that part of herself alive, and who made a conscious effort to keep that time for herself, and she has daily battles with her husband and with work. But then again, she likes acceptable creative activities like needlepoint and piano playing. She has society's stamp of approval—the Navy likes arts and crafts."

Samantha said she had started to think about other passions that she had put away. Curiously, what came to mind was a recent decision about her cat.

As Samantha explained, "I had to make the decision to keep the stray kitten when I found her and I had trouble with it because I realized that having that kitten is painful; it reminds me of a time in my life when I was more myself. I had a cat when I was totally on my own in college; I had several cats until Jill was born. Then I got rid of them. It was like I had closed a door on a part of my life. Mike and I got a dog. But cats are my passion; it's not the same with my dog. I never knew that, but I came to realize that I thought that the relative absence of love for the dog was defined as maturity. It was like when I got married; I thought society said, 'She should be happy—she has a house and kids to take care of.' When I was a child I had a duck. Everyone thought the reason I loved the duck was that I *took care of the duck* but it wasn't that at all. The duck was my friend. The duck and the cats were about a kind of companionship. It's a side of me that no one knows . . . a deep and abiding feeling."

Finding, recovering, this "deep and abiding feeling" is the critical task of Samantha's life right now. What needs to change is her belief that "the relative absence of love is defined as maturity." That belief, that to feel deeply is childish, to have passion is dangerous, can destroy a life.

If Ann Ehringhaus, Mary Nolan, and Lucy Lippard are women who fully own their passions, Samantha is a woman still in search of them. Some of the constraints that block Samantha and all of us from access to our passions are psychological and rooted in family experience to be sure. But a larger factor is the reality that Samantha is caught in a web of cultural chatter about women's ways of loving. If Ann, Mary, and Lucy are atypically free to shape their energies, Samantha is atypically blocked by a traditional form that doesn't really fit her experience.

What traps Samantha are the vestiges of an old cultural story about love. The definition of love in that story follows from traditional notions of family life that, for a woman, assume that love equals "to set oneself aside." It suggests sacrifice of self that is total and unconditional, not situational and dependent on context. That antiquated version of love echoes like a disembodied voice in the back of Samantha's mind, shaping her thinking and her sense of who she is. In fact, she says she was struck in the group interview, ". . . by the women who think love equals taking care of." Samantha assumes that loving can take only certain forms and that feeling that deviates from those forms is "immature" or invalid. She abandons passions and interests that fall outside the story line, or she struggles with conflict at giving voice to them.

THE SPLIT IMAGE AND OTHER MYTHS
OF WOMANHOOD

What is the cultural narrative about women and love and how does it shape us? Virginia Woolf wrote her novel, *To the Lighthouse*, in 1927.[1]

The friendship of the two main female characters in that novel captures the essence of the dual energies that have meant conflict and struggle for women in the domain of love. One is Mrs. Ramsey—she is only a Mrs., with no name of her own. The other is Lily Briscoe, her alter ego, an artist.

Mrs. Ramsey expresses her primary passion in life by giving to others. She is the quintessential wife and mother who presides at the table of her family's life. She adores her husband, and helps chart her children's progress through the murky depths of growing up. Mrs. Ramsey fully subscribes to the definition of love as giving, sacrifice, caretaking, being "for" others, and she believes that "an unmarried woman has missed the best of life."[2]

Her best friend, Lily, *is* unmarried. Lily is introspective and likes to be alone. Her passion is for her art. She takes pleasure in trying to see the relation of one thing to another and in trying to convey this knowledge on her canvas. Her motivating energy is her desire to maintain the courage to say, "this is what I see, this is what I see."[3]

Virginia Woolf metaphorically expressed her own awareness of the dividedness of female identity in these two characters. Mrs. Ramsey is the woman of the common cultural love story. She fully and willingly embraces a traditional female role and she appears fulfilled by it as well. Lily is the nonconformist who goes against the norm. Lily is generative, she creates, she is artistic, she does "her own work." Lily's major problem is to take herself seriously. No one else, not even her good friend, does. She struggles not to feel continually foolish about her passion for art.

In 1927 this view of women's experience was reinforced by a society that believed, much as one of the male characters in the novel did, that "women can't paint, women can't write."[4] Women were only to love. Emotionality and feeling *as prescribed by the roles of wife and mother* were considered to be a woman's domain, doing and creating a man's. For a woman, love meant being the love object, the beloved, and the caretaker of the needs of others.

What Woolf depicts is what we call the "split image" of female experience. The cultural story makes us think that the split is something real, that the energies of nurturing love and love as creative passion are separate and distinct and that they can't be contained in one person. Either one sets oneself aside and loves or one gives up love and creates. If one gives up love for creative passion, one is less a woman and what is created is of little value.

If the split image confines women to loving rather than doing, it also confines us to certain ideas about what love is. The female love story outlined for us by the split image is one that defines caring as *caretaking*, not love as generativity or power or passion—in other words, love with the self left out. Not love as a mutual sharing of passion and interconnection, but love as "I am what he desires, I give what he needs, I create the perfect medium for the satisfaction of others' requirements." Love for women as it is defined by the split image is responsive love, passive love.

It is love that mirrors and reflects, smiles and responds.

Many of the responses to our survey reflect this cultural ideal of love.

What does love mean to you?
"Love means caring about another person's well-being and acting in a way to please them."
"Love is the caring for the growth of another."
"A feeling of being wanted, needed, and accepted by someone special. Being there for all the little things."

Our definitions of love as we understand it rarely reflect the aspect of love that is an active expression of self, love that brings forth. Responses to our survey that did capture this more generative aspect of love expressed a more active sense of self:

"Love means discovering what it is to be human and alive through relationship with another."
"Love means mutual respect and consideration, listening, passion, honesty, acknowledgment, to be heard and to hear, honoring and being honored, being connected in a healthy way."
"Love means making a complete commitment to achieve connection with self, an interest, or another person."

But our training has been to think little of these creative aspects of love, the discovering, the committing, the doing aspects. We think of the shape of our bodies as our art, intimacy as our art.[5] Because creativity implicitly requires self-focus, we learn that one cannot relate and create—the two are separate energies and the one lies outside the dominant definition of what it means to be a woman.

In his 1991 book on creative process, *Creating*, author Robert Fritz begins with the bold statement that "Love is what creating is about."[6] Fritz makes a distinction between receptive or passive love, the kind usually associated with female experience, and love that is more active. In the first, he says a situation happens and one *feels* love. In the second, the love comes first and *creates* the situation. What he suggests is that the energy of love doesn't emerge only in response to someone or something else, it's a force that moves from within us. "In the creative process, love is generative rather than simply responsive. . . .

If the only love we experience and express is the love that happens to us ... then we miss an entire dimension of love. ... With the creative process, creators are bringing creations into being because they love their creations enough to want to bring them into being. Why else would they, or you, create?"[7]

This dichotomizing of the two aspects of female energy, caretaking versus generative action, has been the dominant impact of the cultural narrative about love. We have thought of ourselves either as a Mrs. Ramsey or as Lily—lover or artist—but rarely both. Rarely do we assume that the same process involved in creating must inform our loving, or that in loving we create. Rarely would we assume the *agency* to create, because to have agency means the quality of *moving or exerting power*, the state of being in action, and as women this has not been our common sense of ourselves.

We rarely feel, like Ann Ehringhaus, that "my life is a creative expression of who I am." Rather we fall into discordant and what anthropologist and author Mary Catherine Bateson, in *Composing a Life*, refers to as "discontinuous" roles and functions.[8] We go where he goes, drop our own agenda to follow our partner's, struggle to decide when the optimum time in our careers might be for setting ourselves aside to have children. We assume much of the responsibility for the work of caretaking. We are the shaped rather than the shapers. Frequently our identity becomes totally defined by the roles we have assumed. We rarely stop to think about what love really means to us and whether the forms we choose for expressing it really satisfy.

The point is, we've been fed a line about love, and the forms of our lives are as often constricted as they are enhanced by it. Journalist Bill Moyers recently did a PBS documentary on women's creativity. In it, women artists and writers speak of the conflicting pulls of love and creativity, especially the impact of bearing children. Author Mary Gordon, mother of one daughter at the time of the interview, says, "You just feel this passion for babies." But she also says that being with her daughter "just stops" the creative process. The documentary underscores the point that women have learned to resolve the split they experience between love and creativity by making an art of intimacy. The piece is really a commentary on the split, what Gordon calls the "half life" that women are expected to live.[9]

This split story of women as it evolves through history and popular culture is at its core a story that separates ideas of love from ideas of power. Women's emotions and the capacity for generative love are trivialized. Psychologist Ravenna Helson tells us, "to initiate, change, create are manifestations of power. So it is not seen as natural or appropriate for women to be creative. . . . These problems are accentuated by the fact that femininity is closely associated with being pleasing to men or with pregnancy or childrearing in the years when adult identity is being formed and the fact that women rear children in the very years when, in many fields, young men are exerting their most intense effort toward creative achievement."[10]

Other voices and other stories comment currently on the split image. Jill Kerr Conway, a writer and past president of Smith college, in her autobiographical story about her childhood in the Australian outback, *The Road from Coorain*, talks about being faced with this split in herself as she reaches a crossroads in her life: "I was headed for a traumatic confrontation between ambition, love and duty. . . . So far as my ambitions were concerned I knew they were deviant. Women were supposed to be governed by love."[11]

Psychologist and writer Kathy Weingarten describes her struggle with the split: "Try as I might, I have had an exceedingly difficult time solving, resolving, settling or figuring out once and for all how to combine the love of my work with the work of my loves. I have tried a variety of approaches over the last twenty plus years to handle the tension between wanting to do work of my own and feeling I ought, and want, to spend time with my children."[12]

In our surveys, refrains and variations on the theme of the split image appear over and over. One moving testament to the sense of being split came from a woman who only now, at age fifty-six, describes herself as a sculptor.

"I thought that life somehow really didn't begin until marriage. Marriage was some idyllic state, a state in which you were somehow rescued, finally being joined by a male who you could care for and who would care for you always. Development of self was not a priority—the lives of others assumed more importance.

"I managed to raise four children and three stepchildren who all lived with me until their early twenties. In order for me to survive and grow and not to be overwhelmed, I had to feed myself both emotionally and creatively. So this became a consuming force. Sculpting, writing, photography became more important as the fledglings left the nest."

Julie Flanders, an actress, says in response to a question about which is more important to her, love or creative expression: "Not able to stay with one or the other so I've spent a lot of time in my life trying to get the right blend because I really don't think I'd be happy at either extreme any more. The way I was balancing the extremes was simply to live both of them. I've had a very hard time coming to a middle ground on that. I've spent a lot of my creative energy juggling those extremes and putting my energy in a compensatory way towards the men I was involved with."

The conflict these women describe is a direct effect of the "dominant discourse" about women in this culture. The conflict implied in the story is the same one that affects Samantha who says "It was like when I got married, I thought society said, 'She should be happy—she has a house and kids to take care of.' " . . . as if the traditional marriage should be the fitting structure for all women in any circumstance and it should absorb all of her energies. We tend to think about love and connectedness only as giving to a man and/or children at the expense of oneself. But we all have other energies, other passions, other dimensions to our lives. We simply think of them as split off from what should be our true "priority."

The particular experience of the split is very much determined by age. In our study, older women, those in the pre–baby-boom generation, tended to experience the split in the terms described above. The priority was relationship, creativity was either salvation from it, a kind of escape valve, or something you ultimately gave up and seldom reclaimed. Younger women increasingly feel the split with the opposite emphasis. Many women in their thirties or younger began their adult lives with a sense of their creative power but then become fearful of relationship because they don't want to "lose themselves" to love. One young woman, a recent college graduate, says of love: "I feel as if I get into these situations and I change and adapt and I end up losing a sense of myself. Who wants to get waylaid by love?"

SUBJECTS AND OBJECTS:
VARIATIONS ON A THEME

Before the second wave of feminism, the major cultural storytellers were male. The exceptions, like Virginia Woolf, commented on the inequities of the story as it was being told. But men, through the media of science, politics, and culture, had the power to tell women's story and to render it as objective truth. They had the power to define the meaning of love. Few of us realize how much our ideas of love are affected by what men have had to say about it.

The cultural narrative is deceptive, because it suggests that the split is really only one between relational and creative energy. We're told that relational energy is a "female" quality, creative energy is "male." But the more subtle and more damaging effect of this splitting is the belief it supports that a woman has no inner self, that she cannot be the subject of her own experience, that she is an object whose self is created by the way she is defined, experienced, cares for, and is valued by others. At this level, the split doesn't just polarize loving energy and creating, it tears a rent in a woman's actual *experience* of herself. She comes to feel that it's up to somebody else to describe, analyze, value, or devalue who she is and what she does. To be object is to end up in a *Playboy* centerfold. It's to think like one woman who used to feel: "I never thought was he the man for me, I only thought in terms of was I the woman for him?"

The split image operates on two profound levels. Because love is viewed only as responsive, nurturing behavior for women, there is a split created between our relational energy and our more generative, creative energy that makes us believe that the two are separate, not from the same source. There is a more basic split in the ways that women are defined. As she is defined by others, she is an object. In her potential to define herself she is subject. Because she has primarily been defined by others in the cultural narrative, she most often experiences herself as an object in relation to a more powerful other. Society's preferred role for her is to be object.[13]

This description isn't meant to imply that a woman is always an object when she loves and subject only when she is creative. To care and to relate don't automatically imply passivity or self-effacement, just as expressions of creativity are not always self-defined or self-directed. A woman may equally work outside of her relational life as object, because "doing it all" has become a modern part of the dominant discourse for women. She may work because of economic need, or cultural or family expectations that she be "superwoman," and not because she has a true passion of her own.

On the other hand, many women choose to focus on love very consciously and with great satisfaction. A woman may experience herself as subject equally when she loves and when she creates. The difference is in who defines the shape of her life and how much of her authentic inner energy goes into the shaping. Is the form a good fit and is it fluid enough to change as the woman herself does? A woman can't define the form of her life from an object position, and the more she is subject, the more her life is open to change.

As object, we're more likely to trivialize our own emotions, to think of love only as caretaking—loving of, not passion for. In the object state, we are less likely to create, and we are less likely to think of ourselves as the focus of someone else's attention and care.

As subject, we experience relationship as an active, generative, mutual process, and we're more likely to create as an expression of love. We are powerful and we can form our lives in a way that's consistent with our own "inner imperative." As subject, we're passionate. As subject, we demand equal response from others. We are capable of creating and being the focus of others' attention in the same way that we focus our attention on them. Love becomes a two-way street.

The subject-object split is fundamentally an issue of one's psychological experience of self: How does a woman position herself in relation to others, as a reactor or as an actor, a responder or a generator, as a self-defined being or an other-defined being? What is the story a woman tells about herself, and what factors impact that story?

SMILING WOMAN: THE PRIVATE VERSUS THE PUBLIC SELF

Envision this dichotomy in another medium, a photograph that might capture the split view. There is a woman in the foreground of the photo. She is smiling and engaged. Behind her foreground image (as in the photograph in Ann Ehringhaus's parlor) there is a small oval portrait of the same woman; she is not looking outward but at an easel—we know from the picture that she is painting. The image of the Smiling Woman involved with the world is dominant. She is superimposed over the artist/worker in the background focused inward.

Instinctively, though the images may shift at times in their relation to one another, somehow we sense that the Smiling Woman, the Mrs. Ramsey, the woman who loves first and seeks connection and engagement, typically dominates the picture. The artist who puts her art, her inner vision first, is typically subordinate. Who is subject? Who is object?

Now take a cognitive leap and imagine that the photograph becomes a motion picture. The Smiling Woman turns and enters her house. As she prepares for a dinner party, she not only cooks—she creates an entire environment for her family and guests. From her own garden she cuts rust chrysanthemums, arranging them with black-eyed Susans picked in the field beyond the house. The children are put to bed. She selects music that is unobtrusive as a background for the conversation that she will stimulate. She will take care to provide the conversational bridges from one guest to another, so that the talking includes and introduces each person to the others.[14] Husband and guests become the audience for her "work."

The Smiling Woman is being filmed on location in this scenario—in the private sphere of the home. Her easel is off in another room, hidden, all her energy and creativity dedicated to relationship. Certainly this is a woman of agency, one whose loving is creative. Yet here her loving is confined by the dictates of a role that is defined by someone else. Even though she may enjoy it, this form of self-expression is one that is sanctioned by the expectation that the Smiling Woman creates only in the private world of the home, the setting defined by the story as hers. Is she subject? Is she object?

Imagine one more scene in which the woman as artist/worker is in the other room packaging a painting. She puts it under her arm and strides down the streets of New York toward a gallery. She dares to be subject in the public arena. We follow her from the inner world of her creation into the public sphere, the world beyond the front door.

Here her work will become the object of scrutiny, her inner creative life will go public to be judged. This movement outward will have a very different impact and generate much different response from the performance of the Smiling Woman at the dinner party in the privacy of her home. Now the Smiling Woman steps outside the acceptable plot of the love story—she will be judged harshly for stepping out of role. Her work will be compared to a man's and found wanting. Implicitly she's given the message to go back home—that love as caretaking is her true identity. And if, as artist, she deals with themes that directly represent or express aspects of her experience as a woman, her art is likely to be considered second class.

So what Virginia Woolf commented on in her novel, what the image of the Smiling Woman represents, is the pervasive and insidious split that shapes our energies and the ways we think about ourselves. This culture-bound love story limits us because love is an energy that has both a nurturing and a generative flow. To highlight one at the expense of the other is to ordain that one half of women's powers are rendered invisible. It makes all of us, men and women, one-dimensional characters, halves of whole beings, because if, for a woman, generative power is defined out of the picture, for a man, what gets lost is the power to nurture and to care.

PSYCHOLOGY: THE CREATION OF A STORY OF LOVE

Usually when women consult us for therapy, their major preoccupation is with relationship–love problems. They will predictably talk about their difficulties finding, keeping, making a partner happy, their conflicts with those who disappoint them or who convey that they themselves are failing to love adequately. They will rarely talk about their creative or work interests—somehow it's simply assumed that therapy is about love and trouble and that there must be some other place where people discuss the parts of themselves that are passionately interested in creating and in having satisfying inner lives.

Only rarely does a woman think of her creative life as part of "the problem"—one woman told us, "My creativity is the real essence of my power, but I don't know who I am as a creative self—I've forgotten who I am."

Intuitively, we sense the split that thinking within a psychological framework about our lives sets up—if we are women and we have problems or dissatisfaction, the problem must be love, because we know love to be our appointed psychological domain.

Psychological theory has been the predominant definer of the love story of humanity and it, more than any artifact of modern culture, has been responsible for constructing a story that strips women of agency and strips men of the capacity for taking care. Its language and theories have had enormous power to reinforce the split image, so it makes sense to question how it came to be that in its clinical language, the word "woman" comes to equal love and "love" equals selflessness.

From Sigmund Freud to Jacques Lacan, psychoanalysts have talked about female identity in terms of a split between subject and object. The male is, in all theories of psychological development, understood to be the subject. Woman is his opposite. There can be no subject without an "other," no protagonist without an antagonist. It's not uncommon for women to be thought of as antagonists. In Nancy Chodorow's discussion of Lacan, who followed Freud, she explains that, "A person takes his place in the world as a subject only through entry into the 'symbolic,' into language and culture."[15] In psychoanalytic theory, one becomes subject by identifying with the source of power, the male. So the boy becomes a subject when he eventually leaves his mother and identifies with his father. Exactly what men's movement advocate Robert Bly is saying in the nineties. But, as the story goes, the girl thinks of herself as like mother and seeks her father's love and approval. She remains the love object who awaits the loving gaze and desire of the male to create her and give her life so that she can go on to fulfill her biological destiny as a bearer and nurturer. Freudian theory seems to suggest that women don't have super-egos, and in translation, that means that we have no power. We are weak-willed, we are passive, we are dependent on the male to provide us with a sense of self. This psychic state of affairs renders us morally, sexually, and socially inferior to men and makes us incapable of creating culture, that is any artifact of the world outside the home. We are the symbolic creations of men. We are Stepford Wives, images a man creates to carefully respond to his own projections and his own needs.

What this means is that we're not beings in our own right—we have no "voice," no power to define the language in which we're described. What we lose in the process are our own love stories, our own sense of identity, our own passions.[16]

What was Freud really saying about love? Decades of controversial attempts to translate and understand his work make it appear that he was saying that woman's experience is solely a function of her biology.[17] That for a woman, passivity is normal, the desire for agency is pathological, and that the greatest fulfillment a woman can hope for is to be desired by a man with whom she may fulfill her biological role of childbearing, caretaking, and nurturing. Rosemary Reuther comments that Freud actually defined aggressive, autonomous women as "infantile."[18] Within this framework, when she has conflict about her sexuality, a woman becomes "hysterical." When she tries to "behave like a man" with power, agency, or aggression, she is not only infantile, she is "castrating." The very desire to create, work, be generative is called "penis envy."

To be woman is to be equated with all that is untamed by reason in nature, all that is primordial, bound by feeling, defined by body rather than mind. In the early psychoanalytic world view, women were solely relational in nature while only men experienced the great drama of struggle from attachment to the mother to autonomy and separate functioning in the world. If Freud viewed the dual achievements of love and work as the hallmark of a healthy mental life, then women, who were viewed as incapable of work of their own outside of relationship, were implicitly sentenced in his view to mental impairment.

This love story of Freud's reflected his classical training and the ideas about love that had filtered down from Greek and Roman scholars who were themselves notoriously demeaning of women. It was also embedded in the historical events that surrounded its telling. The economic changes of the Victorian era ushered in a new form of idealization, and with it, submission of women. As a capitalist work ethic developed, work moved from being an integrated part of a family's life to a separate undertaking that happened outside of the home. The differences between the loving, emotional sphere of the home and the impersonal, competitive sphere of work became exaggerated. Love became associated with home and female, work with creativity, agency, competition, maleness. The woman as love object who could function in this capacity had to possess certain qualities that would distinguish her absolutely from the male. As psychologist Juanita Williams describes it, the "true woman . . . had four virtues: piety, purity, submissiveness and domesticity."[19] Motherhood became the new model of love and males idealized women's chaste purity and domesticity.

This tendency to view love as "woman's work" is referred to as the "feminization" of love.[20] Increasingly ideas of love became gender polarized as men and women were each confined to their separate spheres of influence. This division of labor intensified women's economic dependency on men. It also intensified men's emotional dependency on women, but this story was not to be told.

MORE OBJECTS

Ironically having ultimately constructed a theory of intrapsychic life so powerful that it was to dominate the course of Western psychological, philosophical, and literary thought until the present day, Freud was always clear that women's experience confounded him. Yet his influence prevailed, and psychoanalytic thought became the dominant theory to define mental disorder in the psychiatric profession. Newer versions of his thinking that emerged in the fifties were actually referred to as the "object relations" school of personality development.[21]

Object relations theorists thought that all capacity for healthy relatedness in adult life depends on the quality of the infant's attachment to the mother. If before we had penis envy, now women had to examine whether or not they had been "good enough" objects of gratification to their vulnerable infants. Mothers were expected to provide "mirroring," safe holding environments, constant objects. The language of disease if she failed might include terms like "disturbed object relations," "failed object cathexis," "lack of internalized object representations," failure to establish appropriate "transitional objects."

Consider the implications for the cultural narrative of love of a theory that now proposed that women had to be "good enough" in order for their children to enjoy healthy relationships, ones in which female children would grow up to assume their appropriate role as wives and "good enough mothers." Since its focus was almost exclusively on the mother-child interaction, its effect was to heighten the idea in the popular mind that women, mothers, were somehow sick, deficient, and even evil in their capacity to disturb the relations of all persons to one another. Meanwhile there was little suggestion that mothers themselves had needs for support, validation, or constant objects, such as their spouses, in the playing out of their good mother roles. There was little suggestion that children had a need for "good enough" fathers. The fifties saw, both in popular conceptions of personality and in literature and popular culture, a surge of what became known as "momism," the tendency to assume that mothers were to be held responsible for all the love problems of the world.

If women strayed at all from the plot of the "official story," the influence of this powerful social institution, psychological theory, claimed the authority to remind her that she was sick, maladjusted, and what was worse, unfeminine.

CURRENT TRENDS IN PSYCHOLOGY: THE RETURN TO LOVE

It was in the late sixties and early seventies that there was first a call for radical reform in the way that psychology depicted women. While cognitive, developmental, behavioral psychologists all continued to develop theory with little attention to female experience or gender bias, feminists began to critique psychoanalytic theory and to lay bare its patriarchal assumptions. In 1976, analyst Jean Baker Miller published the first psychological study to attempt to view women's development outside the frame of the male story about personality and about love.[22] In an attempt to explain why relationship might be so central in women's lives, she made the point that a focus on relationship is connected to the power differential inherent in society. In fact women's focus on relationship is adaptive—they must learn to relate to others and be carefully attuned to them if they are to survive in a male-dominated culture. Along with other female psychologists at the Stone Center for Research on Women, Miller began to work on analyzing the meaning of relationship in women's lives and began to advocate for a strengthening of female capacities for empathy and caring. Basically she began to reframe women's focus on relationship and connectedness as more valuable to society than the template for "male" development that emphasizes separation and autonomy at the expense of connection and compassion.[23]

In 1982, Harvard developmental psychologist Carol Gilligan challenged earlier studies of women's supposed inferior moral development by presenting a new cognitive perspective on masculinity and femininity.[24] Gilligan claims that there are major sex differences based on a woman's valuing of caring and relationship and that women should not be judged by male standards. Men make moral judgments based on justice and fairness while women value interpersonal aspects of care, concern, and connection. Like many of the psychoanalytic feminists, Gilligan accentuates difference: Male psychology is traced as a progression toward separation and individuality while female development progresses toward greater connectedness and intimacy in the search for identity. What she objects to is using the former as a yardstick of mental health for the latter.[25]

While Gilligan's and Miller's work marked a shift away from the prevailing theories that viewed female experience only in terms of male development and found it inherently inferior, they nevertheless supported certain ways of thinking that tend to reinforce the notion that men and women are "essentially" different rather than having different experiences based on the ways that the split image makes them think about themselves. In their view, men are defined by the need for autonomy and women by the need for attachment. Yet we know that men crave intimacy as much as women and women crave autonomy as much as men. Issues of relationship and connection versus autonomy and differentiation are more *culturally determined*. Men more easily achieve the illusion of autonomy because it has been more culturally expedient for them to do so. Women are more focused on attachment because they've had to be to survive.

In the same way that the split image had created a seeming polarization between relatedness and autonomy in women, newer theories of female development tend to heighten a sense of polarization between women and men, between male qualities and female ones. The more we think in terms of dichotomies of experience, the more we think of ourselves as split.

As psychologists Rachel Hare-Mustin and Jean Marecek point out in their book, *Making a Difference*, "The emphasis on gender roles . . . obscures the commonalities between women and men. The masculine ideal of autonomy may be well out of reach for women, but it may be unattainable for men as well."[26]

By the eighties, the focus of psychoanalytic and psychological debate about love had shifted from a focus on individual development to an exploration of the dynamics of interaction. The language of subjects and objects became less current, at least in some areas of clinical study. Psychoanalytic feminist Jessica Benjamin could talk about concepts of intersubjectivity and could assert that the mother is not just an object or a mirror reflecting the self of the child, that there is a mutual system of response that builds a relationship between the two.[27] Yet the relationship with the mother was still held to be critical to the development of all relatedness in the family. It was still assumed that the female knows herself in a relational context while the male develops identity through a process of separation from relatedness. Much of the popular psychoanalytic feminist literature still pointed to early relationships with the mother as critical to love and self-love in women.

Finally, family systems theory, the preeminent theory of intersubjectivity, entered the discourse and individual problems were viewed as problems within the whole system of family interaction. In systems theory there was no patient, no victim, no villain, but only a pattern of interaction that could be understood and changed by learning how the family thought and worked together to maintain it.[28]

On the face of it family therapy initially held out the promise of freeing us from the dominant love story. The theory seemed to get away from the notion that mothers and women were responsible for all the breakdowns of loving connection that can occur in a family. Everyone was assumed to have an equal and mutual impact on interaction. But examined through a feminist lens, family theory seemed to ignore one essential factor—the larger social environment of the family is defined by an inherent inequality of power between women and men. Mothers in families were still the ones being asked to change, and sometimes therapy conveyed a less than subtle message that they might still be responsible for certain breakdowns of family life.[29]

By not recognizing that males and females start out from very different places of status in the social hierarchy, family systems theory had inadvertently simply reinforced the dominant love story—a father has the power and mother is responsible for love.

GENDER WARS

Ultimately the love story told by psychology has now become focused around ideas about gender. The debate about whether women and men are more alike or "essentially" different has a profound impact on our sense of the meaning of love.[30] If men and women are viewed as different in the ways traditionally defined by psychology, then love will always be the "true" domain of women and work outside of relationship the "true" domain of men. If women are seen as only "relational" in nature and men as only autonomous, then a woman's sense of identity will always be confined by the split image. The Smiling Woman will always have a greater tendency to downplay and subordinate her more creative energies because the sense of agency and power they reflect are experienced as unacceptable. A man will always push away his need for relatedness and his capacities for nurturing behavior because he will experience those behaviors as undermining his power and dominance. The story of love as it's currently told helps us to avoid looking at the fact that it's to society's benefit to reinforce this way of looking at things because the story indirectly suggests that men and women can't change—that we are each prisoners of our natures. What this view does is perpetuate the imbalance of power and the devaluation of women. The current "men's movement" has capitalized on this notion of essential difference and encourages men to reclaim their masculine selves from the oppression of women's attempts to feminize them. While much of the connection with one another that men achieve in this effort is positive, unfortunately, these groups rarely take on harder questions about male status and inequities of power. They rarely question the meaning of love for a male in our culture.

It doesn't help to swing to the opposite extreme of overvaluing relationship more than agency and autonomy or to now overvalue femaleness instead of maleness.[31] What is important is to resolve the split—to know that we are all autonomous only within the context of connection—to create forms in which both men and women are equally relational and autonomous, both public and private workers. The workplace may need to become more homelike and the home may need to have more connection with a larger community as a part of its basic structure. These changes would require fundamentally new political and economic ideologies.

Once the love story changes, men and women can change, and once men and women change, the love story will change. We'll simply have to act more like we claim to feel—that women and men are equal and that love as agency is the domain of all of us equally.

RECOVERY BECOMES THE GURU OF LOVE

Psychological thinking and popular culture are intimately connected. One shapes and influences the other. In some strange interaction that evolved between the two, by the late seventies, the larger cultural story of love had taken a curious turn. While feminists were busy exposing the sexist bias of psychoanalysis yet still demonstrating that the mother was crucial in the evolution of the female's sense of self, while family therapists were busy charting family process, and while other branches of psychology were exploring personality development but still leaving open to question how different males and females might be, something called the recovery movement began to take hold of the popular imagination. It reflected a time in our society's popular relationship with psychology and mental health when people began to feel that self-help was more effective than institutionalized help in resolving certain life problems, most notably drug and alcohol addiction.

If the alcoholic in this story was predominantly the male, what was the woman's disease? She enabled, she loved too much. Love became the newest entry into the lexicon of addiction and disease, and if anybody suffered from this particular disease, it was women. What a curious shift in the love story. While once women couldn't love enough, when their entire value lay in their capacity to put themselves aside and love with purity and selfless devotion, now popular culture, in the guise of the codependency movement, was telling us that our problem is that we love incorrectly, too much, that we put ourselves aside too much.[32] In 1985, Robin Norwood published her bestselling book, *Women Who Love Too Much*,[33] and since that time the recovery movement has inadvertently taken on the mantle of woman-blaming. Just as the idealization of women as mothers in the early part of the century gave way to "momism" and mother blaming in the fifties and sixties, women's basic training to put themselves aside was recast by the codependency movement as the desire to control others and to avoid themselves. While it's assumed that men too may suffer from codependency, the basic definitions of codependent behavior sound curiously like the selfless object woman, the thing woman, that we had always been raised to be. Mary Kay Blakely was to write, in *Ms.* magazine, in 1988, "I was less than amazed to learn that media hearts were pumping over another book about women and love, given the tremendous amount of ink poured over women who love too much, not enough, make foolish choices or love men who hate them. With the possible exception of reshaping women's thighs, there is almost no cause approached more devotedly than straightening out the inept, misguided, unsatisfying ways women love men."[34]

It could be that as we began to hold men accountable for the abuses of power that their addictions supported, it was important to find a new way to implicate women as responsible for them. Now it was suggested that women could be labeled as "sick" because they loved in ways that "made" men abusive.

New language, same old story—whatever love is, women are responsible to take care of it, but since they're fundamentally inferior and inadequate, they never quite do it right. Not only are they responsible for love, but they are responsible for the behavior of others and if others behave badly, it means that it is women's fault for not loving well.

The unfortunate impact of the codependency movement is that our concepts of love became all the more confused. We began to think that somehow the need for connectedness was bad, that autonomy, once again, was a "higher" value. While the codependency movement may rightly comment on our training to love as object, it threw out the baby with the bath water and seemed to pathologize our need to love as subject as well. This new love story is just as disempowering as the old one. It suggests that there is some "ideal" way of loving that we have to aspire to, not that our ideas about love and the structures we have created for expressing it need to change.

Yet we seem only too willing to accept the mantle of dysfunction and codependent disease, as if constantly questioning what love is and not really knowing, it's easier to accept a negative definition of ourselves than to decide what love does mean to us.

What is more disturbing is our tendency to keep taking on the responsibility and blame for the unloving behavior of others toward us, even their abusive and controlling behavior. Perhaps one of the most frightening things we could admit to ourselves is the possibility that we are not *being* loved—that we have sold our souls and our lives for an illusion. The social structure that we live in is predicated on the assumption that if we give and sacrifice self, we are automatically loved and cared for ourselves. Yet as a group, women are devalued and disadvantaged, we are often on the losing side of our social contracts. We often give a great deal and get very little back. It is easier and less frightening to deny that we are abused, overpowered, and that love is often one-sided in our relationships. Better we think of ourselves as sick. Then we don't have to confront the men we feel dependent on for our sense of self, we don't have to hold them accountable. We tell ourselves, "He's a person too." We protect, try to be "loving" and understanding. In the process we keep ourselves victim-objects and nothing changes.

THE RETURN TO THE GODDESS

Since the seventies, women have been engaged in the difficult process of reclaiming their experience of love and creative power from the constricting framework offered by psychology and popular culture. But to reclaim an image of a woman of agency, to understand love as agency rather than caretaking, to overcome the pervasiveness of the split image has been difficult because at no time in history have women existed outside of the influence of the dominant narrative who could serve as models.[35]

On the social level, many of us have tried to imitate male models of agency and power. Our dominant focus has been to achieve equality in the domain of work and we have achieved only minimal success at this, and sometimes only minimal satisfaction. We keep assuming that somehow we can integrate love and work, yet since the unequal structure of society still traps us in the split image and since our social structures haven't changed sufficiently to support this, we suffer from conflicting pressures that leave both our relationships and our work lives and ultimately ourselves stressed and in conflict.[36] In the creative arena, we try to explore the lives of women who have achieved, but we also learn that to the degree that these stories are even available, that artists, writers, women of achievement are still undervalued and have had to make extreme personal sacrifices to support their creative work. Tillie Olsen points out that most women writers in the last century were unmarried, married late, were without children, or could relegate child care to household help.[37] Things have not been radically different for women writers or artists in this century.

So, failing to find any fertile social structure or environment for identifying a model for the woman of agency, many of us have looked to archetypal images to help restore or re-create a sense of ourselves. Writer Patricia Reiss, recognizing that her ideas of herself as a creator had always been based on male images, turns to the goddesses of the Paleolithic era to uncover a spiritual and artistic heritage. She tells the story of her quest for the Great Goddess.[38] More frequently, inspired by the work of Jean Bolen, we look to the goddesses of Greek and Roman mythology for archetypes of our essential femaleness and we particularly look to goddess imagery for ideas about what it means to love.[39] Our sense is that the goddess figures of myth and history can provide us with a model for reconnection to our essential femaleness, to those energies that are inherently female within us.

What is referred to as the "mythopoetic movement" is important to our reclaiming of feeling and identity and a sense of the sacredness and power of our own stories and patterns. But it's important to be aware that the goddess archetypes are not themselves totally outside the dominant story of women written by men. It was Jung who taught us about archetypes and Jung was both a male and an analyst. We might consider him as much the father of the split image as Freud, because he was clear that in dividing psychic representations of inner consciousness into *animus*, male, and *anima*, female, that the anima was always the dark side, the "unconscious" side, the passive side, the receptive side. Jung is as much a part of the story told about women as Freud and his description of the collective unconscious is as much dominated by stereotyped ideas about maleness and femaleness.[40]

When people embrace the Jungian view of human consciousness, the result is often a reinforcement of the kind of polarized, "essential difference" argument we mentioned earlier. Certain qualities are viewed as "essentially" feminine and others as "essentially" male. When a male enjoys or is highly competent at certain stereotypically "female" interests, we say that he has a very dominant female side and vice versa with women and "male" qualities. We view people as split personalities who walk around somewhat desperately trying to integrate what are viewed as the two polarized parts of their psyches. In the backlash against women's agency, critics define our current social problems as ones of women trying to be too male. Instead of assuming that men and women may have different ways of "expressing" universal emotions, experience, and capacities because of their cultural conditioning, we define maleness and femaleness as static, unalterable, predictable "innate" qualities.

As recently as 1988, for example, Dr. Toni Grant, a popular clinical psychologist, wrote a book called *Being a Woman*. Based on her understanding of Jungian psychology, she reinforces the notion that a woman's preoccupation and concern with love is valid and natural. "Biology *is* destiny," she claims. She believes feminism has failed us. A woman can experience true fulfillment of her femininity only when she is fully involved in a relationship with a man, with love, marriage, and family. She treats us to advice about reclaiming the capacity to catch and keep a man—the capacity to "find love." She tells us her book is "for every woman who wants a heightened understanding of her life and for every man who wants an expanded awareness of 'his' woman."[41] This is probably not the love story that we need to return to—men must be men and women, women—it is the Smiling Woman story reincarnated one more time.

So the search for our inherent femaleness in past myth and archetype may not serve us fully. What we propose is that women may need to have the courage to create a new myth—a vision of the woman of passion who taps the power of her vital, caring energy to achieve authorship of her own life, to express and create, and to forge new kinds of loving connections with others and the world around her.

LOVE, PSYCHOLOGY, AND LANGUAGE: MAINTAINING THE SPLIT

In its version of the story of love, psychology, as a discipline, was trying to define some objective knowledge or truth about human behavior and experience. The academic study of psychology is a relatively new phenomenon. It was only after the Industrial Revolution that there was a growing preoccupation with defining "true" knowledge as only what can be observed and proven through scientific study. It is considered a "romantic" notion to assume that there is some pattern of inner energy that can't be seen that is the stuff and substance of the self.[42] But it is equally the case that psychology as a scientific discipline is limited in terms of what it can actually "see" and prove in an objective sense about the nature of human experience. Logically, when psychology talks of love or tries to explain the intricacies of human bonding and care, or even human dysfunction, it's likely to present us, at the very least, with an incomplete picture. The capacity of human beings to love can never be adequately explained within the confines of psychological language. Moreover, psychology may describe what it sees, but it can't really tell us what that observation means. The power to create meaning lies within the person who has the experience.

The arrogance of psychology's attempt to explain and render scientific all of human behavior has caused us damage because in many ways it has been psychology that has robbed us of our passion. Samantha reminds us of this when she says, "I thought the relative absence of feeling was called maturity." Wanting to be "mature," she gave up the pet that she loved and replaced it with one that her husband thought would be a better idea. She could take care of the dog, but it was the cat she loved. She had lost her passion, all in the name of doing the right and "mature" thing.

The dominant theories of psychology do tell a story that discounts passion and the deeper pain and emotion of life. To respond to human emotion it has given us words like regressive, reactive, infantile, object choice, hysterical, histrionic, all attempts to turn what is full of feeling into some objective and controllable state. In family therapy terms we talk about fusion, lack of differentiation. As in most models of health that are based on male concepts of autonomy and individuation, the family therapist might talk of the differentiated person as one who functions unaffected by strong feeling.

As psychologist James Hillman is quoted as saying, "The language of psychology is an insult to the soul."[43]

So, psychology applied its "scientific" principles to the phenomenon of love and somehow the experience of love got lost.[44] Feeling, women's feeling in particular, was subdued and devalued. Culture lost a focus on passion. Love became an institution. We moved away from love as a phenomenon whose realm of study was the airy philosophies of a Plato or an Aristotle, or the passionate poetry of a Keats or a Shelley or a Wordsworth to a psychology of personality types that tried to objectify all feeling, particularly woman's.

The splitting of males into doers and females into feelers in our thought and language speaks to this need in our culture to deny feeling and hence meaning. If woman represents feeling, and if passion works to radicalize and change, then both must be subdued by the forces of patriarchy.

Men and women are not so different. Men feel deeply and women work, act, and create. But because the valued way of being in our culture is nonpassionate, we all suffer from the absence of a sense of what moves us. The result is that we go to movies in which we're treated to perversions of feeling, in which we see rampant and gratuitous violence, daily talk shows on TV in which we see the exploitation of intense feeling that is focused on blaming, humiliating, shaming, and making a circus of the worst extremes of human emotion. For lack of meaning, for lack of love, our popular culture infuses itself with junk feeling, in the same way we infuse the economy with junk bonds.

Our preoccupation with easy psychological explanations and recipes for all the complex emotional dilemmas of human existence has fed this creation of an emotional wasteland. We don't any longer pay attention to our own passion and our own pain. Instead of allowing ourselves to feel, we numb ourselves, we work, we exercise, we self-improve and we self-help. And the experience we have least understanding of and least idea how to direct in modern culture is the power of passion and of love.

Clearly, the split image doesn't affect only women—as a foundation for our thinking about human experience, it has shaped the progress of our ideas about love, about the relationships between men and women. Love is one casualty of our cultural mythology and creativity is the other. The image of the Smiling Woman tells the visible part of the story, her counterpart at the easel, the artist/worker, speaks to what is more hidden in female and cultural experience.

CHAPTER THREE

The Shadow of Her Smile

IN A RECENT ARTICLE on women and art in *Ms.* magazine, writer Arlene Raven was reflecting on images of smiling women. She mentions the Mona Lisa, Leonardo da Vinci's quintessential portrayal of woman. "Mona's smile shows no teeth or tongue, nothing moves. She is static and mute. These features pleased Leonardo so much that he revered Mona Lisa as the essence of womanhood . . ."[1] Later in the same article, Raven describes a modern Mona: "As I rested from my computer screen today, I turned to the 'Oprah Winfrey Show,' where a doctor had surgically turned up the lips of his wife into a perpetually pleasant smile."[2] Oprah and da Vinci are four centuries apart, but the Smiling Woman lives.

This image of women smiling has been peering out at us from the background of history. In some eras it dominates, in others it recedes. Popular culture both creates and reinforces the image and sometimes what looks like change is only the deceptive retreat into shadow.

The Mona Lisa smile tells only one part of the story of woman as object. The rest is hidden behind the smile in the untold stories of women's struggles to own their creative power and to express agency and generativity in their lives. What can be discerned of women's subjectivity emerges in bits of our social history recovered by feminist scholars. Psychological theory sheds light on one aspect of women's subordination, but cultural, economic, and political history all contribute important evidence of the impact of women's blocked creativity.

HIDDEN STORIES: THE SMILING WOMAN CREATES

Since women have been defined psychologically by their capacity for relational love, the range of their creative power has been a well-kept secret. The topic has been largely erased from the cultural narrative. Historically, female creativity was assumed not to exist, even when the evidence for it stood in plain view. For years, aspects of gender and creativity weren't even examined. In the fifties creativity was briefly a research topic because when the economy was expanding, the government wanted to see if women had skills that could be used to maximize economic growth potential. But the research efforts of that era dismissed women as more interested in their families. Psychologist Ravenna Helson concludes that this outcome tells us more about women's conformity to the love narrative than it does about their creative abilities.[3]

And yet women have always created and been present in the production of culture, but never in a starring or even obvious role. As the title of Germaine Greer's book, *The Obstacle Race*, suggests, the path of the creative woman has been fraught with difficulties not faced by men. Even as women reclaim the capacity to make their art visible in the world, the male narrative often co-opts it. Female creative productions are often referred to disparagingly as "women's art." Men presume the power to comment on, criticize, and ascribe meaning to women's work. Women's creations are relegated to a separate but unequal sphere, the importance of what they produce is trivialized. There is "folk art" and then there is "fine art." There is art that is public and there is art that is private and domestic. Quilting, crafting, needlework, the private, domestic arts are rarely valued for the quality of the artistic and creative energy that goes into producing them.[4] As Greer says, "Women have always excelled in the production of the 'merely' beautiful, remarkable for fineness, delicacy, elegance, small work taking up little space, much time in its making and no duration in its observation."[5]

In the complex interaction between love and creative energy, the real truth is that women's creativity was and often is co-opted by family or romantic love. Before the nineteenth century, women seldom expressed their generative energy. They were essentially extensions of men, their models, assistants, objects for male artists to utilize. Nearly all pre-nineteenth-century women painters were related to male artists, since no other women had any practical opportunity to find training. Women's creativity was validated only if it mirrored the male art that was the standard of greatness. Artists' daughters made copies of art, prepared materials and engraved work. Often the best male students of great artists would marry their mentors' daughters so that the artistic legacy would be "owned" within the family. The wives then trained male children but not daughters to paint.[6] "Daughters were ruled by love and loyalty; they were more highly praised for virtue and sweetness than for their talent, and they devalued their talent accordingly."[7]

It became commonplace for women artists to fall in love with their male art teachers. If the infatuation developed into an affair, often women were completely absorbed and the relationships were generally dominated by the artistic personality of the male partner.[8] This may explain why many women artists had their work ascribed to men. For instance, the sculptor Camille Claudel's work was ascribed to Rodin.

This trend isn't confined to the arts. The *New York Times*, as recently as 1990, reported that the theory of relativity may actually have been developed by Einstein's wife.[9] It is Erik Erikson, not his wife Joan, who is remembered for his contributions to developmental psychology. Greer tells us of artist Frida Kahlo: "As it did for many women, a desire for art led her to the artist; creativity was personified in the master and she was prepared to build her life around him and dedicate her art to her love."[10]

Or as Tillie Olsen says, "Remember the young women writers, their aspirant lives clogged in Love's ambuscade—those who let their work go in the belief that they would become one of the tradition-hallowed 'inspirer-beloved'; and those who had every intention of going on writing—and tried; both usually subsumed into the server-enablers; wives; mothers of children."[11]

It's little wonder that the story of the smiling, passive woman dominates the picture of female experience. Woman as artist/worker has been given no narrative line, her story has not been told or even explored. For a woman, biology was to be destiny, creativity confined to the reproduction of the race.

Women have had to unearth their own creativity stories and it has taken at least two decades for feminist scholars to begin to do this. Tillie Olsen writes about women's silence in literature, Greer, Chadwick, Munro about art.[12] A recent history of women's music by Christine Ammer is titled *Unsung*, referring to our meager awareness of women composers.[13]

We could as easily have focused on the accepted story of women in music (patrons not composers), the story of women in theater (performers not playwrights), or the story of women in literature (muses not authors). Or we might have focused on women in science

(Madame Curie), women in business (other kinds of madams), or women attorneys (Katharine Hepburn relinquishing power for love with Spencer Tracy in *Adam's Rib*). They are all stories whose major characters are either in hiding or, if central protagonists, openly tainted with suspicion of ruthlessness, masculinity, wanton sensuality, desperate loneliness, madness, or, worst of all, triviality. The feminist scholarship that is rewriting them reads like a detective story. "Who killed Athena and Aphrodite, goddesses of intellect, career, passion, and the arts?"[14]

Often the stories we do hear are only those of exceptional women, the Georgia O'Keeffes, Golda Meirs, and Lillian Hellmans. As former Representative Bella Abzug (D-NY) has been quoted as saying "We don't so much want to see a female Einstein become an assistant professor. We want a woman schlemiel to get promoted as quickly as a male schlemiel."[15]

AGAINST ALL ODDS

The absence of a narrative about women's creativity sets the stage for invisible or vanishing aspirations. The woman who does persist in expressing herself creatively despite cultural prohibitions does so in the face of ongoing discrimination. Families, schools, and the workplace continue to select and encourage males in their creative pursuits. Training opportunities more often go to men, male children are more often viewed as being specially talented. In one study, when daughters scored in the ninety-eighth percentile on performance in math, the parents usually attributed the score to the girls' "hard work." But to the male child they said, "You're working hard and you're so talented." Inevitably the daughter comes away with less self-confidence in her native talent and ability.[16]

The qualities necessary for passionate possibility in either love or creativity aren't fostered in women. We're taught to be passive, submissive, dependent, and traits like courage, risk-taking, love of solitude, nonconformity are considered taboo. More serious are the economic limitations most women face and the prohibitions against anger, separateness, all intense feeling, and the desire to take oneself seriously.

Finally, a woman who tries to create and relate will still face the burden of society's belief that she should be the principal care giver. She will face the absence of institutional support, child care, elder care, flex time, paternity leave, all those political changes that would suggest that the responsibility for care is one to be shared with male partners. As quilter Susan Schroeder tells us in *The Quiltmaker's Art*, "I needed a medium that could be taken up at will as I cared for my baby."[17] Most pervasive is our fear as women that if we create it necessarily means that we *lose* the possibility for relatedness.

HIDDEN CREATIVITY, LOST PASSION

When we question why one half of our experience has been rendered in the foreground while the other is relegated to the shadows, we have to understand ourselves in the context of history and culture. Story builds on story. What we tell ourselves about our own values, feelings, abilities can't be separated from the trends and currents of popular social constructions of reality. We are the products of our history and of the current social mores that tell us how to think about our lives. In both those arenas, images and metaphors of women as lovers rather than creators dominate and fix us in certain patterns of thinking and behaving.

We think of the story of Carol Smith, a woman caught between eras, a child who came of age in the sixties whose mother handed down an older version of the split experience. Freer than her mother, Carol was nevertheless inducted by the Smiling Woman image. We were particularly struck by her story of lost passion.

Forty years after Virginia Woolf had created the characters of Mrs. Ramsey and Lily Briscoe in *To the Lighthouse*, Carol sat in a college library writing an essay about Virginia Woolf and about that novel. She was a graduate student in English literature at the time. She remembers vividly her passion for what she was doing. Literature had always been her "first love"—her dream was to become a college professor.

But at that moment, the cultural myth of love undermined the passion. A nagging voice took hold in her mind. The voice said, "But what good does it do anyone for me to be sitting in a library writing learned papers about a dead author? What about all the real problems out there in the world?"

It might have been the clarity of the split image in Woolf's work or some other hidden influence, but in that moment Carol told herself that what she loved to do had no meaning because it was not about the needs of other people. She made a choice that was to shape the course of the next twenty years of her life. She left graduate school, married, and became a specialist in child development. Ultimately, though it gave her a sense of connection to "the real problems" of people, her work never really satisfied: She had lost her creative passion.

Carol finished college in the early seventies, a time when the women's movement had begun to make its impact felt, a time when she had already begun to read the literature of "awakening" from the bonds of love as it had been constructed for us by centuries of cultural narrative. So why, as it had for so many women of that era, did the split image remain fixed in Carol's psyche? How is it that the mandate to love in traditionally female ways became stronger than the passion to do the work that she loved to do?

Carol, as a young woman in her twenties, lived in an era of change, but she had developed her most critical ideas about herself during a time, the late forties and early fifties, when ideas about love were deeply nostalgic and conformist. Those ideas were reinforced by a family structure that in turn was founded on the need for conformity, the need for women to retreat from any autonomy they might have gained during the war years back to the domestic sphere. Indeed, when asked about her mother's life, Carol recalled that her mother had been a very traditional housewife who had been entirely controlled by her father. Her life had been focused around the needs of her family. Carol says, "One time I remember asking my mother about a couple who lived down the street who had no children. I suppose I wanted to know if it was alright to be married and childless. 'Those people are very selfish,' she said."

When it came to the prevailing story about love in her life, Carol had learned that love meant love of family, love of children, love of a man. It was little wonder that at twenty, when she could say to herself, "literature is my first love," that passion had to be put aside. It must have seemed that to remain loyal to that passion would have been like being a partner in her mother's definition of a childless marriage—selfish. For lack of any different way of thinking about love, for want of a different story, Carol had assumed that relational love was more valuable and more important than creative passion.

The story Carol's mother had heard about love was the story of woman as object. By the time she heard it that story had already been embellished and sanctioned by the long arm of psychiatry and psychological theory. And in the time that intervened between Carol's mother's childhood and Carol's, the image of the Smiling Woman had already emerged and receded and emerged again in the peculiar dialectical pattern that has dominated our social history.

Exploring the Dialectic of Love

While the basic themes of the love story remained consistent and embedded in women's minds, the roles of women from the turn of the century to the present have evolved in a curious dialectical process that brings the split image into sharper relief. An emphasis on love and family yields to an emphasis on self, and an emphasis on self returns full cycle to an emphasis on love and family.

We do well to remember that it was only in the twenties, some seventy years ago, fewer years than a lifetime for some of us, that women were granted the right to vote. Women also entered the work force in great numbers in the twenties and an emerging image of female independence held sway.[18]

By the end of the twenties, there began to be a renewed emphasis on domesticity, although women continued to go to work during the thirties and forties. By the fifties, domesticity had become the prevailing image of a woman's role one more time and women went back home. This back and forth movement sounds remarkably like the beginning of the nineties, when women, after a hard-won fight in the seventies and eighties to enter formerly male-dominated professions, then set their careers aside to follow the "mommy track," or to have children later in life.

In the years that intervened between the twenties and nineties the world saw another dialectical movement that affected men and women equally. The bland conformity of the forties and fifties gave way to the angry turbulence of rapid social change that was a hallmark of the sixties and seventies.[19]

This change and counter change, movement forward and movement back, however, represents relative movement within a historical box that imposed certain limits. Change in women's roles could only go so far: Woman still could not construct her experience as subject. Movements toward independence for married women were framed as "You're lucky that he 'let you do that.' " The rules prescribing women's roles could be tampered with, altered, somewhat departed from, but there was still no question who made the rules, and even whose language described the experience. Change seemed defined primarily by economic expedience. Whenever the economy needed workers, women could leave the house. Whenever the economy faltered, women were sent back home.

By the nineties a woman could vote, she could enter the corporate boardroom, have one-woman shows of her work or see her novels, poetry, essays published by major media giants. But the appearance of change was greater than the reality of change. She still wasn't elected to office in great numbers, still hadn't passed the "glass ceiling" to become CEO very often, nor did she command the prices of a Rauschenberg or a Picasso for her art. And by the nineties what she still could not do was walk the streets safe from male violence, become president, or even take for granted her right to control her own body or the law enforcement that would guarantee the payment of her child support. She could not see a popular film in which her experience was represented fairly or in a way consistent with the subjective experience of her life. She was hard-pressed to free herself from the guilt, conflict, and shame of not smiling. What she still could not do was claim to have any knowledge of her own of what it meant to love.

So the image of a Smiling Woman cast its shadow over every apparent change in women's roles, even when the figure at the easel seemed to move into the foreground. Each era dominated by the smile tended to be followed by one in which women struggled more forcefully to assert their creative control.

It was in the forties and fifties, the era of Carol's childhood and her mother's coming of age, that women were perhaps most powerfully co-opted by the mandate to smile. There are very few of us who weren't affected by the fifties portrayals of the Smiling Woman, in fact most of us, like Carol, grew up in families where she was the mother. It is toward this fifties version of society's ideas about womanhood that the dialectic currently swings in the backlash against women's subjectivity.

REINFORCING THE SPLIT IMAGE

The forties and fifties were decades that followed the Depression. Jobs were scarce and there was resistance by both men and women to the idea that a woman's role should include work outside the home. As the Depression deepened, the media pressured women who had previously been in the work force to "go home" and be wives again. Married women who worked were looked on with hostility—they were taking jobs away from men. The nuclear family came to be idealized as it had in Victorian times as a place of refuge from the harsh realities of the outside world.[20]

But World War II intervened and suddenly, instead of "Stay home" the message to women shifted to "Go to work." Rosie the Riveter became the popular media image of the female who was now the woman behind the man with the gun—she was suddenly woman as worker, but this was work for a cause, not work of her own.[21]

The fact that women were now called on to work and that many liked it created massive conflict in the popular mind. The number of working wives doubled during the war.[22] Women's aspirations became a growing social problem—many didn't want to go back to working at home. It seemed important to reinforce the message that even though women were now visible in the public sphere, love and home were still more important. Social attitudes didn't change, and the cultural discourse remained the same. "In a *Fortune* survey . . . most Americans accepted female labor force participation if it did not conflict significantly with wifely or maternal duties."[23] The experience of being subject for woman became "an unavoidable, if temporary expedient."[24] By '45, as the war was nearly over, media propaganda began to support a shift back to domestic life. The sexual division of labor was back.[25]

Split attitudes expressed in popular culture were most visible in the movies of the time. Patriotic women were seen keeping the home fires burning, and bravely learning to live in a world without men. They were shown as nurses, and women in combat, as courageous war widows.

And some women were portrayed as subjects. Films like *The Corn Is Green*, *When Ladies Meet*, *Lady in the Dark*, and *Take a Letter, Darling*, with Bette Davis, Joan Crawford, Ginger Rogers, and Rosalind Russell, finally depicted women as novelists, business executives, and advertising moguls. *However, the central point of conflict in all these career women films was still love.* It was clear that women's divided energies still weighed most heavily in the direction of love, home, family.

If women were reminded during the war that love was still more important than work, after the war images of women increasingly reinforced a return to their traditional roles. The marriage rate and the birth rate soared, and the years 1945–57 were the height of the baby boom. The term "homemaker" was coined to keep the smiling woman smiling, to dignify residence in the private sphere.

Writer Joan Ellis notes, "Women were silent and dutiful in the postwar wealth as their husbands worked and they stayed at home to raise the children. Women were enablers, nurturers, and teachers."[26]

The baby boom, the suburbs, and the corporate culture of the fifties were also the guarantors of the prevailing pattern for a woman's life. Babies kept her home, the suburbs kept her isolated, and the corporate culture determined not only her husband's work life, but where the family lived. The American Dream was an ideal of domestic life that was heterosexual, middle class, suburban, and family centered.

Music as well as film reinforced the traditional love story. Song lyrics conveyed a clear message that love was the meaning of life. A woman did her job but just until love came along. In song, a woman was longing for a man, meeting a man, enjoying being a girl, wandering about talking to the trees about love, having her heart clang, wandering through orchards in a film of cherry blossoms and love, or sitting on a bench in the same apple orchard being true to her man.[27] The Smiling Woman was in her prime.

It was during this period that the institution of the "family" reemerged as the dominant form for the expression of love. Nobody questioned the form itself. Its rigidity ordained a kind of imprisonment for women in which they were to have lesser social status and importance than the men they supposedly loved. As a culture we were only too willing to stress and dismantle this idealized social form when it was expedient—we would send fathers off to war, men would send other men off to work away from families in support of our nationalistic and capitalistic goals. The family could change forms when there was good reason for it to. But women's needs, their ideas of love and creative choice were never a good enough reason. Their role was to stay in their place. Women may have had the vote, but we never really had a choice.

ONLY MEN HAVE THE WINGS FOR ART

The forties, the fifties, and the entire post–World War II period saw the emergence of an American avant-garde in art. Abstract expressionism began to take hold. It was the height of what is called modernism, the age when we still believed in absolute values and a pure aesthetic. Before then, during the Depression of the thirties, American artists had started to formulate a social role for the visual arts. Several women artists, such as Lee Krasner, Louise Nevelson, and Alice Neel first got their financial support from programs supported by government patronage.[28] According to one author, during the thirties there was "extensive public hostility toward working women but there was also government patronage for artists."[29]

Temporarily it was as if the belief that women couldn't be creative, which had persisted since Freud and before, was suspended. Necessity was the mother of invention. Just as World War II had offered employment opportunities for women in the early forties, the Depression offered an entrée for women into the art world by government funded projects. But when the Depression was over the story changed.

Artist Lee Krasner's career exemplifies some of the shifts back and

forth from woman as subject/artist to woman as object/wife. Lee Krasner was already an artist in her own right when she became Jackson
Pollock's wife, meeting him in 1941 and marrying him in 1945. As she
had to move from the world of government supported nondiscriminatory art projects to that of private galleries and dealers there was a
corresponding transition in the art world's view of her. The image of
"Mrs. Pollock/wife overshadowed Lee Krasner/painter in New York's
art world."[30] Once nondiscriminatory government support ended for
the arts in the 1940s and 1950s, Krasner and her colleagues confronted the widely held view that women couldn't paint. Freud's dis-
ciple, Havelock Ellis, said "only men had the wings for art." And the
highest compliment Hofmann, a noted painting teacher, had for his
women students echoed Ellis: "This painting is so good you'd never
know it was done by a woman."[31]

After Krasner and Pollock had a joint exhibition in 1949 entitled
"Man and Wife," the negative reviews and the experience were such
that Krasner did not exhibit again for two years, and she destroyed
many of her own paintings. One can only assume that she was devastated and temporarily renounced the part of the split image that was
herself as artist. Elaine de Kooning, another important woman artist
married to a noted male artist, Willem de Kooning, had a similar
dilemma. Eventually both Krasner and Elaine de Kooning signed
their works only with initials in an effort to avoid being labeled "feminine."[32]

The critical reaction to many important women artists of the
period was to trivialize their contributions, thereby establishing a different way of talking about their art. O'Keeffe and other earlier women
artists were spoken of only in terms of the special category established
by the art world as "feminine" art. This attempt to marginalize women
artists by establishing special categories of criticism for their work had
its parallels in literary criticism, music criticism, and all other arenas of
female artistic expression.

So the shape of a woman's life in the forties and fifties, even that
of the woman artist, most potentially subject in her own life, was still
inexorably molded into the model of a woman devoted to home and
family. The attempt at reconciling the split image was powerfully
expressed by Louise Bourgeois's "femme-maison" paintings, first ex-
hibited in 1947. They are paintings with houses perched on top of
women's bodies in place of heads. Critics of the time said that the
paintings affirmed a "natural" identification between women and
home. Chadwick says, "In these disquieting works, domesticity, im-
aged through blank facades and small windows, defines women but
denies them speaking voices."[33]

FROM CONFORMITY TO RAPID CHANGE

We mark the sixties as the point in our collective history when things began to change. They were a turbulent and chaotic time in this country, characterized by assassinations, war, and urban riots. With the seventies came a wave of new movements: consumerism, environmentalism, and feminism. Inflation and unemployment rates went up, as well as the divorce rate. The traditional form of family was challenged and began to crack. The term "displaced homemakers" was coined as women were forced for the first time to find work outside the home in the wake of the high rates of divorce.

Women emerged from the conformist fifties into these turbulent times to face the issues raised by second-wave feminists. The split image began to change dimensions as self-expression and independence, equality in the work place, all became issues of concern to women in certain segments of the society. Yet change was not very far-reaching in terms of the cultural narrative. Except for a much publicized and reviled group of feminist separatists, and "political lesbians," women were still expected to incorporate self-expression and self-direction within their relational lives.

The sixties and seventies marked the beginnings of what was thought of as sexual and political liberation for women. Sexual freedom became a new norm. Women were encouraged to reclaim their sexuality from the inaccuracies of male psychological dogma. The myth of the vaginal orgasm was replaced by the celebration of the clitoral orgasm. Many of us turned from a preoccupation with romance or mothering to social activism. We insisted on our status as rightful owners of our own bodies and our own sexuality. Yet the conventional love story really didn't change significantly—free love meant only free sex, and the minute a woman succumbed to the traditional structure of marriage, she became once again an object, a mother, a wife, guilty and oppressed.

In fact, sexuality in the form of pornography became the heightened forum for the new exploitation and objectification of women. It was a curious return right back to the biological determinism of Freud—a woman was a body. The sixties spawned encounter groups, casual sex, hot tubs, and decreased privacy; what films of the time depicted of women's changing experience was increased nudity, porno, and prostitution. Some would claim that the new sexual liberation on film was symptomatic of a new intimacy. But others would argue that the sexual revolution led to a kind of cultural alienation. On film we saw characters who were sexual but not sensual, emotionless and devoid of romance. The love story seemed obsolete.[34]

By the end of the seventies, powered by the feminist movement, women's energies were forging new patterns. Some women demanded the chance to integrate their own inner vision with the challenge of actualizing that vision in the public arena. The Smiling Woman image became part of a collage of identities that began to blend relational energy with the energy of a heightened sense of self, the energy of a woman who had begun to be the subject of her own life.

But predictably the social dialectic swung back. The swing was once again influenced by economics and by crisis. Yuppies who sought achievement and personal success in a material culture replaced hippies. The AIDS crisis slowly gained more media attention as the epidemic reached further.[35] In the backlash gays and lesbians became at once more visible and vocal about their rights and more harassed and reviled as a threat to the "family" and standardized notions of love. In the face of increasing challenge to the traditional love discourse, the political tide turned back to fundamentalist notions of family, home, church, even though the conveyors of those values generally failed miserably to live up to them themselves.

The eighties were called the era of greed, the height of the "me" generation as the "baby boomers" came into their own. Fitness centers spread across the country and addiction and recovery from addiction became big business. Self-help groups based on the Twelve Steps of Alcoholics Anonymous proliferated. In this growing climate of consumerism and crisis, and a "have it all" mentality, women gained increasing visibility in the public world but their contributions were still less valued economically and there was no corresponding increase in men's presence in the private sphere of the home. No one could decide whether the changing roles of women were good or bad, but when in doubt, the tendency was to try to push them back to the way they were.

America elected Ronald Reagan just as the rapid social changes of the sixties and seventies were peaking. Reagan's election marked a return to traditional values and a vision of a Rockwellian America.[36] We watched Nancy Reagan "stand by her man" and suddenly, the shadow of a smile crept into our collective consciousness one more time. While women were gaining ground in the public domain we were also fed images of the good woman who embraced "family values" once again as she stood smiling adoringly up at the "Gipper."

For women, the split image was more split than ever. The pull to return to the forms of the past was and continues to be seductive. In fact women, even those who had benefited from the liberation achieved for them by the women's movement, began to reject the definition of themselves as "feminists." Having gained a measure of subjectivity, there was a growing trend among women to depoliticize it. Fearing that the term "feminist" really means "man hating," many women of substantial power and achievement were rejecting what they viewed as the implications of polarization between men and women on a private, personal level that "feminism" seemed to suggest. Mayumi Oda, a highly successful Japanese-American artist whose work focuses heavily on goddess imagery and concern with female images and archetypes, says, "I do not consider myself a feminist, but I believe in the strength and vitality of the female. . . . The reason that I could not become completely involved in women's liberation during the sixties and seventies was that I found their attitude was to blame men and society. Society has mistreated women for many thousands of years. I felt that men themselves were mistreated too. Rather than blaming the problem on others, we can find our resources and strength in ourselves."[37]

Few of us realize that it is the way society is structured, the way attitudes about women are structured, that is the problem and that those structures were created and defined by men. If to be feminist means simply to believe in the equality of women, then we cannot afford to forget the source of the problem. The solution is not a return to old forms, but the radical work of creating new ones. Finding our resources and our strength within ourselves is only part of the job, because much of the problem lies outside of us.

THE CURRENT STATUS OF THE STORY

In the decade of the nineties, women fortunate enough to be free of certain economic and class constraints have more options, more choices, and do not have to feel the intense conflict between love and creativity that characterized the lives of women in earlier decades.

In the arts, women have made visible but still limited gains. In 1969, when New York's Whitney Museum Annual opened, only 8 of the 143 artists represented were women.[38] There is now a feminist movement in the arts known as "the Women's Action Coalition," but women artists are still grossly underrepresented in major museums, and their art still sells for substantially less than men's.[39]

In the mid-seventies two comprehensive surveys of American music listed just one woman composer. In a recent personal conversation, a music writer for the *New York Times* was ruminating on why there still were so few important women composers. Even a 1991 book entitled *Feminine Endings: Music, Gender, and Sexuality*[40] has been accused of so marginalizing women composers as to make them "virtually invisible."[41]

It wasn't until 1981 that there was even a published history of women in American theater. However, women playwrights seem to have fared a little better than artists and composers. Today most theatergoers recognize the names of Wendy Wasserstein, Caryl Churchill, Tina Howe, and Marsha Norman. But they are still not the big money-makers on Broadway.

Ostensibly, women's film since the late sixties has explored a broader range of female experience. Films like *Personal Best*, *Entre Nous*, and *Desert Hearts* deal with the complex relationships between women. More recently, *Thelma and Louise* and *Fried Green Tomatoes* comment on women's struggles to find and be themselves outside the domain of male power and oppression. But David Geffen, producer of *Personal Best*, denied that it was a lesbian film as did the producers of *Entre Nous*. The lesbian relationship was minimized in *Fried Green Tomatoes*. And *Thelma and Louise* provoked outrage among both men and women for its antimale message, although it was a box-office hit.

Women's humor seems to have come into its own. "Murphy Brown," "Designing Women," and "Roseanne," have replaced "I Love Lucy," and Edith Bunker in "All in the Family." But Dan Quayle tried to make Murphy Brown's single parenthood a major campaign issue in 1992 presidential politics. As Regina Barreca says in her book *They Used To Call Me Snow White ... But I Drifted*, women's humor can be used strategically as a weapon against the powerful and privileged. If Dan Quayle had a fit about Murphy Brown, what might he do with the following Elayne Boosler routine (as quoted by Barreca)?

"When Elayne Boosler talks about the right-to-lifers' attitudes: 'You ever notice that the same people who are against abortion are for capital punishment? Typical fisherman's attitude, throw 'em back when they're small and kill 'em when they're bigger.' "[42]

Women's creativity has begun to take on solid form, to emerge from behind the shadows of the split image. And yet most of us still feel fractured. We are unclear about our right to a self that owns the subjective power of a man, the power to be generative and to produce something new. We don't know whether we are subject or object, whether we can sing our own songs at the top of our lungs or whether our self is most whole only when ours is the supportive voice in a composition of someone else's making. We struggle daily with paradoxes and juxtapositions, never knowing fully who we are or what we are to be and do. Do we focus on self or other, doing or caring, creating or loving, knowing or feeling? When we love, do we do it out of choice, as subject, or do we love out of a reactive anxiety about not being a Smiling Woman?

These juxtapositions and divisions of experience are part of the socially constructed state of being a woman. They are not our personal conundrums, failures of our individual psyches. History has posed particular problems for us, it has ordained this split. Today perhaps more than ever, we have the tools at hand to begin to reconcile it. But it has not always been so, and the path to our current level of consciousness has been fraught with peril.

The cultural story is one that forbids women access to power, the split functions to maintain the status quo. Love as nurture and creative expression combined is a powerful force. Should women continue to shape it more in their own image, the balance of power in the world might shift. As women integrate more subjectivity they change.

But as Susan Faludi tells us, there will be no progress forward for women without a "backlash" that tells us to go back home to the traditional pattern ordained for women's lives.[43]

True, the shape of a woman's life has begun to change. Increasingly, we have had models of women who have big lives of their own while still struggling with relationships.

But the shadow of the Smiling Woman is still there, embedded in our psyches. The image of the nurturer as the dominant definition of "woman" still has impact and still emerges as a major theme in the cultural story. We have only to look around us to see to what degree society is still uncomfortable with any change in women's roles and definitions of themselves.

The statistics on the incidence of violence against women tell part of the story. They are staggering and a symptom of the backlash against women who begin to think in terms of their own power. The Anita Hill/Clarence Thomas hearings, the whole issue of sexual harassment, tell more of the story. So does the acquittal of William Kennedy Smith on charges of rape. In current films we see little but violent, gratuitous slaughter, as if the notion of love were some anachronism left over from the peace fests of the hippie generation. Each day now threatens women with the loss of hard-won rights, specifically the right to make choices about their own bodies.

The nineties reflect the ongoing changes, the dialectic pulls of the love and creativity story and its corresponding attitudes toward women in popular culture. The messages are no less contradictory than they have been since the turn of the century—have a self, but stay in your place.

CHAPTER FOUR

The Subject Is Herself

WITH STORIES OF FEMALE CREATIVITY SO HIDDEN, with passion so suppressed in our lives, it's hard to imagine that most of us could have the courage to define and pursue what moves us. Women can't begin to think of change if they have no access to the stories of women who have challenged cultural stereotype and dared to shape their own lives. It's only by seeing what a woman has really experienced in the depths of her subjective pain that we understand the constraints of her life and the meanings she secretly gives to her own experience. It's only through having this kind of access that we can feel connection, empathy, and identification. The kind of courage it takes to fight convention and define what makes one feel passionate can't happen in isolation. We need the supportive voices of our peers to make our own stronger. Until the development of feminist scholarship and the new perspective we gained during the women's movement, we didn't really have a context for understanding our own experience because women's stories could not be told and they equally could not be heard.

REWRITING THE STORY, BREAKING THE SILENCE

What feminist scholars have learned as they've begun to reclaim the stories of women from the dominant cultural discourse in the past two decades is that the forms of storytelling available to us were never really adequate to the task of recording women's lives accurately.[1]

Even the *manner and style* of women's speaking has been proscribed and limited. Women's autobiography is an example. According to Carolyn Heilbrun, before 1973 women's autobiographies recorded idealized lives. Women spoke the language of the Smiling Woman. This was the case because women were denied anger and the public expression of power. "If one is not permitted to express anger or even to recognize it within oneself, one is, by simple extension, refused both power and control. . . . If women did write of the real pain and anger of their lives, their text might be criticized as shrill and strident or partaking of too much "feminist ideology."[2] Virginia Woolf's *Three Guineas* was dismissed for its angry tone, but Woolf, one of the few, went on to publish real stories despite the criticism.

The fact that women couldn't express certain feelings publicly explains the great popularity of journal writing. But if we operate within a certain set of public constraints, it's possible that we won't even express our deepest feelings to ourselves. Fear of criticism and self-criticism limit us. According to Heilbrun, accomplishment and achievement do not dominate the narratives of women. Even May Sarton, the famed journalist, published one journal in 1968 and in 1973 published another that integrated all the anger and despair she had left out the first time. Both books deal with the same period of her life.[3]

Most significant is that women feel constrained from speaking about themselves without linking their identity to the presence of some "other." Unless it's within the context of relationship, many women don't feel able to write openly about themselves, they don't feel *entitled* to take themselves seriously. What this describes is the process by which women find it difficult to be subject in their own lives.

In chapters 2 and 3 we've outlined the themes that are the backdrop for women's stories in this book. The larger "discourse" of cultural history has created the illusion of a split in women's experience. Because of it, women tend to think and speak in terms of self *versus* other, love *versus* creativity. Everything we know from working with women in therapy reinforces our belief that this sense of divided identity permeates women's stories about themselves. It shapes their beliefs about love, and it shapes their sense of freedom to express themselves creatively. It has a profound impact on the degree to which we can own our passions and direct our lives in response to them.

The purpose of our study was to hear what women had to say about these issues. We hoped that we were creating the potential for a different story to emerge, one that could shed some light on the ways women struggle to define their own lives.

THE STORY OF OUR STUDY

Our process in developing this project started out split, we ourselves perhaps still victims of the split image. We thought of writing first on love, then on creativity, two separate books. We were fascinated by both aspects of women's experience and wanted to look at them from a new perspective—how did women think about love in their lives and then what did it mean to them to be creative? After lengthy discussions with friends and colleagues, we realized that the real question that we were posing lay in the relationship between the two—that for women, one could not look at creativity without looking at the ways that it was impacted by our thinking about love.

Once we decided to pair the subjects of love and creativity, we talked to almost every woman we met about the passions of their lives. A night clerk at a motel told us about her passion for writing children's stories, and for making handmade dolls out of old wedding gowns and the brocades of old curtains. When magazine interviewers called to interview us, we would turn the tables and also interview them. We talked to our aunts, our mothers, our sisters, our friends, our clients, waitresses in restaurants, women we saw perform, women in our workshops, over lunch, on breaks. Always we were asking, "Did you have an early passion that you put away? What happened? If you had all the money and all the talent in the world, what would you have been, what was your secret dream, your greatest passion? Who was your first love? Tell us your love story."

We saturated ourselves with women's stories. Then we developed a fifty-three-item questionnaire that took between forty-five minutes to three hours to complete. Next we asked friends and colleagues, seminar participants, any woman we met who expressed an interest, to fill them out. The questionnaire changed form as we learned which questions didn't work to give us the information we needed. We collected forty-five questionnaires.

The challenge now was to boil the questions down into a format that would give us some quantifiable data for analysis. We hired two research assistants. They recorded and coded every response to every question on those long forms. We met weekly for four months and taped or transcribed our meetings, brainstorming the issues, developing our ideas. From the coding we collaboratively developed a forty-nine-item (referred to as the survey) multiple-choice version of the longer questionnaire. We were now faced with the task of collecting a large sample of responses.

Undoubtedly we surprised many women with our zealous questioning. Sometimes we were just plain intrusive. Acting on the advice of a well-known researcher, our assistants scouted the countryside looking for locations where we'd be likely to find women waiting—where they might have time to respond to a questionnaire while they were waiting to do something else. We finally settled on gynecologists' offices. Our assistants went themselves or sent packets of questionnaires to friends all over the country who sat in doctors' offices waiting to capture waiting women. Our assistants also went to meetings of displaced homemakers groups, to offices, to town greens in summertime where people were gathered for music festivals, to college campuses. Everywhere any of us went, we handed out surveys. In all, we collected two hundred and twenty-two of these surveys. Then the four of us spent hours with the data spread out on the living room floor puzzling over the responses.

The puzzling was energizing, exciting. The project took on a kind of life of its own—we were learning so much about the ways women think about their lives and in the process we were also asking, comparing, questioning ourselves and our own lives.

Finally we went into the interview phase. We wanted not just quantifiable data for this project, we wanted to talk with women directly, to know their subjective experience of their own lives. We did group interviews, dyadic interviews, mother/daughter, husband/wife, lesbian/partner interviews; we talked with single women artists, with writers, songwriters, entrepreneurs, actresses, musicians. Every interview, most of them in person and some by telephone, was taped and transcribed.

If we had been moved before by the results of our data, the long interviews provided some of the most enriching experiences of the whole project. We chose women we thought would have unique things to tell us about the balance of love and creativity in their lives. We chose a high proportion of creative women engaged directly in creative work in the public arena because we felt they might have more to tell us about how they worked out the inevitable conflicts of the split. We hoped we would learn more from them about how women who are subject go about becoming so. Some of the women are well known; we found all of them extraordinary.

We drew enormous energy from these women. More and more, as therapists who often ask about people's difficulties, we began to realize the positive impact of having people talk about their resources, their solutions, and their joys rather than focusing on their "problems." The more we talked about passion with women, the more passion we felt for the project. The more we talked about creativity and love, the more creative and loving we were inspired to become. It was as if we and our interviewees served as muses and mentors for one another.

Finally we read through responses on the long forms, the short forms, and the verbal interviews. In all, we had data from over three hundred women. They ranged in age from fifteen to eighty-eight, they were from all geographic areas of the country, they represented some measure of cultural and class diversity, they represented a range of relationship patterns, about 146 had children and another 76 did not. We noticed that women seemed to have clear patterns to their responses, that the energy of some was much more highly relational in its focus, that for others, creative outlets and self-expression were more a focus. For other women, these two threads were more evenly integrated in their lives. So we grouped women in terms of high relational energy or high creative energy and then energy that was more integrative with a trend either toward the more relational or creative. From these categories, we developed the concept of the four basic forms that shape a life. We call them: Lovers/High Relationals; Artists/High Creatives; Leaders/Relational Integratives; and Innovators/Creative Integratives. The categories refer to the patterns of energy that most shape the through-line or spine of a woman's life at a particular point in time. In the case of the women we interviewed, the categories refer to a woman's dominant energy at the time of our interview as well as the way she chooses to express that energy.

When we analyzed the survey data and put it together with our more subjective understanding of the interviews and the questionnaires we found a high degree of consistency, or what researchers call "face validity," in the responses—that is, our questions measure what we think they measure. The survey and the questionnaires are available in the Appendix.

Of the 222 women in our sample who responded to multiple choice questionnaires, we classified 171 as primarily relational, 51 as primarily creative. Broken down more specifically, 87 were Lovers, or High Relational, 84 were Leaders, or Relational Integrative, 30 were Artists, or High Creative, and 21 were Innovators, or Creative Integrative. Because the women who responded to in-depth interviews were deliberately selected for their potential to contribute to our understanding of how women balance love and creativity, most fell into the Innovator or Artist category.

Some questions that we posed don't distinguish between groups as much as others. Sometimes the differences were greatest between the more general categories, relationals versus creatives, and sometimes they were most notable between women combined in the more divergent groups, Lovers and Artists, as compared to the women combined in the more integrative groups, Leaders and Innovators. In focusing on difference and similarities in the discussions that follow, we'll report percentages where they are significant. Other trends and patterns that we discuss will combine results from the surveys with more subjective material from the questionnaires and the long interviews.

We were acutely aware as we analyzed the data and thought about the results of our interviews that the categories we have developed are not static ones. They reflect the basic form and energy of a woman's life *at the time of our interview*. Our most basic finding was that women's energy changes and that there is a fluidity to the balance of one's involvement with relationship and creative energy determined by many factors. One is age, another is the ages of children.[4] In some cases, the four categories represent almost a developmental schema. Some women who begin in the High Relational category progress through the more integrative patterns to eventually become High Creative. Some women progress in the opposite direction. They start out more focused on creative energy and end up more focused on relationship.

What was most revealing were women's reactions to being asked this particular combination of questions. When we combined a focus on *both* relationship and self-expression, the vast majority of women seemed uncomfortable registering clear preferences for creativity, career, and other more self-focused choices without also including relationship. Some were uncomfortable at having the questions posed for them at all. Many women got angry at the questionnaire, some cried. Those who were primarily relational felt guilt that they hadn't embraced more creative outlets. Those who were more creative still qualified most of their answers to include relationship.

Some women talked easily and at length about these issues, others didn't really know what to say. Some didn't even think in terms of a split because they had never considered that there was an option for them to have both love and self-expression in their lives at the same time. Often, responses were so contradictory that we could clearly see the continued struggle women were having even to tell the truth about their lives to themselves. These reactions speak to the continuing invisibility of models and stories of women who actively embrace both loving and creating in their lives.

In the seventies, many of us had consciousness-raising groups as a methodology for establishing a different ground for our experience. But in the nineties, memories of "CR" groups have faded from our collective experience. Most of the women who responded to our survey, in fact, had never experienced one, and our questionnaire had inadvertently challenged them to think in a new way about their lives.

HOW WOMEN THINK ABOUT LOVE

The questions in our interviews and survey were designed to help us understand how women think about and experience love in their lives. As much as possible, we tried to ask questions in a way that would free women from the influence of the dominant discourse—we wanted to know not what they thought they should feel, but what was actually true about their experience.

Responses to our questions taught us most about diversity—different women value different kinds of love and experience it in different ways.

What does love mean? The use of language in response to this question was interesting. Some women tended to define love in terms of feelings, some in terms of action or behavior, and still others in terms of qualities of relationship.

Typical action types of responses included:

- "Love is the caring for the growth of another."
- "Love means caring, holding, being held accountable."
- "Making a complete commitment to achieve a complete connection with self, an interest/passion, or another person."
- "Listening, hearing and being heard, honoring and being honored, caring about another person's well-being, and acting in a way to please them."
- "A deep level of mutual understanding and commitment."

Action-oriented responses focused heavily on the notion of commitment and often included a reference to self-love, "being good to myself," or "taking care of myself." One woman said, "Love helps me best explore myself at my best." The action descriptions were generally the only ones to mention sex or eroticism as an aspect of love. "Love is support, caring, tenderness, intimacy, sex, touch." In general, whether in the long questionnaires or short surveys, sex and physical passion or intimacy were of much less importance to women, or at least mentioned much less frequently, than other aspects of love. Again, does this reflect our cultural conditioning or is it a function of finding it difficult to choose between sex and other definitions of love?

The more feeling-oriented responses described love as an emotional state. They included:

- "Warm, friendly feelings, affection, commitment, sometimes devotion, a feeling of being wanted, needed, and accepted, complete happiness and warmth, security, contentment, harmony, connection, serenity, tenderness, wanting what is good for the other person."

- "Love is warmth and security to me. Love means trust. Love becomes a big part of my happiness. Love, when mutual, is very safe."
- "Love is completeness, fulfillment, sharing, sensitivity."

Emotional responses focused heavily on ideas about trust, safety, contentment, happiness.

Other women tended to describe what they viewed as qualities of a loving relationship, defining love not as an internal state so much as a process that occurs between them and another:

- "Love is a powerful force each of us generates in response to others. Love's power moves us to make decisions we might not otherwise make. We feel full of energy, risk-taking, hope, fear, expectations for the future, acute sensuality."
- "Love is bittersweet memories, idealized persons."
- "Love is mutual respect and consideration, honesty, acknowledgment. Love is gentle, nurturing, open."
- "Enjoying each other as we are, feeling tenderness and gentleness for the imperfections in the other person. Being free to grow and change. Valuing each person for what he/she is, rather than what I want him/her to be."
- "It's like being in a moment of grace with another person."
- "Being there for all the little things."

Often women seemed to write their idealized versions of love. If these descriptions of relational qualities seem somewhat detached, it may be that they represent women's ideal beliefs about love rather than their direct experience of it.

On the short surveys where multiple-choice answers were provided, the highest percentage of women defined the qualities of love as a sense of being accepted and understood, knowing and being known, vulnerability and openness. Sexuality and sexual expression, intensity of feeling, appeared to have much less importance to women in our sample than a sense of being accepted and embraced—in short, safe—known and recognized by the others in their lives.

In general, women expected honesty in their relationships, were pragmatic about the work of loving, and, while there were some who did, the majority of women tended not to idealize love. They demonstrated a range of feelings, no two responses were alike. They were honest with themselves about the disappointments as well as the fulfillments of love. Interestingly, the highest percentage of women said they felt most loved and loving in a relationship with a spouse or intimate partner, and they equally felt most disappointed by these relationships. The second most fulfilling love was that for children and consistently the least fulfilling relationships for women were those with family members and parents. The youngest women in our survey were the most pragmatic and realistic about love—they speak of it in less expansive, less emotional terms, and in many of our in-depth interviews, we sensed a hesitation and a fear of being co-opted and of losing self to relationship. This perhaps reflects the growing disillusionment in our culture with the fulfillments of relationship and family life. Clearly it reflects beginning changes in the love story for women—changes that undoubtedly have both positive and negative aspects.

HOW WOMEN THINK ABOUT CREATIVE ENERGY

Because we wanted to suggest that creativity is more than artistic expression, the questions having to do with creativity in our questionnaires don't necessarily directly use the word, *creativity*—the language of the questions suggests more a concern with the focus of a woman's energy. We ask questions such as, "What other aspects of your life do you love, what activity or situation makes you feel most alive, most involved, most engaged? In what ways do you feel you most express who you are?" Answers on the long forms could be expressive of a woman's creative energy simply by virtue of their uniqueness. One woman writes in response to "What other aspects of your life do you love?":

"Small, silly dogs, chocolate-covered cherries, the ever/never changing mountains of New Mexico, the feel of sand under my feet at Laguna beach, flowers blooming through the snow, the fragrance of the forest, the aroma of leather, Jessie—a pet goat."

Another writes: "Horses, most animals, writing, learning, reading, biking, talking, listening, eating good food, taking hot baths, swimming, music, art, textures, editing, getting mail. All these things I love because they help me experience myself more fully."

One woman writes of her spiritual consciousness—a frequent preoccupation of women in our surveys: "I love God and my life. I love witnessing or participating in the love of God, activities which are healing, nurturing. I love nature, feeling the changes in nature—a storm, strong wind, sunlight and losing consciousness of myself when aware of grace." In general, women associate creative energy with strong experiences of the sensual, the spiritual, and the aesthetic, as well as the active pursuit and nurturing of relationship.

The responses to these types of questions helped to tease out the distinctions between the creative and the relational paths. Women who were more relational generally responded to a question like, "In what ways do you feel you most express who you are?" with responses like:

- "In being loving to another, in helping another to become his/her best self, in drawing people out in a personal way, in being kind, tender, thoughtful, caring."
- "Talking with a friend about important issues in my life one on one."
- "In the little things I do for people."

Many women viewed their greatest expression of creativity as their love of conversation, a theme that emerged over and over again in the responses.

The woman with a more focused creative energy might respond to this question with something like:

- "I feel best expressed through my sports and writing."
- "Through teaching, tennis, and skiing."
- "Taking pictures."

The more integrative woman generally combines relational responses with creative ones, "What activity makes you feel most alive?":

- "Biking, singing, my own therapy work, my own body work, love-making."
- "Playing in an orchestra, teaching a well-prepared student, nursing my infants, involved conversation with my grown children."

Responses to the question, "When do you feel you most express who you are?" often suggest the same kind of integrative energy:

- "When I allow myself to dress as who I am and play with *bright* colors and jewelry; when I participate creatively in church liturgies and women's rituals."
- "Reading, spending time with my son."
- "Teaching—whether it be the violin, knitting, cooking, or parenting—conversation with my children."

It was on the basis of these kinds of response patterns that we identified our four basic categories. As we've noted, some women's responses were purely relational, some focused almost exclusively on creative energy and others talked about both with the weight of one dominating. In the survey, in general, women in the integrative categories believed that the energy put into relationship *enhances* creativity or vice versa. But women who were Lovers or Artists stated clearly that focus on one arena detracted or interrupted or conflicted with the other. When we combined responses to this question about enhancing and detracting energies with other specific determining questions, the patterns that became the four categories emerged clearly from the data.

LOVERS, LEADERS, INNOVATORS, ARTISTS

The categories we describe as an outcome of our study each expresses a woman's dominant sense of herself on the continuum of energy for relationship versus energy for creative expression. The shape of her life has consistent and predictable qualities depending on how dominant each energy may be.

Women who are *Lovers*, the High Relational category, are primarily concerned with relatedness, their greatest energy goes into caring for others. They are more likely to put themselves aside in the interests of others' needs. Like Samantha's in chapter 2, the structure of their lives tends to be more traditional, more confined. While Lovers frequently embrace others as subject, and can be highly fulfilled and productive if they do, they are the group most prone to becoming or starting out as Smiling Women. If they slip into objectivity in the sense that they focus on others because they feel deviant if they don't, they are highly likely to suffer from addiction, depression, eating disorders, and other discomforts that reflect the impact of lacking a passion of their own. Their creativity, if accessed and not "put away," is usually structured around their relationships and is always secondary to it. Of women in all the categories, they experience the greatest split between relational and creative energy.

The *Artist*, or High Creative woman, at the other extreme on the continuum, focuses her energy primarily on creative work and relationship is secondary. She often experiences relationship as detracting from her focus on self. She is the woman who enjoys solitude, may remain single by choice, and who does not allow relationships in her life to compromise her own work. Relationship and work are maintained almost in separate compartments. While the tendency is to think of the High Creative woman as most subject, it's possible to be as much object as a worker as it is as a Lover. The woman who "does it all" or works compulsively or chooses a singular life in reaction against the cultural narrative does so with as little sense of choice as the woman who sets herself aside for relationship. The "career woman" who decides to prove that she doesn't need relationship is as much a prisoner of the current cultural mythology as the Smiling Woman—she's the woman attempting to be subject in a male way. As subject, the Artist is a Lucy Lippard. She revels in her own creative power, has more immediate access to her talents and to her inner life, and produces much that puts her own stamp on the world around her.

The integrative forms are similar, only the emphasis of energy is different. Leaders and Innovators integrate relational and creative energy, both are important to them, they most overcome the split image. The difference is that, for the Leader, relationship is foreground, creativity background. Forced to choose between accessing the two energies, the Leader would always focus more on relationship. For the Innovator, self-expression, creating, is more important, more foreground, and relationship is background. Mary Nolan is a particularly good model of the Leader, and Ann Ehringhaus the Innovator. While the Leader is more likely to fit her creative work *around* her relationships, the Innovator is more likely to fit her relationships around her own work. For the Leader, work almost always involves a concern with relatedness on a larger societal level, for the Innovator, input from relationship enhances work, provides deeper access to the self.

To a degree, we all fit in all groups, we fit in them differently at different points in our lives, we access different aspects of our personal energy in different ways at different times with different people doing different things. Many of the women we interviewed were clearly struggling with a transition from one form to another. In explaining the distinctions between each pattern in part 2, we'll describe women, who, *at this point in time*, clearly reflect the characteristics of one dominant category.

A final point about this schema of energy we've evolved is that it does not find relevant distinctions in terms of patterns of energy and passion between lesbian, bisexual, and heterosexual women, aging women, women of color, and white women. While our sample was limited in terms of diversity, we did talk to women, especially in our in-depth interviews, who represented a range of different life-styles and cultural backgrounds. We have all been socialized as women. The larger differences we face have to do with the constraints imposed by homophobia, heterosexism, ageism, racism, and classism. These external forces dramatically affect the shapes that our energies take because our struggle for subjectivity may be greater depending on which types of oppression are more or less present in our lives. Sometimes the more oppressed we are, the more determinedly we demand subjectivity.

Most of us, all of us, seem to overcome great odds in our paths toward claiming our passions, finding forms that fit the nature of our emerging selves. The differences rest in the inequities imposed by the political realities of our society. As women, we may speak with different voices, but we sing with one heart.

BACK TO THE SPLIT IMAGE: GENERAL TRENDS

If women are becoming more pragmatic about love, they equally view it as what makes their lives most meaningful. "Being loving and giving to others" was the choice for 64 percent of our respondents when asked what makes life most meaningful. Creative activity ranked second with only 20 percent choosing it above relationship. Clearly women still think of relationship as the aspect of their lives in which they express themselves most fully.

But responses to creativity questions on the short, multiple-choice surveys revealed an interesting discrepancy. When asked what made them feel most alive and engaged, in other words, most passionate and energized, 74 percent of women checked creative activity or some other self-focused pursuit or hobby such as sports or spiritual practice. Only 26 percent of women felt most engaged when involved in some relational activity. But asked "In what ways do you feel *you most express who you are*?" the percentages reversed and 71 percent of women said they most express themselves relationally while only 29 percent felt most themselves when engaged in creative or self-focused pursuits. The suggestion here is that although women enjoy creative expression and feel alive and impassioned when engaged in it, they still find their sense of self-definition and meaning in relational rather than self-expressive situations. While they may feel more alive, they feel less secure in their identities when self-focused or engaged in creative activity.

The question is, does this reflect a real choice for most women, or does it reflect the influence of the split image? Are women telling us what is really true for them, or are they telling us what they think they should feel?

When asked what they need more of in their lives, 40 percent of women say they need more time to pursue creative interests or a better connection with themselves. Fifty-eight percent of women said they had a talent or creative outlet in childhood that they later gave up. While women still choose relational paths, they equally note the absence of the creative parts of themselves. This suggests that the longing for more creativity is there for many women but is overshadowed by the relational imperative that defines a woman's identity.

Time, Talent, Love

For many women, *time* is the biggest variable in their choice to give up a creative pursuit—love and/or money, earning a living are the priorities, and self-expression always takes a back seat. Women also feel that they can't make a commitment to a creative pursuit unless they are highly talented at it. We're taught to value product over process in this country so that simple enjoyment is not a justification for expending energy on a self-focused activity. A consistent theme that emerged throughout our interviews was the "I'm not creative" assumption that most women make about themselves. Mistaking *artistic talent* for creative ability, women assume that they have no true talent and therefore can't justify pursuing their love of some activity, such as dancing or singing. Some channel their energy into other hobbies or careers, but many just leave their passions behind.

This choice seems to lead to overfocus on relationship for some women and to a chronic sense of loss and disconnection from self. The responses of women who gave up creative pursuits tended to be more traditionally relational and to express less enthusiasm and energy for interests other than relationship. In short, they seemed less satisfied and less alive in their responses.

SHAPING A LIFE: THE IMPORTANCE OF FORM

When we grouped women's responses into the four categories, Lover, Artist, Leader, Innovator, we were really attempting to develop a useful description of the forms women seem to evolve for expression of their energies. The categories are a commentary on the ways that women overcome or deal with the split image. The patterns differ primarily in terms of the *proportion and emphasis* of relational or creative energy. These forms may either constrict a woman or enhance her capacity to be subject. A woman whose dominant energy is really for creativity may choose a High Relational form and the result may be dissatisfaction and constriction. If a form enhances her sense of passion, the form is a good fit. If it constricts, then she may need to make alterations within that pattern or shift to an entirely different one. Again, as subject she experiences choice, she is fully engaged; as object, she conforms to someone else's expectations and her creative passion is blocked. Both states are a matter of degree.

After reading this book, one woman might say to herself, "Right now in my life, I have High Relational energy, but unless I alter the form of that pattern as it works in my life currently to fit me better, I can see that I'll continue to be frustrated and more focused on others' feelings than on my own. I need to get more of my love of photography and creative design into my life."

Another woman might say, "My life is structured as if my energy is purely High Relational, but if I'm honest, I really prefer things that I do alone and I really need a lot more solitude and time for myself. Actually, I think I may really have more High Creative energy. Being in the kind of relationships I'm involved in doesn't really fit for me anymore. I want to focus more on my work."

And, equally, a woman might say, as so many women as well as men are today, "I've been in the fast lane, achieved my creative goals, but where is the time for love? I want a child." Or, "There's something wrong with my life if I can't attend my friend's son's bar mitzvah." Or, "My grandmother is sick; I want to spend time with her."

Changing forms doesn't have to represent a major life change—it can mean taking a class, doing volunteer work with people to balance a highly solitary career, creating a space for oneself in one's home and spending time in it. It can mean simply putting more of what you love into your life.

But the larger forms we choose tend to have a large impact on how fully we express our passions. Those forms evolve through the interaction of several factors. One is the intrinsic strength of relational energy and of creative energy each woman possesses. Some of us knew from a very early age that we had a passion for some creative, intellectual, athletic, artistic pursuit. Others have always been highly relationship oriented.

Another factor is belief—how we're taught to think about the forms available to us and whether they have been defined as acceptable for expression of our energy. Culture, our families, our economic status, our access to education, and our particular life circumstances all affect our beliefs about what we can and cannot do and to what degree we must be split or can integrate our various loves. Our beliefs about what we can and cannot do, more than any single factor, tend to determine whether we follow a passion or give it up. It was fascinating to listen to the many very successful women in our long interviews who said that when they identified a love for a certain activity, they proceeded with absolute "inner" confidence and determination that they could be successful at it. Women who ultimately gave up passions tended to feel that "they wouldn't be good enough at it."

Finally, our capacity for overcoming fear is critical to being more subject and changing forms when they don't provide us access to ourselves. Or, better stated, it takes courage to know oneself, to follow one's own vision, to overcome the inevitable shame, terror, and discomfort of self-expression in any medium, relational or creative. It takes courage to change forms when one has been convinced that certain ways of expressing oneself are unacceptable or that certain ways *are* acceptable and therefore expected by friends and family.

A woman will find herself adopting a certain pattern based on all these interacting factors. When she thinks of changing forms, or making alterations within them, it may be in small or large ways. First she needs to identify what her deepest energies are, what her passions are. Within the four dominant patterns there are myriad ways of shaping a life that satisfies, a life that embraces passion.

Form can mean sexual and emotional preference, it can mean single versus married, it can mean having children, not having children, it can mean communal living, it can mean living with extended family, it can mean living with your sister. It can mean making adjustments within the basic form of a marriage or partnership, like having certain prescribed areas of separateness in physical space or routine, taking separate vacations, or working out arrangements about the balance of work time and intimate time that may be a better emotional fit.

Form can mean small but important choices. Do you feel closed in if you live surrounded by trees or do you prefer open spaces? Do you like windows open or closed? Do you need a space of your own, a time in the day all to yourself, or do you love the activity of a busy household with ten different things going on around you?

What do you need to eliminate from your life to prune it to its right shape? Do you need to live in the city or in the country? Do you need to give up committees, take on more, see less of your friends, or cultivate new ones? Do you like to do many things at once, or do you need concentrated focus on one thing at a time? Do you like the structure of a nine-to-five job or do you prefer to control and direct your own time?

One woman who had begun to experience the traditional form of marriage as too confining for her told us, "You've got to have some- thing else besides a marriage to do a relationship in." This woman is at a point of transition—she knows she needs something different in her life, but she isn't clear yet what options are open to her or what her relational life would look like if she were to create a better fit. But she highlights something anthropologist Margaret Mead commented on years ago in a talk at the Metropolitan Museum of Art. Mead sug- gested that as a civilization we would need to find a wider acceptable range of forms for relationship because the growing complexity of our lives cannot be sustained or nourished in only the traditional form of heterosexual monogamous marriage.

The larger point is that the structures and shapes of the lives we operate in affect our well-being even more directly than who or what is inside them, because the structure determines how much of what's inside can effectively be accessed. The issue is to know and understand what your energies are and to follow them as faithfully as possible. When a form that you choose doesn't fit, have the cour- age to change it.

THE CHANGING CULTURAL NARRATIVE

What was clear to us from our study was that there are times for most women when energy can be available to us for our own lives, but rarely at the expense of energy for others. The question this left for us was, to what degree do women, even in the nineties, feel free to speak what is really true about their feelings? Are we witnessing the ongoing impact of the cultural narrative—that women feel deviant if they com- mand more energy for themselves than for relationship, so that they can't really admit to it? Or is it the case that women *do* experience themselves as subject when relationally focused—that for certain of us relationship and creativity are not split, they are both part of our experience of ourselves as loving, whole women?

Our conclusion was, *both*. In the nineties, this is where the dialectic rests: Many of us are, at times, still the Smiling Woman, but more and more we are subject, passionate and engaged with our lives, we love and we create. We do these things at different times and in different balance, the force of our energies shifting at different points in our life cycle, shifting depending on our age and the constraints of the times we grew up in, shifting, depending on the practical demands of our lives. We are a diverse, talented, and energetic half of the human race who are moving more and more toward subjectivity both collectively and individually. Many of us are in the process of transforming our lives to be more passionate. We are inspiring, we are generous, we are courageous, we embrace change. But we still struggle against the unconscious influence of the dominant story, the split image, and if we're not careful, its influence can still induce us to silence ourselves.

In this era of enormous social problems and cultural transition, we can't afford to sacrifice the passion and dedication of any individual woman, of any group. We need to learn to value our diversity and to express it—it is the source of our creative energy. In identifying with the lives of other women, we can come to value our own struggles and our own strengths.

The framework we've evolved in this book is meant to be a celebration of diversity, an affirmation of sameness, a celebration of the capacity of women to overcome the constricting cultural influences that have oppressed us for centuries. In understanding that we all are creative and loving in different patterns, we don't any longer have to value one way of loving more than another, value loving more than creating, value any one form of creative expression more than another. We can begin to look to the structures and forms of our lives and repair whatever it is in them that blocks us from being as passionate about our lives as we can be.

The stories of women in part 2 provide us with models, give us glimpses into the ways that women who are our contemporaries and our peers have struggled with issues of creativity and love. They are the stories of women who are "working things out." We hope that they are inspiring and instructive. We can each find ourselves in the stories of one of these women, and, in that identification, perhaps move more confidently toward a deeper sense of the value of our own lives.

PART TWO

THE PATTERNS OF WOMEN'S LIVES

CHAPTER FIVE

Lovers: The High Relational Pattern

IN A VIVID PASSAGE FROM HER BOOK, *The Writing Life*, Annie Dillard tells a story about the Fourth of July that captures the essential difference between a Lover and an Artist, even though both may write. Dillard the Artist says, "On the Fourth of July, my husband and our friends drove into the city, Roanoke, to see the fireworks. I begged off; I wanted to keep working. . . . The horizon of my consciousness was the contracted circle of yellow light inside my study . . . —at last, unthinkingly, I parted the venetian blind slats with my fingers, to look out.

"And there were the fireworks. . . . It was the Fourth of July, and I had forgotten all of wide space and all of historical time."[1]

There are, in the world, two other wonderful, but as yet unpublished manuscripts, both written ten years ago by women who are now in their sixties and who both chose the path of the Lover. The first book is *Voices from the Silent Generation*,[2] the second is *Rehab*.[3]

Both writers had happy marriages. One is now divorced. The other is still married. The first is writing movie reviews for several newspapers; she also manages thirteen rental properties. The second woman is reading ancient Chinese literature and writing a second book. The first has three successful children. The second has two. The books are unpublished, but neither writer ever missed the family's Fourth of July.

The movie reviewer would say she loved the first act of her life. It was the second act that necessitated the divorce. She and her husband are still good friends. The Chinese literature buff took a detour into addiction in the first act of her life. In the second act, her marriage and her sobriety provide the foundation for her writing and her intellectual life. She and her husband are still good friends.

Joan, the movie reviewer, entered college in 1947, married in 1950. Ruth, the Chinese literature buff, entered college in 1941, married in 1953. The first act seemed a form that fit for Joan. The fit was more uncomfortable for Ruth.

Joan tells us, "My greatest anger is, nobody in my entire life ever said to me, What do you want to be when you grow up? It was just, of course, assumed that I would be married and have children and that there wouldn't be an afterlife. People who had an afterlife, *knew exactly what they wanted to do from early on*."

In other words if you were to dare to be the subject of your own life, you had to know unequivocally from the beginning that that's what you wanted. You had no right to pursue a passion that selfishly expressed your inner vision unless you were so deeply committed to something that you couldn't deny it; otherwise you were not entitled.

THE SMILING WOMAN: WHAT SHE DID FOR LOVE

Joan's and Ruth's stories highlight the enduring power of the cultural narrative about love. Both are women whose lives were unalterably influenced by the Smiling Woman image of the fifties. They conformed to a form of love that both fit and didn't fit, and they each developed their own style for integrating creative energy in their lives. Since a majority of women in our survey fall into the Lover category, their stories are particularly significant—embracing a traditional definition of love and family has its advantages and disadvantages, and Joan and Ruth came to know both intimately.

Joan was the younger of two children born to Alfred and Janet Ferguson. They were quintessentially WASP, and, as Joan puts it, "always distrusted passion."

One of Joan's stories about her family is set in her mother's parlor. Janet Ferguson has been visited by a social worker who has come to her home to discuss the ways family life will need to be reorganized in light of limitations imposed by her husband's recent stroke. They sit, Janet, regal at eighty-six, perched on the edge of a chintz wing chair, her husband Alfred, in a rumpled brown tweed suit, in his wheel chair. Their son, a prominent attorney, rebelliously wearing madras shorts and ill-matched striped shirt, is there along with Joan, who has arranged for the social worker's visit and is sitting uneasily on a footstool.

Janet calls to Alfred's nurse to serve iced pineapple juice and macaroons, thus defining the social worker's visit as a social call. The social worker asks a question about feelings.

"Feelings?" repeats Janet, somewhat puzzled. "Oh, yes. Alfred, do you remember? We were here in this living room during the hurricane of 1938 when the big elm tree went through the roof at the end of the living room. We were frightened, weren't we, Alfred? I remember we got the hurricane lamp and we all confessed that we were frightened."

Joan chuckles retelling the story because it captures the emotional atmosphere she grew up with so accurately. "I was always surrounded by WASPness. I had a mother with a lovely spirit who attended to her flowers and gardens, and her husband and children. She and my father stayed to themselves pretty much. There was no reaching out. There were no books in the house, there was no music in the house. There was no intellectual curiosity at all. And I was very, very young when I knew that I didn't like any of it and that there must be something more. I had to develop a kind of self-starting mechanism."

Joan discovered the "more" when her family moved to Ohio from the East Coast during World War II. She was suddenly thrown into a big public high school, and due to early promotions, was two years younger than anyone else. Her world now included people from many different class and ethnic backgrounds and she remembers loving the diversity.

But the adjustment to difference was hard because she was unprepared for her family's reaction to it. She relates an experience that was to imbue her with a lifelong passion for social justice. "The one person who befriended me was a Jewish girl named Joan. One day mother drove me over to Joan's and we sat in front of the house. She waited until Joan's father came home in the car and she said, 'Look at him, look at that nose. He's Jewish. And I want you to understand that.' And I didn't articulate it to myself then, but I knew that I would go on being friends with Joan the whole time I was in Dayton, and that nothing was going to change that."

In contrast to the constriction of her WASP world in childhood, the world in Dayton, Ohio, seemed to open up for Joan. At sixteen she went to Vassar and now the world did more than open up—it split wide open. She took courses with a constitutional scholar, became fascinated with the Bill of Rights. Her academic interests coalesced with her awareness of and valuing of diversity. "When I was a freshman at Vassar, I came home for a holiday and my grandmother was sitting out on the porch at my mother and father's house and she used the word *nigger* and I ordered her to leave. Get out of this house, is what I said."

Joan continued to channel her passion for social justice into her academic work. She loved ideas and intellectual debate. It's hard to imagine that in her junior year, she decided to leave Vassar, the most exciting part of her life, to get married.

We asked her how she thought about her decision to leave Vassar, to follow Corson to Yale.

"It wasn't even a question."

"You just knew you would do it?"

"I knew I would do it. There isn't much of a way to tell somebody who didn't live at that time how overwhelming it was."

It wasn't that Joan didn't struggle against conformity. Not surprisingly, part of what drew her to Corson was his unconventionality. On their first date they went on a canoe trip, rather than to a fraternity party. Corson didn't drink, he was uninterested in following the crowd.

But when the dean told Corson he could marry if Joan gave up Vassar, Joan followed the conventional form of the day, giving up her separate life and never questioning it.

"Did you clearly want to make this choice?" we wondered.

"I have no idea how much of this was duty, no idea how much of this was conforming to my culture, but it would be very wrong to say that I didn't love him. I really did. I know I did. For a long time."

"And you loved many aspects of your life as well," we said.

"Oh, yes."

"What did you love about your life?"

"Well, we spent eight years moving around in different cities. And every place we moved, and he never told me . . . I mean, he'd come home and say we're moving to Chicago. And every place we moved I'd make a home of some kind in whatever apartment we would find."

When Joan and Corson had children they moved back to New Jersey, settled next door to Joan's father and mother, built a small ranch house on several acres, and Corson started his own company. The world that had split wide open at Vassar was constrained now within the conventional suburban cultural story of her time. But Joan loved this life as well.

"We started having children. I had three. The second I saw the first child, boom, that was it. I never looked back. I loved having that child."

"What did you love about it?"

"It was so helpless. There it was. It had only me; it certainly wasn't going to have him, he was going to be at work the whole rest of his life. But it lasted for me for fifteen years since there was nobody's company that I enjoyed as much as I enjoyed the company of my kids.

"They were just so alive and there was just tremendous fun and excitement in the things that we did. If it snowed we built snow horses, and snowmen, and snow forts, and mazes, and if it was ice skating we played with wooden sticks and hockey pucks. It was just an endless wonderful thing. I loved it. That I have no doubt about. What I really loved was Friday night when we'd all sit around the fire and watch 'Rawhide.' The boys would take turns rocking on the red rocking horse. Home was where I wanted to be on weekends. I really hated leaving them. Just for their good company. Cork played with the kids. We did everything together on the weekends, we built a rope tow and we taught the kids to ski out there and he'd spend hours and hours building those kinds of things for the kids. He was very much a part of it."

Love for her children, Joan said, "was the most primal and intense love that I've ever had. But I have a hard time talking about love. I don't think it's because I'm inhibited, I think it's because I've decided that love is absolutely irrational, period. And I'm not sure that that isn't just fine. What is troubling to me about it is the degree to which you give yourself over to it."

Joan totally gave over her life to her family. She helped her husband build his company, she entertained a constant stream of visitors from around the world. She describes living with him as like "living with an engine." Project followed project and together they literally cleared the land and built their own house. She loved creating the environment and Corson and she were a wonderful team for years. They were partners. They became very self-sufficient. And it was here, in part, that Joan's creativity in altering the typical suburban patterns tailored her life to her own energies. Joan was, in many ways, no suburban housewife, despite living in suburbia.

"When you dig your own well, and clear the land, and push back the forest, you feel very self-sufficient. Each weekend, we'd do that for a few hours and then we'd play football with our kids, and then we'd all push back the forest some more, and then we'd eat lunch and it was just a family way of being when the kids were home from school. Then we got into all the ways of using the land. Wherever there was a hill we made it a coasting hill or a skiing hill and the place became a center for all our kids' friends."

During all these years Joan had no time to think about herself. She didn't even have a space in her house that she could call her own. That didn't matter to her then. The shape of Joan's life, with the alterations she was able to make, provided a wonderful form for her energy during those years and she was often joyous. But she knew that the euphoria of her life would end when the kids left and she had to face the second act.

THE VICE PRESIDENT OF CBS

Clippety, clippety, clippety clop
Yonkers Raceway—that's the stop[4]

Ruth was part of the creative team that wrote this jingle for the New York Racing Association. Friends remember her as a five foot tall coil of energy with wild red hair and a Philadelphia accent. It was 1950, she was twenty-seven, and she was one of the first women in television.

She can describe the scene as if it were yesterday.

"The sound man turns to me to ask me a question. All of us, cameraman, director, other copywriters, fellow that holds the canvas film bag, have gone three days with no sleep, chain smoking, drinking cold coffee from plastic foam cups, the grease floating on the top. We are young and we love the excitement and intensity of working under pressure. If this jingle flies we will secure the account of one of our firm's biggest clients."

Ruth's energies were clearly focused on her career goal at twenty-three. She knew she wanted to be vice president of CBS.

But by 1970, Ruth was creating a different kind of jingle, ironic and self-mocking. This one was written while she was in a rehabilitation center for alcoholism and pill addiction:

Tuinal
Nembutal
Seconal
Sodium butisol
I've had them all
and washed them down with
alcohol.[5]

As Ruth said, "A deadly rhyme, a killing dose."

Ruth grew up in an intellectual Jewish family. She was always creative. From the time she was a little girl, she was unconventional, independent, highly imaginative. She can't remember a time when she didn't see herself becoming a writer.

"I wanted to be a writer from the time I was five and I wanted to be an editor when I was a little kid. All I wanted was an editor's rolltop desk. My much older cousin, my favorite out of twenty-seven first cousins, was a copywriter and I wanted to be like her and I wanted to be like Dorothy Thompson, a famous reporter, and I loved the summer because I could wear shorts. I remember being ten years old when I got to go to Girl Scout camp and wear shorts. I said to my mother, 'Gee, I want to wear pants. It's really comfortable to wear pants.'

"My mother says, 'Well, if you become a famous writer like Dorothy Thompson, you can wear pants.'

"I thought, 'Okay.'" And she determined she would become a famous writer.

Ruth never envisioned marriage or a relationship with a man as the primary goal of life. She challenged all of the established forms of the day. During World War II, as an undergraduate, she challenged the charter of the University of Pennsylvania. Creativity, as Samuel Coleridge acknowledged, presupposes destruction of the old forms.

"When I first went to Wharton, women students were not allowed to use the main staircase even though we were having the same classes, same professors, same everything. We had to walk up the fire stairs on the outside of the building. The College for Women was seen as totally separate from the University of Pennsylvania, although it was really the same school. So, when the war came along and male students, in general, were gone, the women became a little more important to the institution because our tuition was keeping the university afloat. We had our own dean; it was garbage. Anyway, the charter of the university was for male students so I was really upset with the situation because I wanted journalism. I had worked at a newspaper as a teen and I'd worked in radio and I knew what I was doing. But women couldn't be on the *Daily Pennsylvanian;* we had to have our little women's newspaper. We couldn't do anything. It was gender segregation to the umpth degree. So, the charter of the University of Pennsylvania said."

Ruth was angry. "One of my professors said, 'Well, if you're so annoyed about the whole damn thing get the charter changed.' You had to see trustees, you had to go through all this legal stuff and I did. I spent my junior year and most of my senior year and we got the charter changed for the university to say men and women."

Ruth's challenge of the established segregation of men and women began early.

"When I was a kid, my mother sent me down from the women's balcony to the main floor of the shul to tell my father it was time to go home. A man stopped me at the sacred wooden doors and said, 'You can't come in. Get your brother.' That little schnook was fit to walk into the sacred center and I was not, even if I was older, smarter, and a better basketball player? Why was he equipped to go to Hebrew school and learn the magic language, to study the Talmud and learn the rules? No wonder I feel I never know the rules. Why was he honored with a bar mitzvah while I sat behind the grille with the women, noticed only when the rabbi said a woman's voice should not be heard in synagogue because they sounded like clucking hens?

"Even when Jackie grew up and became a Civil Rights activist, I could never make him see there wasn't much difference between sitting in the back of the bus and sitting behind a metal grille in the balcony of the shul. Both are wrong. Does that say something about God or about the mentality of men who believe in the valuelessness of women? When Moses asked God what His name was, He answered, 'I am.' He didn't say Sol or Benny or Irving."

Ruth graduated from Penn in 1945 and started out by writing radio copy for a department store in Philadelphia. The vice president of the firm became her first mentor. "Think like management," he told her. "You're not going to get ahead unless you think like management. You can't think like labor."

Thinking like management meant producing ten times the amount of work she was used to producing, and always focusing on doing what was necessary to reach a goal.

"So I took over the department at twenty-three, then television came along and we tried it. We got the program started on TV in front of a live audience. We turned the store restaurant into a studio. If we needed furniture, we borrowed it from the furniture department. It was great. Jackie Gleason's guys used to come down and watch our 'Hump and Mary' skits before 'The Honeymooners' went on the air. Television at that time, 1948, cost $400 an hour. To support the costs, we wrote copy and sold the commercials ourselves to manufacturers. We sold it as an experiment and one day, the first manufacturer said, well I'll try this new medium. We advertised swirls, tie-in-the-front house dresses. What else do women wear? And we sold 700 dozen dresses in one day with a one-minute commercial. It was so far beyond what we had ever dreamed or imagined."

By 1948 Ruth had become one of the first and most successful women in television. By 1950 she was working in New York as a television copywriter, by virtue of submitting the first successful commercial to a million-dollar client who had turned down the prior twenty-seven submissions. The Yonkers Raceway jingle was to be one of several well-known advertising slogans she helped to create.

She wrote, she filmed, she directed. She was there at the start of color television. She loved the drama, the intensity, the pace. "You needed both a good stopwatch and a good deodorant if you were going to work in television."

Ruth's energies were flowing in a direct line toward her career goals undiverted by a focus on love and marriage.

We wondered what she had thought about love, if she had ever felt, up to that point, that a man was necessary to her life?

With characteristic wit, Ruth replied, "Yes, necessary if you wanted the normal life. But I wanted fame and fortune. I wanted to be vice president of CBS. That was my goal."

"Why vice president?"

"Because there weren't any women vice presidents. That was as high as I could imagine I could get."

Waylaid by Love

Then Ruth met Phil at work. In fact, for a short time, she was his boss. Initially, she didn't have to grapple with the Smiling Woman split. She loved Phil but she never considered giving up her career. She saw no reason for love and creativity to conflict. Neither did Phil. "He and I made statements to each other. I don't want any relationship, we said. I don't want any commitment, we said. We each said, 'I have no intention of getting married until I'm thirty-five years old.' Both of us. Every day, every day. And I don't know what happened. Marriages are made in heaven. That's what I think. All of a sudden, boom. We both changed our minds."

After marriage, Ruth kept working. The energy of her love and the energy of her creativity were pretty evenly balanced. But she and Phil wanted children and for seven frustrating years she was unable to bear them. She was even part of a research study on sterility.

Her gynecologist then gave Ruth what was extremely typical advice to working women unable to have children for many years. " 'You know,' said my gynecologist, 'you have a very tense high-power job. Commuting to New York every day, you're under a lot of pressure. You should really quit your job or take a leave of absence. Take the summer off. Just don't have all that pressure and we'll see if that will work.' . . . It worked."

Having children was a turning point for Ruth.

"Did you want children during all those years of the visits to fertility doctors?"

"Oh, yeah! Yes, we did. Phil wanted a lot of children. I wanted a lot of children, until I had one. But I didn't want to give up my career.

"At the office there was a pool on when I'd be back at work and the longest date was thirty days. Elizabeth was born at the end of July and they all thought I'd be back for the fall commercial season. That was twenty years ago."

We asked, "Did you fight staying home? Did you and Phil argue about it?"

Ruth says, "Did I fight staying home? I didn't know you could not."

Phil is sitting in the kitchen listening to the interview. He interjects here. "I didn't want her to go back to work."

Ruth says, "Oh no. He did not want me . . . but I didn't know that I had a choice." Oddly enough, although she had challenged the form of a university charter, she didn't challenge the form of the fifties family. Unlike Joan, she didn't make the alterations that would have made the form a better fit.

And also unlike Joan, for whom mothering became an exciting way to express her creativity, Ruth's creativity suffocated in the boredom of being a mother and housewife. Ruth says, looking back, "I just didn't know how to handle leisure time. Non-working time. I didn't know there was a way out of boredom."

She expected herself to be a perfect mother and that included maintaining a total focus on her children.

"I gotta tell you, I was determined that I was going to listen to what my children had to say. It was not going to be a family in which children are to be seen and not heard. And my eyes used to glaze up [with boredom] because Jenny [her youngest] would come home from third grade and tell me *every single thing that happened all day*."

Ruth began to see a series of doctors for depression. Two of them told her she'd be fine if she went back to work. Of course they meant work outside the home. But she did work, at home, and she loved that work too. When the kids were in school she tried to find a way out of her malaise by throwing herself into volunteer work, but it didn't help.

There were also compensations for staying home. Ruth enjoyed her family, and the energy she channeled into her children's lives spilled over into open relationships with them as adults. In fact, she describes herself as passionate about her family. She still calls Phil "Mr. Wonderful" and means it. But her passionate involvement with her family depleted her of psychic energy.

Ruth suffered from the arduous reality that breaking the accepted norm for her time was not so easy. She would not have been comfortable working at a job that took her two hours away from her children. "Today I would be able to fax copy in. But not then. And Phil figured that the kids would be better off having a mother at home."

Finally she tried to talk to psychiatrists about the conflict between staying home and going back to work. "When I first had anxiety and talked to my doctor, that's when they started making me into the cultural norm. By giving me Valium and taking away all my energy. The war was me against the culture and the culture won." As she says, "Fatigue makes cowards of us all."

Ruth's response was rage turned against herself. She increasingly abused alcohol. She hated herself for disliking her role. As the character in her novel says, "People who live in a nice house with an in ground pool and two cars are supposed to be happy. See the nice suburban matron smiling at home, happy and sincere. No dirty ring around her respectability."

Sober for many years now, she is no longer angry, but ironic. She says, "I realize I had totally lost my identity. I didn't know what to call it back then. But nobody knew I was a successful, television commercial writer. I was Elizabeth and Jenny's mother."

LOVERS: THE PASSION FOR RELATIONSHIP

Edna St. Vincent Millay may have articulated the passion of the Lover best in one of her sonnets, when she says:

> Love can not fill the thickened lung with breath,
> Nor clean the blood, nor set the fractured bone;
> Yet many a man is making friends with death
> Even as I speak, for lack of love alone.[6]

We locate Joan and Ruth in the High Relational category because their dominant energy for much of their lives went into relationship. It was the compelling and driving passion. Even though both had great creative energy as well, they diverted or channeled that creativity to meet the demands of the High Relational form. For Joan, being a Lover was a choice, she experienced herself as subject because she could mold the form to fit her dominantly relational energy. She found ways within it to channel her intellectual interests and creativity. But Ruth really had more the energy of the Artist or the Innovator and she could not alter the form to fit her. She experienced herself as object. For Joan the High Relational form was a choice that fit, for Ruth, it was an accommodation that did not.

The High Relational pattern does work for the woman whose primary passion is for intimate, nurturing love, for intimacy that is private, bounded by the pleasures of caring for relationship in its most physical and daily expressions. The Lover's signature characteristic is her clear knowledge that relationships come first. The Lover would agree with one woman in our study who says, "love is *it!*" Relationship is the medium for the expression of her deepest passions, and it's within this form that she experiences love as most fulfilling.

To say that a woman is a Lover doesn't mean that she doesn't also have creative or intellectual energy, and it doesn't mean that she doesn't have work outside the sphere of the family. It does mean that, like Joan, she is more likely to channel the creative energy into relational activity. She may choose avenues of self-expression and creativity that make room for her relational energies, support them, or complement them. But creative work never supplants relationship, never takes away from it. The more High Relational a woman is, the more she is absolutely clear about putting relationship first. In meeting the needs of family and friends, she experiences herself as subject. Her sense of self depends on her role in relationship to others.

The most typical structure for the expression of High Relational energy is the traditional family, although it's not the only one. Any relationship characterized by a strong sense of devotion and commitment to the other's needs may constitute a High Relational form.

Many Lovers feel great satisfaction with traditional roles, particularly if that role is a choice rather than an accommodation or a sacrifice to anxiety about their sense of self. They throw their creative energies so totally into relationship that their own individual imperative becomes submerged in the relational context of their lives. If the annual convention of her profession takes place during her child's first week in kindergarten, a Lover chooses to skip the convention. If she is taking art classes, and has a chance to go with her class to an intensive painting workshop for two weeks, she won't go if it leans too heavily on her family. She will pursue her art only to the level or point that it doesn't cause any major disruption to her relationships. She rarely says, "Do not interrupt me. I'll talk to you later, when I'm through with this project." Instead she prides herself on being available when people need her. Her child, her friends, her network, a mutually respectful and caring relationship with coworkers and colleagues, take precedence over ambition, or "getting the job done."

Lovers made up the largest of the categories in our survey— eighty-seven women. The Lover is the woman who most often says that choices having to do with relationship make her feel most whole, the woman who, as a child, always knew she wanted marriage and a family.

As much as Lovers value relationship, however, they do not always find it fulfilling. An interesting trend in our data revealed that of all the groups, Lovers are least likely to describe the story of love in their lives as "love fulfilled." Sixty-one percent of Leaders felt fulfilled, 57 percent of Innovators, but only 34 percent of Lovers responded positively to this question. Lovers were the group most likely to describe their "love story" as "love hoped for but not attained." In fact a higher percentage of women in the combined relational group report themselves to be separated or divorced than women in the combined creative group.

It's difficult to interpret the meaning of this data, except to speculate about a number of possible interpretations. Perhaps Lovers overvalue love and then find it disappointing. Perhaps they find themselves too constricted by the form, they accommodate too much and lose a sense of themselves. Perhaps they misread their true energies and fail to move into more integrative patterns. Women in the other more divergent form, Artists, were almost as likely to feel unfulfilled by love. While this would seem a more likely characteristic for this group than for Lovers, the suggestion is that women in the more integrative patterns achieve, in general, a more satisfying balance in their lives between love and self-expression.

As a generalization, the Lover is the most likely not to choose to work in the public domain to the degree that that remains economically possible. If she does, her work is usually not her primary source of satisfaction. Lovers indicated that they rarely sacrifice love for practical reasons, yet they were the most likely to say that they had given up a creative talent or outlet.

If she is single, a Lover can experience an ongoing sense of frustration and loss that will require creative solutions. Relational needs are strong, intense energies that have to be channeled into a form if one is to feel whole and fulfilled.

On the other hand, the Lover who has more creative energy will have to work hard to redirect the shape of her life if she has chosen a High Relational form before she has understood her need for creative expression.

Relational energy can change. Some women start out being High Creatives, focused on career, and gradually find themselves wanting more intimacy in their lives. Some start out with families or being highly relationally focused and move to more integrative forms. Younger women today commonly start out focused on their creative energies and move more toward relationship; older women who felt they had little choice about marriage and mothering become more integrative after their children are grown.

What most characterizes Lovers is the intensity of their focus on others. The disadvantages of adopting this pattern involve the great danger of objectification, of conformity rather than choice, of feeling trapped by economic expedience into an unequal, nonmutual relationship. Lovers are more at risk than women in other categories of being exploited in relationship because they often accept economic dependency in order to focus their energies exclusively on relationship.

If a woman needs to make alterations in the pattern to meet the demands of changing needs and interests, this form is difficult to alter because, more than the other forms, one version of it has dominated the cultural narrative. Women who have High Relational energy often, without question, assume that they must play out a version of that story, the story of heterosexual marriage and childbearing. As a married but childless woman recently said to us of the common cultural assumptions, "I get asked, 'How many children do you have?' not 'Do you have children?'" The form itself has been almost assumed to be a story of the Smiling Woman, and in that sense women themselves have a harder time bringing their creativity to bear on changing it.

COMMON HIGH RELATIONAL THEMES: CONFORMITY VERSUS CHOICE, CHILDREN AND CONSTRAINT, A CONTEXT FOR CREATIVITY

Conformity was very definitely a part of the love story for both Joan and Ruth, but how could it not be? Conformity was synonymous with the era in which they fell in love. Conformity is directly opposed to creativity for men as well as women. It requires a surrender to the norm, an abdication of the novel, a loyal willingness to march in step with the others. Creativity requires courage, independence, and an ability to take risks and at least the glimmer of a new way to do things.

Both Ruth and Joan stressed that they didn't see that they had options to do things differently. Joan never thought twice about giving up Vassar and her intellectual passions to marry Corson, "it wasn't even a question." Her lack of questioning is all the more remarkable considering that she challenged convention, and fought for social justice.

Ruth held out longer. She was pretty sure the "normal life" didn't include what she wanted, which was "fame and fortune." She saw no reason to give up her career just because she married Phil. That far in her plot, she was able to rewrite the story line of traditional marriage. But children proved the guardians of conformity for Ruth. When the children came, she never returned to work in television.

Author Sarah Ruddick asserts that "there must be distinctive kinds of maternal thinking that arise from and are appropriate to the demands of maternal work."[7] Speaking of the kinds of thinking that arise from the need to "foster growth" or nurture, she says, "Whatever mix of happiness and sorrow it brings, a commitment to fostering growth expands a mother's intellectual life. Routines of responsibility, ex-

hausting work, and, for some, the narrowing perspectives of a particular profession or academic discipline conspire to undermine most
mothers'—and most adults'— active mental life. But children are fascinating. Even as caring for children may reawaken a mother's childhood conflicts, *in favorable circumstances* [emphasis ours] her children's
lively intellects rekindle her own. The work of fostering growth provokes or requires a welcoming response to change."[8]

The recently divorced woman, or even the married mother in a
heterosexual marriage, might have difficulty imagining the lively rekindling of intellectual interest in between doing loads of laundry,
repeated trips to court to fight for child support, and working two jobs
to meet the mortgage. As many experts have pointed out, social legislation still does not provide adequate supports for women, and men
still don't participate as equal partners in child rearing.[9] Given the
pragmatics of survival, intellectual energy may become a moot point
for the High Relational woman with children.

Ruth, even with a supportive husband and a good marriage, was
bored to tears intellectually, and felt quite literally like a "misfit" in
her suburban life. Although she loved her children, stimulating their
intellectual growth felt discontinuous, not continuous with the high
creativity of her writing days in television.

Perhaps if Ruth could have brought her creativity to bear on the
form itself of marriage and family she would have struggled less with
the effort to conform. The feelings were there, and were somewhat
conventional ones for a woman. She loved Phil passionately. She loved
her children. But the whole package was a difficult fit for her.

For Joan, on the other hand, raising children proved a comfortable
match for her intellectual energies. She would agree with Ruddick's
analysis. She easily channeled her intellectual passions into challenging her kids. Even when she began the second act of her life by
returning to Princeton in 1978 to finish her undergraduate degree, she
made a bridge between her own intellectual life and that of her kids,
now young adults.

Imitating the assignments given her by one of her professors she
tells us, "One Thanksgiving when the kids were all away I sent out this
letter that said, 'You are all warmly invited to address the family on the
subject of your choice at Thanksgiving dinner.' And those kids, they
never mentioned it. I didn't know whether they were going to do
anything or not, but when we sat down for Thanksgiving dinner, all
three of the kids, some of them also with girlfriends and boyfriends
present, and my parents, and Corson and I, each pulled out what they
had prepared. Young Corky addressed us on needing some space from
the family. Laurie chose to talk about how angry she was that she

hadn't been brought up with any religion. Kevin chose to talk about constitutional amendments. They had given a tremendous amount of thought to it and we had a wonderful time."

So, although Joan conformed, she also altered the fit in significant ways and was able to do so not only because she was creative but because she was not constricted by the practical economic constraints that many women face. She experienced herself as creating her life. Rather than feeling constricted, she saw the form of her life as an opportunity to express her ideas.

The kind of conformity sometimes required by the High Relational pattern can provide a positive context for creativity for many women. When a woman concentrates her energies on the private sphere of home and on relationship, she doesn't have the burden of conflict or choice in terms of what to do for a living. Nor does she have to figure out an acceptable arena for her creativity outside of the home. To paint, act, or cook professionally, to write for publication, to pursue a career, all bring one face to face with questions of talent, ambition, competition, commitment. Finding outlets for her creativity within the context of her home and family may be more satisfying for a woman than trying to find an avenue of creative expression that can exist parallel with a full-time job, or, for that matter, to find a job or career that is as creatively fulfilling as the work of creating a home environment. Creativity and career can be in conflict. The economics of the arts are discouraging. And certainly the corporation can be as stifling as the home.

High Relational women are apt to express creative energy through the domestic arts and through crafts, like cross stitch or quilting, that can easily be set aside, can accommodate interruption. Many High Relational women don't pursue creative activities that might divide their priorities because they believe, as Joan did, that one is only entitled to pursue a creative dream if she is willing to sacrifice everything for it and knows exactly what she wants.

This hesitation was echoed by many women in our study like Kathy, who, in her response to our long questionnaire, says she knew she had a strong creative energy earlier in her life but believed that she did not have sufficient talent. As a child she had a dream of being an astronaut. She traded the one dream in for the current dream, "a quiet life in a midsize town with my husband, dog, and a couple of children." She says, "I don't really consider myself creative. The only 'creative' things that I feel proud of are the sweaters that I've knit. I'm generally pleased with the way I've arranged my house (the colors work together), the little touches that 'make a house a home.' "

THE IMPACT OF THE CULTURAL STORY
ABOUT LOVE

When the High Relational pattern can be a context for creativity as it was for Joan, it can work well, it can be satisfying, it can transcend the constraints of the subject/object split. What most blocks women when they do limit their creativity in this pattern is the impact of the cultural story about love.

Ruth didn't question her creativity; she had already succeeded at work in the world and she knew she could excel. Her problem was that she didn't experience herself as having a choice about the relational form. She was more affected by the love story of the time, one of the major traps for the Lover. She bought into the part of the psychological love story that said that all capacity for healthy relatedness in adult life depends on the quality of the infant's attachment to the mother. In spite of her sensitivity to issues of male privilege, some part of her also believed the Freudian notions of the day. She thought that her love of work was in some way deviant, that she suffered from something she called, in rebellion against the more sexually determined jargon, "job envy."

Psychiatric help at that time didn't offer her a choice—its goal was to make her fit, "force her into the cultural norm," "work through" her job envy, accept the passive, receptive female role. When alcohol allowed her to express her rage too much (she relates one incident in which she took Phil's forty-five to the psychiatrist's office and laid it belligerently on the doctor's desk), the doctors prescribed tranquilizers to calm her down. Or to keep her down. Ruth, in fact, had strong ideas about the Mona Lisa smile. She says, "I always thought the Mona Lisa's smile was really saying 'Fuck you.'"

The love story applied to Joan in different ways.

It determined her belief that Corson, with his intellect and his work, was more important than she. Because she and Corson were active partners in building a home and raising their children, Joan did not experience herself as the object of someone else's definition although, reflecting back, she now sees the degree to which she had accommodated to the traditional forms of the time.

Ruth and Phil didn't have the same kind of partnership that Joan experienced. Although Phil was a very involved father, the form of his marriage to Ruth was even more traditional than Joan and Corson's. He was the doer, active in the public sphere. It didn't occur to him or to Ruth to alter the traditional form of their marriage once children arrived. Ruth was increasingly confined to the private sphere and her excursions into the public sphere in the form of volunteer work only whetted her creative appetite and left her hungry for more substantive work.

THE CHANGING STORY LINE

It's tempting to think that the constraints and dangers of the High Relational pattern have been modified by our more sophisticated ideas about love and relationship. But passion is passion, not rational, and it seems we are all vulnerable to slipping back into being object rather than consciously directing our lives in ways that are a good fit. We're all also vulnerable to falling into a particular pattern because the pressures of tradition are intense.

During the eighties, Sarah Richman, at age twenty-nine, became the CEO of an international conglomerate. Her lover William, a photographer, initially moved into the brownstone she owned in Manhattan. When they married and decided to have a child, however, Sarah moved away from New York with William, gave up her career, and put her creative energies into local politics and into loving him and her son, Kent. Within five years, their marriage was in trouble, William accusing Sarah of having "lost passion." Forty years separate Ruth's and Sarah's stories. But when problems evolved in the structure of her relational life, Sarah blamed herself for "not fitting" just as much as Ruth did.

Choice of a partner is important to the satisfaction of the Lover. Given the complexities of our lives currently, a partner has to be willing to participate fully in creating a workable relationship without reverting to traditional patterns that are equally constricting for men. William and Sarah's story looked different on the surface. She was the initial breadwinner, he the artist who stayed home. But when Kent arrived, it was still Sarah who had the responsibility of child care, and William who "helped out."

On the other hand, we heard many stories of Lovers for whom the form is a workable and good fit, who make small adjustments to traditional patterns and experience themselves very much as subject. Penny Mather is twenty-five, married, and has two children ages four and six. She lives in a house that she and her husband, Steve, built on the coast of Oregon. Our interviewer, who is a friend and has visited her there, says it is the most beautiful house she's been in. It's filled with plants and skylights and windows that look out over a drop to a creek below.

Penny takes great pride in the house, particularly the huge white kitchen equipped with restaurant ovens and stoves. Penny is self-employed as a caterer—she caters everything from affairs for a thousand people to small, elegant dinner parties. Her passions are her husband, her children, her house, and her catering work. She says what is most deeply satisfying to her is being in her home with her family and she thinks love gets more fulfilling for her as time goes on. Part of the reason she loves her work is that she can do it from her home. She describes the way she'll cut up vegetables in the evening where she can sit and be with Steve. When she's very busy, she hires babysitters but has them come to be with the children in her own home so she can maintain contact with them while she's working.

Penny altered the shape of the traditional marriage by expecting more participation with the children from Steve. They struggled to learn to compromise with each other. "Steve didn't used to help out before but this year he's done a lot. He comes home now and says, 'What time do you need from me this weekend?' We try to make it easier for each other."

When we ask Penny what makes her feel creative, most expresses who she is, she says, "Catering, everything that has to do with being in this house with this family, trying to mold my kids the way we want them to be."

So, in the nineties, the more traditional focus on relationship and family that characterizes the Lover still works well for many women. But this generation of women and those who will come after us are also beginning to write new stories that open up the possibilities for new forms for love.

Stories today include women both bearing and raising children alone, women who live in partnership with men who have no intention of marrying. A woman may choose to remain single, as more and more women do, and still live a life high in relational energy. A primary relationship, whether with a man or a woman, is *not* a prerequisite for expression of relational passion.

Many women today are unwilling to force themselves into the old High Relational forms and express relational energy in different ways. They may, like a colleague of ours, choose co-housing, buying a beach house with friends, and expressing much of their relational energy through their building of community. Or, like several of our colleagues and acquaintances, a woman may adopt a child when in her forties or bear one outside of marriage. A lesbian partnership may be the best fit.

Then again, like Alison, whose story concludes this chapter, a woman may alter the archetypal form very little, but find it still a good fit for her passion.

A PASSION FOR LIVING

The lunch that follows the funeral service of Jonathan Black has been catered by Walter, whom Jon knew from his days in musical theater. Walter has managed to have chocolate-covered strawberries flown in from Balducci's in Manhattan. There is champagne. Jon arranged the menu weeks before his death. His widow, Alison, is twenty-seven years old. Hers is a modern love story.

Eight months earlier, Jon is center stage in the local theater. From a handsome red wheelchair he sings "My Death," from Jacques Brel. Alison says, "I was there for every rehearsal and performance, and was allowed to share the joy at his ability to do one more time what he loved to do so much." She sits in the front row watching the performance. Few others in the audience know how poignant the song is that he sings, how he knows his own death waits.

"When I married," Alison said, "I understood the words and I meant the words I said. But what I understand about love now is its essence—that with it I can do anything. It is my greatest source of power, my greatest strength." Marriage to Jonathan required a kind of love that she could never have anticipated she would share, and a capacity to express and receive love that she never knew she had. Nine months following her marriage to him he began to have trouble walking. Neurological testing followed. He was diagnosed with a terminal illness.

Until college, Alison was a somewhat traditional young woman. Raised in both Europe and America, she was born to a life of seeming privilege. She knew the rules. Women were to channel their energies into marriage and create a well-functioning home, in which they raised clean, intelligent children with good manners. Success and goals were always to be big, always visible. Her first year at Barnard radicalized her. She became an ardent feminist whose closest friends were deeply involved with women's issues. She explored what was beyond the boundary of her known world, the world that had told her only part of the story about women. That exploration challenged many of the values she had been raised with.

Then she fell in love with Jon who was studying history at Columbia. With him she found a profound emotional connection she had never known. "Finally someone was there who really cared for *me*." She married him in February of 1988. She continued to work. They lived on the upper West Side, went to the theater, frequented good restaurants, entertained at home.

Alison was not a submissive wife, though Jon wanted a more traditional marriage than she did. They fought over housework. She thought it was ridiculous for her to focus on being a *hausfrau* and she wouldn't do it. They argued over money. She, with family money behind her, set limits on the way they lived. They were working it out.

By the time neurological problems necessitated Jon's wheelchair, Alison had given up her job. Despite the fact that she could easily afford nursing care, she made a choice to do most of the physical caretaking herself for the two and a half years that he lived after the diagnosis. They moved to New England for a quieter life once New York became too physically stressful, although Jon loved to fly back for the weekend while it was still physically possible.

Jon said four days before he died that the themes that lent shape to his life were Beauty and Love. There was no self-pity in him. After March 1991, he couldn't stand anymore even with a cane. Alison often said that the hardest part was that the wheelchair was always there; they could never sit side by side again. But she had shared the love that completed Jon's short life.

And the wheelchair that became so much part of their daily lives became also their prop for the black humor that helped them get through the worst times. They delighted in shocking onlookers with a routine they would pull in a public place, like a delicatessen. Jon, from his wheelchair, would imperiously demand in a loud tone, "Get me those black garbage bags from the lower shelf." Alison would say, "When's the last time *you* took out the garbage?" Jon would imitate Blanche in the film *What Ever Happened to Baby Jane?*, querulously whining, "You wouldn't treat me that way if I weren't in a wheelchair." Alison, doing Bette Davis, would say, "But you *are* Blanche, you *are*." Alison said, "Love allowed us to use whatever we had to make it good, to say to the world: Look at your lives, you fools; you think you're so safe."

Did she regret giving up her job? Did she regret pouring all of her energy into Jon and their life together? "No. Sometimes. I wish I could have had both. One time I canceled a trip to New York to see friends because he was so terrified of my going. We had a terrible scene about it but I knew then that it wasn't just dependency, that his terror was very real; that it was terror at the recognition of how helpless he had become. So I stayed home. I have no regrets. When it came to making choices I just always understood that I had a limited amount of time with him and that it wasn't something I was going to get back. I wanted every day to be the best it could be. Jon was the only person in my life I ever battled it out with to get my needs met. But it was also my need to give him the love he had never had. That just always took precedence. And it was my need to have his love for every day that I could." For Alison, loving first was a choice she made, an expression of her deepest energies, not a diversion of them.

It is easy to think that Alison had little choice about her commitment to Jon. She knew it was time-limited, and, after all, Jon was dying. But not everyone wants to, or can, respond to crisis in that way. And more, the choice to pour most of our passionate energy into a partnership, or children, or family, or friends, or community work, can be the right choice at certain points or maybe all of our lives even without the specialized circumstances Alison faced. Creativity can be expressed through relationship.

COURAGE

Many women who currently adopt the Lover pattern could have more access to their creative energy than they're likely to realize. We're still bound by the illusions of the split image and we fear that creativity must necessarily mean loss of relatedness. It takes courage to walk past that fear and create the new models that will free us.

There is no question that being a Lover can provide either rich satisfaction or exact terrible sacrifice. Within the same forms and their variations we can experience ourselves as either muse or lover, as either surrendering to conformity or affirming choice, as leading lives that are discontinuous with our first loves, or continuous with our earlier passions. The way we alter the archetypal form of the Lover will determine whether we find a good fit for our energies, or one that chafes uneasily, constricting our deepest dreams.

CHAPTER SIX

Artists: The High Creative Pattern

KATHERINE BRADFORD'S PAINTING, *Good Girl, Bad Girl*, captures the split image of women perfectly. The painting, done in blue tones, outlines two identical heads of women, almost cartoon drawings, facing each other. A dotted line divides them and a dotted line connects their eyes.

Katherine says about the image, "I wanted to do a painting about the tension that exists among women about who's a good girl and who's a bad girl—who's willing to play within the rules of society and who's willing to break the rules. By high school everyone knows who the good girls are and who the bad girls are. They eye each other— there's a dividing line between them—so I drew the painting to illustrate this. I used the formal abstract vocabulary I always use only this time I wanted to examine a feminist idea.

"By making these girls look almost exactly alike and by putting them forever in one painting, I wanted to probe the possibility that they are two parts of one self, that we have these two opposite sides within us. The interesting part to me is simply why we tend to divide up this way. I think a good painting sets up these kinds of questions— probes a paradox."[1]

Parenthetically, Katherine tells us, "This is the only painting I've done that my daughter wanted to own, so I gave it to her last year when she started her senior year in college."

The "paradox" of the painting, *Good Girl, Bad Girl*, mirrors the split image that dominates the story of women. When an Artist emerges from behind the shadow of the Smiling Woman and takes center stage, society castigates her as a bad girl. A woman such as

Kathy Bradford, whose High Creative passion shapes her life, symbolizes a woman who is fully subject. What Katherine seems to question is why it is that, because the woman as subject breaks the mold, society views her as bad.

THE ARTIST: PUTTING CREATIVITY FIRST

Women who choose other patterns prize balance and learn to compromise to achieve it. But the High Creative woman, whether she is an artist, professional, or career woman, is capable of being highly single-minded. This single-mindedness necessitates a break with convention that makes her path the least traditionally "female" of the four forms.

Women in the Artist category comprise 30 of the 222 in our sample, roughly 13 percent. Artists are women who tell us that creative activity makes them feel most whole and that relationship makes them feel most conflicted. Artists feel that creative activity makes life most meaningful and that they feel most alive and engaged when involved with it. As children, Artists were likely to have dreamed of being successful in the workplace or of having a life of travel and excitement. Interestingly, they are as likely as women in the Lover pattern to say that the story of love in their lives is unfulfilled, even though women in the creative group combined (Artists plus Innovators) are as likely to be married as relational women.

The singular characteristic of this pattern is clarity—knowing what one wants and needs to do and doing it with an unwavering, undiluted energy. In the data, Artist responses were consistent across measures, there was little conflict or discrepancy about the fact that creative pursuits were their priority.

Such clarity requires independence, confidence, selfishness. The woman in the Artist pattern must deal with issues that men have been bred to, but that are less familiar to most of us as women. These issues include competitiveness, goal setting, ambition. Our society has mistrusted and punished women who are too intense, too single-minded, too self-seeking.[2] But creative women are highly intense women, highly passionate women. And that intense energy can be a force strong enough to resist compromise, so that the woman as Artist sets priorities fairly easily. It is not that she never suffers conflict or guilt. But she is clear that she will put her vision first, so she does not struggle over figuring out what her priorities are, and her conflict is less within herself than with society's reaction to her.

Her very clarity, the self-focused passion, the determination to be the Artist rather than the art object puts the Artist at odds with cultural expectations. Society may hurl its final epithet at her by calling her "selfish." That selfishness, the being subject, is what most marks her as a "bad girl."

If she is to honor her creative impulse, the woman in the Artist pattern must have the courage to rise above that judgment of selfishness. She must dare to appropriate her own power, act with agency, so that she can say of her life, "I've gone out and done what I've needed to do." This confident embracing of her own power contrasts with the self-doubt we found in interviewing most other women.

The judgment of selfishness is just that—something imposed by external standards without any real appreciation for the experience of the individual woman. Many High Creative women pour intense energy into love, friendship, and raising children. The energies of love and creativity are inextricably intertwined and energy, if flowing from our own center, tends to expand rather than diminish. So love may come but love is not allowed to waylay the High Creative's vision. Perhaps her finest creation is the creation of her own life, a form that fits for her.

Beth Anderson, an important woman composer, puts it this way, "Your passion is the thing you reach for first." She reached for piano. Today, like other women in the Artist category we have talked with, she follows the rule that relationship, passionate and necessary though it might be to her happiness, must not, in the end, be allowed to intrinsically compromise, sabotage, or destroy creativity.

KATHERINE BRADFORD: PAINTING HER LIFE
AS CONSCIOUS CHOICE

Katherine Bradford is an abstract painter with a concrete and clear sense of who she is and what her life is about. Clarity is her trademark—the energy that shapes her is as clear as winter light on a bare landscape. Hers is, now, a consciously constructed life, built to the measurements of that energy, relating always to the central theme that lends her life coherence. "I am a painter," she says. "Life is enormous and chaotic. There is great satisfaction in whittling down to what is essential."[3]

She lives her life exactly as she wants to live her life. And she is highly respected as an artist.

From the brochure of her 1991 show at Victoria Munroe, we read:

Katherine Bradford's vocabulary of primary colors and basic geometric forms recalls both game boards and the work of early American modernists. Her colors and forms are not so much composed as "listed" on the surface of her painting. Words and numbers are also presented in list form, and while this evokes a strong sense of logic as in a game, the final statement is primarily poetic.[4]

Kathy Bradford says, "When I decided seriously, and it wasn't in one day, but the period of my life when I really felt that I wanted to be a serious artist, commit a great deal of time to painting and maybe put it at the center of my life as much as I could, I was in my early thirties. I was married and I had two kids who were just starting school. So as far as I'm concerned I was in one of the worst positions to be a really professional artist. There are many women who paint or write or whatever in that position, but I was frustrated. I wanted more. I wanted to devote the best part of my energy to my work. I wasn't interested in being someone who made watercolors of flowers in their spare time. I wanted to be an artist who could realize herself in painting."

She looked for models. Speaking about Georgia O'Keeffe, about whose life she read extensively, and Katharine Hepburn's life, she says that they are "interesting to everybody because they did seem to have a sense of themselves, that they were worth it, that they could take up a lot of room." For herself, she said, "I think that attitude has been hard for me to take on. I looked at O'Keeffe's choices and you know the fact that she dressed all in black and didn't wear jewelry seemed to me that she wanted to be very focused. She didn't bother with what she didn't want to bother with."

She also watched male artist friends. "It has helped me tremendously because women have a long tradition of being hobbyists as painters, but men take themselves so seriously. They're so ambitious. I watched how they worked, I watched the choices they made. What they put first . . . what they spent their money on . . . lots of paint. I mean they set themselves up. They had a sense of entitlement that I really had to learn by watching them. They also made huge paintings and that just seemed natural to them to do something big."

Bradford set out to make the focus of her life her painting. "I made all these changes, and I consciously went toward these things so I could paint." First she went through a painful divorce from her husband. "I felt I could never be the person I wanted to be and stay in that relationship." Her marriage consumed more energy than she could afford to expend if she was also to paint. "Love and creativity have always been at odds; one took up a lot of room that the other might take up. I think of them sometimes as being very mutually exclusive. I definitely went for creativity at the point that I became divorced."

She was in her early thirties. She says she had tried for a while to see herself as the "wife of an important person," her husband, but she felt it would be suicide. "Oh, maybe I'd buy art or something, and I'd probably think I was happy, but I wouldn't really have done what I wanted to, followed my deepest wishes. I would have just buried those wishes. I think by staying busy you don't pay attention to what you really want. He was a fine person, and we had a wonderful family; it's just that I was kind of going in a certain direction; I couldn't really handle both."

She says she was "really scared" to act on that choice. "I was scared that it was bad and I'd really be punished."

After the divorce, when her paintings began to sell, she rented her house to provide extra income, and she moved to New York, to be at the center of the art world. She chose to move to New York to live in a setting that would support her energy. It was a choice in favor of having the stimulation and serious criticism that would come to her by living in a community of artists.

Kathy had two children, a set of twins, at the time of the divorce. She "seized" the time that they spent with their father, who had joint custody, to paint. For other income, she depended on child support and on writing an art column for a local weekly paper.

But once divorced, in graduate school in fine arts, she continued initially to divert energy into relationships with men. At about thirty-nine she describes a turning point: "I just saw that the relationships I was having with men took up so much time, and the men were interesting but always looked to me to help them. Many of them were other artists. I couldn't possibly concentrate on myself and what I needed and be in those relationships. So I just kind of happily dropped out of that whole game and I had really some wonderful years where I worked hard, I stayed up late, I didn't spend time cooking meals, I did exactly what I wanted to do with my time. My kids were teenagers and were away a lot. I feel they were just as glad I wasn't in a relationship. I read a lot, I felt great, and I had plenty of time to think. I think it was then that I finally got in touch with what I wanted to make ... good paintings. Relationships just took up too much time and energy. You just couldn't be as 'selfish' as I think an artist needs to be."

Bradford was rare in recognizing that it was not just the marital structure but the preferred form of all heterosexual relationships, in which the man is the performer, the woman his audience, he the important one, she the support system, that drained energy from her central vision. Rarer still was her discipline in making the choice to resist the distractions of those relationships.

The thing about Bradford is that her choices have all been conscious ones. She has been proactive not reactive. Even amidst the energy and stimulation of New York that she sought, she has made choices about the potential distractions of being in a large city. She doesn't go to every new film, or lecture, every party. She exposes herself only to those aspects of that community that feed her rather than drain her. "I try to exist in New York, which is a very competitive professionally oriented place, and not get too drawn into the emotional uproar . . . everybody's gossip and disappointment and triumphs and financial this and that."

She is careful about all distractions, even money. She doesn't make economic security a prerequisite for pursuing art. She does sell her painting, but she also teaches part time. "I've never done a nine-to-five job," she says. "I think that's bad for creativity."

In her thinking about what is essential, she has whittled away too much extraneous focus on external reward. "A lot of artists get bitter. They don't find success and they lose hope and they lose their optimism; they lose that energy that they need to grow from." Talking about the hubbub surrounding her recent show in New York, she says, "It gets you way off center. You're hustling and talking to people, and I'm looking forward to calming down and being quiet, getting back to the life in my studio, painting."

Again Kathy Bradford has put essentials first. She knows "how much is enough."

MAGIC AND INTENSITY

If Kathy's experience captures the commitment and clarity of the high creative pattern, Julie Flanders's speaks vehemently to the intense and enchanting quality of living a life engaged with one's most imaginative and creative self. Julie is twenty years younger than Kathy Bradford. She is passionately involved in theater and in songwriting and she has no intention of letting twenty years elapse during which she puts them on hold.

We asked her, "As a child did you ever have a vision or a dream about something you would do or be?"

"Magic," she said without hesitation. "I always dreamt that I would practice magic. I am really intense and I like things that I can come up against. All the passions meet in something where I can engage all of my energy."

Our interviewer's energy is already high when she meets Julie in a noisy café in Greenwich Village. She says, "Just meeting Julie is an intense experience. One is drawn into her excitement."

Julie, a native New Yorker, talks at a speed that is twice as fast as normal conversation. Her long straight black hair falls to the front of her face as she talks, and she frequently scoops it up with both hands and places it on her back, behind huge gold hoop earrings. She is tall and slender, dressed in a stylish black stretch dress accompanied by an oversize black leather sack of a handbag. Her lipstick is bright bright red. Her outward persona seems to match the inner experience she is describing.

Songwriting and acting both fully engage Julie. They are still magic to her and she compares them to alchemy, transformation.

She says, "I love, I love putting music together. I love creating the sound, having a cohesive voice to the music . . . I love getting an idea, having a vision of something and then rendering it with people I want to be around. I put together a band recently and it is music that I have written that is rendered exactly the way that I want to hear it." She loves the collaboration, the relational aspect of music.

She also wanted to pursue something separate, a part of her life that was separate from her main collaboration. Acting provided a separate avenue for involvement. "I really love acting. I love it. I am just totally completely crazy about it. It is really intense discipline and if you work on your technique there is a moment at which you . . . well it is like you are getting sucked down into another universe. I mean it is like a trance thing so you work and you work and work and then it takes off. It is like you set up a container for yourself. You dive through something and you go into some sort of time warp, you just kind of go somewhere else. You come back and wonder, 'What happened?' You dive and you know that if any part of you holds onto the ledge you get rapped against the wall or you get splinters in your hand if you don't dive all the way out."

When Julie says she likes things she can "come up against" and then talks about diving through to another dimension, the emotions she describes are those that the psychologist Mihaly Csikszentimihalyi has called being in a state of Flow. He describes Flow as arising in a situation in which you are challenged enough to have to use your full energy but one in which your skills are equal to mastering the challenge. It is a kind of optimal experience, a full focusing of attention in the activity, and lack of self-consciousness. Psychic energy is invested in reaching the goal, rather than in ruminating about any threat to the self, any fear or doubt. People frequently describe the Flow experience as a feeling of oneness or union with their surroundings, a suspension of ordinary time, a profoundly deep concentration that involves one's total being.[5]

Flow describes what a woman feels who is in tune with her own energies, and fully engaged in expressing them.

Julie's recognition of her own intensity and her clarity about the moments and activities that allow those intense feelings to flow precedes her creation of a form for expressing the feelings.

She must be and remain very passionately interested in herself to be aware of those feelings and needs. Yet, this passionate interest in ourselves has been pathologized for us as women, because the split image story has told us we are supposed to intensely and fully engage with relationships, not with ourselves.

Perhaps no word forms a more integral or damaging part of the psychoanalytic language of love than the word "narcissistic." It is used to shame us for focusing on our own experience. Yet as women we are so required to focus outward on our relational worlds and the practicalities of daily living that support other people's self-involvement that it will inevitably appear "narcissistic" to the rest of the family and social system when we dare be fascinated with our own rather than their reflections.

Totality of engagement with oneself is a necessary part of the magic and intensity of the creative process. The dialogue with self can take many forms for women. For Lynn Wilson, another composer, meditation as her spiritual practice has many of the same elements of composing, and both are similar to the full engagement of passionate sex. "When one is in a sexual climax you have this sense that you lose track of time. When meditation or anything is completely involving (for instance I was washing lettuce, washing every leaf of lettuce, that was my yogic instruction, just looking at every single leaf the way I would be with every breath), it allows you to go deeply into something. You trust that you won't, or that you can't, go so far in that you get lost, or you will get lost, but it will be alright."

Lynn's sense of time when composing is not at all different from her sense of time when washing the lettuce. "I am pretty damn good at being conscious of time in my left brain. I can hear a piece of music and I know whether it is sixty beats to the minute or eight, but when I am in that other place that is the reality, and when I am composing I don't know how long it has taken, whether it has been a half hour or one and a half hours or two hours. I lose time but I am in deep relationship with myself."

PROBLEMS FOR THE WOMAN AS ARTIST:
CHOICE, FEAR, TALENT, MONEY

The woman in the Artist pattern is confronted daily with the necessity to focus and to choose. Kathy Bradford spoke of the distraction that relationship can create if one needs to focus exclusively on one's work and creative inclinations. But love relationships are not alone in their potential to divert energy. As scholar Kenneth Gergen points out in his analysis of the postmodern life, multiplicity of choice becomes one of the greatest pressures we face today. "The world of friendship and social efficacy is constantly expanding, and the geographical world is simultaneously contracting. Life becomes a candy store for one's developing appetites"—we become "saturated selves."[6]

Gergen goes on to say that today a person can hardly achieve self-respect unless demonstrating proficiency or participation in everything from food and wine sophistication, fitness training, money management, to being a family person.[7] We can react guiltily for not measuring up, we can experience an optimistic sense of enormous possibility, or we can make clear choices.

The necessity to make choices is critical for the Artist, no matter what her preferred medium or the focus of her work, because she needs to create the time and space for herself to dive in and get lost in herself. This diving in and getting lost, the full engagement that Julie Flanders describes, is critical to the creative process. Many women in other patterns can do it in relationships, in athletics, in spiritual practice. But many of us have a fear of giving ourselves so totally to the moment, becoming so passionately engaged that we "lose ourselves" in a creative interest. One friend gave up her love for watercolor painting because she knew if she let herself "go" she wouldn't want to do anything else. Men and women both fear this immersion.

Otto Rank, in one of the first and most influential psychological books on art, *Art and the Artist*, foreshadowed the split image for all artists, even men, in 1932.[8] He thought that life energy or sexual energy might detract from the aesthetic or creative sensibility, and due to this split, characteristic of the dualism inherent in much of patriarchal Western thought over the years, he thought that the artist struggles to liberate himself from the sexual and biological. Rank also talks of the problem of total absorption in creation. "One means of salvation from this total absorption in creation is, as in ordinary life, the division of attention among two or more simultaneous activities; and it is interesting in this connection to note that work on the second activity is begun during work on the first just at the moment when the latter threatens to become all-absorbing."[9] The second work may be different in kind from the first or a continuation of it on another level.

The fear of total absorption in creative activity is comparable to a fear of death; if one totally expends one's life energy in a single-minded intense focus on an activity does that energy essentially burn itself up? We think that for many women, total absorption in creative activity would threaten the relational structure of their lives. But most of us don't have to worry. Total absorption isn't possible for us anyhow. As women we lead interrupted lives, our own agendas are continually interrupted by the needs of others, or even by our own awareness of inattention to those needs. Interrupted as we are by others, we often don't have to worry about limiting or interrupting ourselves. It is hard enough to focus on our own agenda.

The process of immersion varies among High Creative women. Some of them engage with their creative energy in a way that is linear, goal-oriented, single-minded. Their passionate involvement is "all or nothing," and will brook no interruptions, no detours. Others work on four projects simultaneously; their process is more spiral, circular, everything is grist for the mill.

All women tend to avoid immersion in their creative process to some degree and it's typically fear of the outcome, fear of having too little talent that blocks them. Immersion suggests taking oneself very seriously. Many High Creative women have energy that goes unexpressed because of this fear, and as a result they often don't discover their passions until late in life. They find themselves instead in patterns that fit less well for them.

In spite of the fact that many of us experience ourselves as happiest when we connect to our moments of aliveness, our childlike creativity, without regard for judgments about how good our "product" is, creative immersion is rarely easy for us.

The risk is the challenge to our perfectionism, the shame we feel when we can't be the best or the only. The risk is that the world will invoke the shaming messages of "selfish, unladylike, incompetent, unattractive, unloving" to get us back into line.

Or worse, our aspirations will be trivialized. Someone will say, "Oh I didn't know you wrote poetry" casually, offhandedly, and move on to the next conversational subject, not noticing how central our poetry is to our life. We will feel embarrassed, foolish.

We don't need others to shame us. We are good at doing it to ourselves.

Norma Marder, a writer and novelist who once sang avant-garde music, was faced with a rare opportunity for professional advancement that would have required her to say no to others and yes to herself. She invoked a sense of shame to limit herself. The way she put it: "There was a knot inside me, tight as the knots my father tied on boxes. Each loop of twine was a truth—I was a responsible mother, I had a traditional marriage, I learned notated atonal music slowly. I could have cut the knot, I thought, *if only I had perfect pitch*. Perfect pitch is a natural ability—like being an idiot savant—which enables people to sight-read anything. Without it I wouldn't be able to perform adequately in case of a domestic emergency."[10]

In our survey, this theme of having too little talent and fear of not being good enough was significant in women's responses. We've said earlier that 58 percent of the women surveyed had a talent or creative outlet in childhood that they later gave up. What distinguished the creative group, Artists and Innovators, is that none of them said that they gave up creativity, when they did, because they didn't have enough talent.

When it came to the fear of not being good enough, the focus being on fear of inadequacy, Artists, along with Leaders, were *least* likely to cite fear as a reason for giving up a creative pursuit. But Innovators, the other creative category, along with Lovers, were *most* likely to cite *fear of not being good enough* as a reason to give up creativity. These results suggest an interesting question. Do Lovers choose love because they fear being inadequate to pursue self-expression, or do they have insufficient experience of their creativity because they have channeled their talents into relationship? Most Lovers said that they didn't have a creative talent or outlet that they subsequently gave up, suggesting that many of the Lovers never felt they were creative to begin with.

This mantra of "I don't have enough talent to justify taking myself so seriously" has been reinforced throughout the history of music, literature, and art as we saw in chapter 2. We not only have believed the cultural story that there are few great women in the arts, few great women entrepreneurs, few women in the professions that make their mark as deeply as do men, but we also believe that product is more important than process and that only a great talent and a great success justifies putting our energies into our own vision. Or we say, "I'm only a potter or a quilter, a craftsperson, not an artist."

Sheila Keats, a pianist, teacher, and writer on music addresses the issue of talent this way. "I have an inner drive to do whatever I do well. Luck plays a part in everybody's life. If you happen to meet up with the right person at the right time and they offer you the right thing to do, that's luck."

On the issue of talent she says, "Talent is only as good as what you do with it. You work with what you've got. There are people in this world with much less talent than mine and there are people with a great deal more. And it's beside the point. I've made happen what I could make happen with the ability that I have. There are people, and I knew them as students at Juilliard, who arrived there having been the best pianist in their home town or the best violinist from wherever they came from. They discovered at Juilliard that everybody was the best of where they came from. Some of them got extremely discouraged, because they had visions of being the top solo performing artist, and since they couldn't have that they wanted nothing. That is counterproductive.

"All I wanted was to go to a music school and learn everything I could about music. Let me tell you a wonderful story. Guess who played his graduation exam right before me? Van Cliburn! Now, I don't play like Van Cliburn now, and I didn't then. The man is a big talent. I walked into that exam and handed my program to the dean, who was chairman of the jury, and I said to him, Do you folks *really* want to hear me play the piano? Because I knew perfectly well that I was not going to have the same kind of career as Van, and I didn't expect to. But to me it was more important to do anything in music than to do something else."

Sheila knew that she wasn't going to play Tchaikovsky like Van Cliburn. She resolved the issue of talent by making process more important than product. She was clear about what she loved. She transcended perfectionism and shame because the need to do what she wanted to do was stronger than the need to be extraordinary at it.

The woman who follows the Artist path needs to take responsibility for figuring out how important achievement is to her and what role ambition and money play in her life scheme.

We live in a society that equates money with value, and as Lucy Lippard points out, "Women's [art] work still sells for a tremendous amount less than men's, although there are now some really incredibly successful women artists." This equation of money with value can lead us to discard our creative path unless we produce a product that is economically viable. Even most men can't make a living in the arts.

Beth Anderson is described in the *New Groves Dictionary of American Operatic Composers*[11] as having done conceptualist avant-garde theater pieces, text sound, musical theater, chamber music, songs and chants for voice, and instrumental music for bands. She has also received numerous awards and commissions, from the National Endowment for the Arts (NEA) and National Public Radio, among others, and written the scores for three musical comedies and one musical theater piece, all of them produced in New York City.

Still, Beth doesn't make the money that would allow her to be more single-minded about her music. The economics of music defeat her. She would agree with the writer Katherine Anne Porter who said, "I think I've only spent about 10 percent of my energies on writing. The other 90 percent went at keeping my head above water."[12] Very occasionally, Beth gets a rare week free to focus entirely on her music, as she did this summer as Bennington College's composer in residence.

Certainly she would like to say "no" to other commitments more often than she does so that she can focus more on her music. But it just isn't always possible when one is scrambling to keep body and soul together. Nor does Beth make those compromises in her music that would always render her commercially current. "The idea that beauty is revolutionary is a revelation to me. I once believed that the concept of the music was more important than its sound . . . I've rediscovered the part of my brain that can't decode anything, that can't add, that can't work from a verbalized concept, that doesn't care about stylish notations, but that does make melodies that have pitch and rhythm. . . . Beauty is enough."[13]

How different this vision is from the compromises made when one succumbs to what Tillie Olsen calls in *Silences,*

> *The overwhelmingness of the dominant.*
> *. . . The insoluble.*
> *Economic imperatives.*[14]

Beth is ambitious but when asked whether she would take money or fame if she had her choice, she says clearly, "I would take respect, respect for my life work."

Interestingly, when we asked what factors blocked women from pursuing creative activity more than they do now, the women in the Artist group all responded that they needed money more than they needed time (30 percent said they needed money more than time compared with 14 percent for the Innovators, 20 percent for the Leaders, and 22 percent for the Lovers). *All* of the other groups reported that they needed time more than money. The Leaders in particular overwhelmingly needed time more if they were to be more creative (46 percent), and the Innovators were close behind with 43 percent. In general, all the women who chose integrative paths, Leaders and Innovators, predictably experienced the pressure of time more than either the Artist or Lover groups.

Integration and balance have become the new measures of success, but often women who integrate don't recognize limitations and try to "do it all," so what they lack is time. High Creatives, though, have trouble having enough money to support their self-expression. Since we tend to value artistic creativity so little as a society, they find very little in the way of social or financial support for their work and often sacrifice economic stability to pursue it.

NOURISHING THE CREATIVE VISION

External supports and resources for the creative woman are very difficult to access, there are few of them available. The High Creative woman searches for ways to nourish her own passion. She has to be creative in overcoming the obstacles. The most critical effort is to stay in touch with the driving force of the energy. In 1935, quilt maker Nancy Crow said, "I make quilts because I am driven to. I have no control over the drive . . . I love trying myriad colors, together up on the wall of my studio while searching intuitively for answers that will fill my soul with excitement."[15]

Many women we talked with have experienced such a driving inner necessity to express themselves that they ignore or overcome obstacles. But many of us give up, don't know how to keep creativity and hope alive. "Filling the soul" seems less a priority given the practical demands of our lives.

How does a woman nourish her vision despite the absence of social supports? Women count mentors, spiritual life, community, and the ability to tolerate marching to a different drum while being criticized for it among the crucial nutrients for vision.

Lynn Wilson, the composer, at one point doubted her commitment to music. Lynn had been singing and composing since she was five. But she dropped out of graduate school after a male professor said that she just had to be more passionate about music than about anything in her life. She says she looked in the mirror and felt, "No, that's not it. I'm not passionate enough. I mean he almost said, 'It's not worth it.'" She got off track, leaving music to take a job as a vocational counselor.

For almost four years she struggled, with the help of another mentor, a woman therapist, to finally come back to music.

Often the kind of personal contact and modeling a mentor can provide is critical to our internalizing a sense of the importance and value of our work. The results of studies on personal, academic, and career development consistently emphasize the need for mentors, particularly female mentors.[16]

A mentor can point us toward the limitless horizon, even while we are deluged by doubt. It is the mentor who says, "Sure you can."

Perhaps the popularity of vision quests, shamans, spirit guides, reconnection with the goddesses, and search for archetypal images speak to our paucity of mentors. While these mystical traditions feed our imaginations, sometimes they mask our real need for the warmth and encouragement of contact with strong women who can support and encourage us in the dailiness of our struggles to express ourselves.

Ellen, who let her dream of being a performing artist, musician, singer, painter, poet reemerge a few years ago at mid-life and mid-career as a family therapist, believes that her career choice alienated her from her passions. Struggling to nourish those passions now, she had abandoned them for years because she had "no family support, no financial support, no cultural support, and a self-image that didn't permit her to think of herself as an artist."

On a trip to Hawaii she found a mystical connection to her own creative spirit. She says, "I connected with my birth capacity there. It's the Big Island in particular—where the volcano flows like blood. I can be completely feminine in that context."

But nowhere in Ellen's life is there a consistent mentor figure who is avidly interested in and encouraging of her creative journey.

Another support to the creative life is a strong spiritual practice. Lynn's spiritual life is extremely critical to her dialogue with herself, and she feels that she needs a healing loving relationship with herself so that she won't be thrown off course again. Essentially she affirms herself, constantly reinforcing her need to take herself seriously. Her spiritual practice is Buddhism.

Susan Osborn, the former lead singer for the Paul Winter consort and a popular teacher of the power of song, says that singing *is* spiritual practice. Susan once experienced a fifteen-year period of laryngitis. She explains it this way.

"When my throat shut down I was denying emotion. You gotta be out of your mind to sing. When I began to let more of the truth of who I am out, my throat opened up again. Singing offers me the possibility of transforming energy, where I can have an experience of my whole self. Singing is about taking a stand for myself, about the power of telling the truth. It is the thing that's moving from the inside that cannot be denied."[17]

Editors of the "Northern Lights Studies in Creativity, 1986" also make the strong connection between creativity and spirituality: "We believe that creativity is not merely a matter of esthetics. As art is neither inert nor apolitical in its effects, creativity . . . is not just the possession of a few gifted individuals called artists. It is a name for the spiritual potential within consciousness waiting to spring into action in the world, not only in the form of works of art, but as a means of disentangling the conflicting threads of experience."[18]

Our data support this view of creativity and spirituality as interdependent. Forty percent of Artists said that the choices they made about spirituality were critical in making them feel whole, compared with only 10 percent of the Innovators, 26 percent of the Leaders, and 28 percent of the Lovers. As the feminist theologian Mary Daly says,

"It is the creative potential itself in human beings that is the image of God."[19]

Community is critical too in supporting the creative vision. Creativity of necessity implies seeing things a new way. New views and visions are not always popular and women can be frightened. The courage to see things in new ways can be maintained more easily when one has relationships to support it.

Both Lynn Wilson and Susan Osborn have a community of other creative women and men that supports their vision. Our data suggests that friendship was of striking importance to the Artists. Forty percent of them ranked friendship with spirituality as a critical choice in making them feel whole, while only 14 percent of Innovators, 26 percent of Leaders, and 23 percent of Lovers felt similarly. Another interesting trend suggests that geographical location is more than twice as important to a feeling of wholeness for Artists than it is for other groups. By contrast, the Leaders overwhelmingly said children were the most important choice in making them feel most whole. Creative women, whether Artists or Innovators, tend to have deep aesthetic attachments to certain places, finding location twice as important to their sense of wholeness as the relational groups do. Artists also tend to choose places where they can find the kind of communal support so critical to maintaining their vision.

HIGH CREATIVE ENERGY: THE DARK SIDE

Sandra, a writer who does carpentry to earn a living, is in her thirties. When asked how she experiences herself when she feels love she says, "I cry because a rock is so gray."

The excruciating piercing of the soul by beauty, the opening of the heart to the pain of the other, the knowing that we are "the cloud, the leaf, the tree"[20]—these connections are the source of the love that will save the world. Because vision inevitably carries with it the capacity to see pain, and because what is true is often painful, the woman as Artist suffers a more acute sensitivity and with it, often, a deeper sense of compassion.

As Holly Near says, "Part of being an artist is being willing to be shocked, being willing to be surprised, being willing to be hurt, by things we've been shocked, surprised, and hurt by for years."[21]

Matthew Fox asserts that creativity and compassion are "in fact the same energy. . . . The artist, true to the primary process which includes connecting all memories and traces of experiences, is involved in 'taking it all in'—and in making the connections. And all justice-making and compassion are a making of connections between the oppressed and oppressor (who is also oppressed), an intuition that the sun falls on all alike . . ."[22]

Facing pain means facing fear. In her extraordinary biography of Georgia O'Keeffe, Roxana Robinson talks about the fear of the artist and what it takes to overcome it. "Imagination is integral to courage: the sensibility that imagines no risks does not knowingly take any, and there is no bravery in a landscape without danger. Georgia's enormously powerful imaginative capabilities resulted in a great capacity for fear of every sort. . . . The experience was always worth the risk. 'I'm frightened all the time,' she said, 'scared to death. But I've never let it stop me. Never!' "[23]

The fear that confronts a lover as one senses the invitation in the eyes of the beloved, or the questions in the eyes of a child who has just seen death, are like the fear of the writer before the blank page, the fear of the singer facing her first opening night audience. The danger is an authentic encounter with the choice either to celebrate the indomitability of the human spirit or capitulate to despair. The danger is the fear of suffering and loss. It is fear of failure.

Often, for the Artist, the fear is a dual one—a fear of the loss of self, on the one hand, and loss of love on the other. Sandra, whose mother died when she was eight, says, "When I'm first in love I express my identity more fully, then I become rigidly protective of emerging aspects of my identity as if they will not be allowed. . . . Fear of loss always accompanies the euphoria of my falling in love. . . . It is risky and exhausting, but my fear of depression (my fear of creating loss because I don't want loss to happen *to* me) is a strong moving force."

The fear of the intimacy of relationship, of "losing oneself to relationship," is both painful and typical for the woman in the Artist pattern. Sometimes, because of the inherent necessity in the High Creative pattern that a woman put herself first, or be a "bad girl," women have to vanquish a belief that something is wrong with them, that they are incapable of intimacy. Actually they just need a form of relatedness that doesn't detract from their creativity, but there have been few models for this. Those that exist, like O'Keeffe, often had to live separately from their partners for extended periods of time.

What's more, our families of origin tend to unthinkingly reinforce the Smiling Woman narrative. When violinist Sarah Minton went to Japan for six months to study violin in her forties, she says her family and friends asked, "How will your husband manage?" not, "How exciting for you." In fact, with a touch of humor, she made a videotape for her otherwise totally competent and brilliant physician husband to watch in her absence. It featured flash cards with phone numbers for all the services he might need, from massage to conversation, and an audio-visual tour of the family refrigerator so that he wouldn't starve.

THE REWARDS: THE BEAUTY OF A COMPLETED GESTURE

The Artist experiences passionate involvement with herself. Like all women who are subject, whatever their path, she is the antithesis of passive. Patterns of involvement may differ for women in this group. But all know what makes them happy, what activities contribute to their sense of wholeness and aliveness, and what conditions must be met to set the stage for pursuing those activities. They know which distractions will take them in a tangential direction, away from the expression of their central energies, and they are willing to suffer the discipline of saying "no" to the extraneous, willing to endure the sometimes tedium of endless hours spent repetitiously perfecting their craft. They are able to set aside questions of talent and reward in pursuit of excellence. They are capable of loneliness but know the joy in solitude. And they sometimes need to temporarily set aside values such as balance and doing for others that have been so important a story line in the cultural narrative for women.

What all of us can learn from the woman as Artist is that a passionate, wholehearted "yes" always requires us also to say "no." Saying yes to ourselves sculpts a life whose shape expresses our passions rather than constricting them.

What is it that we have to say yes to? Essentially to passion, to our first loves. Like High Creative women, we can take our passions seriously and honor our energies. Like them we can have a heightened aliveness, an intense involvement with our own lives, a quality of still being able to experience the newness of "first love" and the beauty of a completed gesture.

CHAPTER SEVEN

Leaders: The Relational Integrative Pattern

IN THE FOREWORD TO THE BOOK, *Women and Families*—
edited by her good friend and colleague Monica McGoldrick, along
with Carol Anderson and Froma Walsh—family therapist Betty Carter
writes: "Every revolution has its firebrands and martyrs, its trailblazers
and historians, but only successful revolutions are blessed with leaders
creative enough to grasp and shape new ideas and, at the same time,
help us to implement them at every level ... in our personal and
professional lives ..."[1]

Monica McGoldrick is one of the creative leaders Betty refers to.
What makes Monica so distinctive is that as a Leader, she has modeled
a path that integrates relational and creative energy—not only is relationship important to her personally, but it is the driving passion of
her work. Her preoccupation has been to understand and enhance
human connection. One of her outstanding achievements is her capacity to bring people together to work at new approaches to family
problems. For Monica, work of her own and relational life are integrated energies, one flows from and into the other.

As a revolutionary in the field of family therapy, Monica is a
theoretician, teacher, clinician, writer, trainer, mentor. She is or has
been at the helm of many of the major organizations in her field and
she spearheads some of its most innovative movements. She was recently awarded an honorary doctorate in recognition for her work in
the field. Feminism, loss, life-cycle development, ethnicity, the development of the "family genogram," are only a few of the areas of study
she has published on.[2] She has ventured into new career paths recently
by establishing her own training institute.

Her career keeps her traveling. She flies in and out of airports like most of us drop in at the dry cleaners. She is also a mother and a wife and she has a passion for the opera, for Ireland, and, she tells us, for singing arias on the way to work in her car. Before becoming a social worker and ultimately a family therapist, she studied for a master's degree in Russian studies at Yale.

There was only one problem with Russian studies. "I was raised to believe I should be a wife . . . and mother. The further I went in my career, the more I began to worry how I was going to do that because it didn't seem to fit with Russian studies. I remember thinking, if I really do Russian studies, that's going to take me to Russia. How am I gonna find a husband . . . ? I was raised to have a career, but it was somehow to be fit into marriage and kids."

There were other reasons for Monica's ultimate defection from the world of academia to the world of mental health. But bottom line it was her feeling that, in academia, "the further you go, the less you can relate. I was getting myself further and further into the upper chambers of the Sterling Library all by myself."

When she discovered family therapy, Monica knew she had found her passion. It was a "fit" for her because it integrated the deeply intellectual side of her with the need for relatedness and connection. "That you could relate whatever you could do intellectually to something that would connect you. From the beginning, I have never had the slightest thought that I was in the wrong field." She describes her passion for her field as "absolutely the same thing" as her passion for Russian studies. "It was a continuity . . . I didn't really change fields, because I was in love with Dostoevsky and this was Dostoevsky, just translated." One thinks of the grand panorama of human complexity and emotion depicted in *Anna Karenina* or *The Brothers Karamazov*. The passion for opera, for Russian literature, for intellectual intensity, and for people all have a common thread—they are full of the depth, richness, and emotion of human experience—the kind of emotion that begs to be focused and expressed in interaction with other people.

Monica was a product of the baby boom. She pursued a career first and thought about marriage along the way. Though she could contemplate a form for her life different from the one her mother may have chosen, she was still heavily influenced by the prevailing story of love.

At a point when her career finally seemed mapped out and she had placed herself where she wanted to be, Monica met and married her husband, Sophocles, a physicist who was born and raised in Greece. There was only one problem for Monica—he wanted to go back there. "I kept thinking, how could that work? That's not gonna fit with what

I'm doing. . . . I don't speak Greek and I don't want to live in Greece, and no way. And he would then accuse me of not loving him enough and I would think, he's right, I guess I don't love him enough. I guess I'm an inadequate lover. And then it was only later that I thought how stuck I was in that set of definitions where loving your man means you give up your life."

They didn't go to Greece. As Monica says, "Luckily, it didn't work out." Sophocles didn't get the job. Had she been faced directly with making a choice, the story would have been more complex.

Having been raised never to question that she would be a wife and mother, like most of us, Monica struggled to free herself from the dominant ideas about just how much of herself she had to give up. Many of her conflicts have been resolved, many are a source of on-going discomfort. For many years most of her relational energy went into work, not only because work was a passion, but because repeated attempts to get pregnant failed. Her son was born and she became the legal guardian of another child, a daughter, at a point when her career was already well-established. Monica says relationship became even more important after John was born. The focus of her energy shifted somewhat more to her family life. But she was not inclined to sacrifice her work life to a more traditional image of being a mother. Both her children and her work are critically important to her, and if one looks at the issue of meaning in her life, there is absolute continuity between her personal sense of relatedness and her professional vision. Her conviction is that relationship, the connections between people, are what matters.

Watching Monica operate in the professional arena can be deceiving because she is so busy, so prolific, travels so often, is so engaged by her profession that one constantly wonders how she has time for her family. On the surface it appears that her energies belong more in the Innovator category. It takes more personal conversation to understand how she really experiences her relational life.

There is no area in which relationship doesn't figure prominently. It's not by accident that this chapter opens with a quote from her friend, Betty Carter, because Monica's professional life is played out always in the context of friendship and supportive collegial relation-ships. Friendship seems an absolute priority to her, and with one or two exceptions, her work and friendship networks are not separate. All her major books have been collaborations with her friends. When much of one's time is spent at professional gatherings, the people one repeatedly sees there become one's close connections. Monica says, "Those relationships are very meaningful to me. I wish I had more time." One of her biggest regrets is that she doesn't see people more on personal visits. She looks forward to more of this kind of contact when she's older and work is less a focus.

The passion for her work, the passion for relationship, the need to balance and integrate her energies, makes for complexity and conflict. Monica is realistic about her limitations, the conflicting demands on her time. "Sometimes I feel here I am the big shaker and mover on people's being connected and I haven't had time to go see my sisters, or to call that relative, to go talk to my son today." She is not always as close to important people in her life as she might like to be. She describes a conversation with her mother that is marred by her own impatience, her preoccupation with other things. "And then I catch myself and say, 'Geez, Monica, you were just talking about how you are going to miss her when she dies, and now when she had that conversation you were sort of uh huh, uh huh, and you were reading the paper.' But then some things have worked out a lot better. I guess you don't ever get it right. I wish days were longer and that there were more time. I worry about my sisters dying and will I have taken advantage of those relationships. I worry about when Betty Carter dies, and what will the world be like without her, and I worry about if I died, who would take care of my children." Thinking about the limitations of time she muses, absently, "If I died, that would be the worst problem!" Monica would probably say that her preoccupation with death is an Irish trait. Or she probably doesn't like the idea of dying because it will stop her from doing everything she loves to do. She even dislikes sleep. "Sleep is pretty wasted time," she says.

A perfect day for Monica would involve doing all the things she loves to do. There would not be enough time. "I love to see families, I love to teach, I love to relate to John [her son]. A really great day would be brunch with a friend, two movies in the afternoon with cappuccino and a brownie in between, a great dinner, and go to the opera." Yet another perfect day would involve time with her children and Sophocles. Though she and Sophocles are very different and have completely different work passions, they share a love of opera. They are likely to love the same arias. They have a connection that is sustaining, almost like the physical foundation of Monica's life. Of Sophocles she says, "The fact that I sleep with him, that I end up in bed with him at the end of the day, is important. He's very cuddly somehow. Bedrock support."

When asked what she values, what is her most passionate conviction, Monica says, "What's going to matter when it's all over and I'm dead, and I'm not sure I really live up to this, but I really think that relationships matter. That you should have no unfinished business with your family. . . . What really gets me going in teaching and clinical work is people who lose connections with other people who need them. Sometimes in therapy I'll recommend to people that they listen to music or something because I think it gets people in touch with what really matters, so I'll give them Mahler therapy. I think nobody could listen to this and not feel touched, and not feel like they shouldn't bother with that stupid fight they're having with their wife, they should just go tell their family they love them."

Of her personal family relationships Monica says, "I hope that my children would feel I was there for them and didn't get in the way of their flourishing. I want them to feel like I support them in being everything they can be—and that we have a good time."

No matter how busy she may be, Monica will always be interrupted for calls from her family—her sense of being there for them, of supporting them, is central to her ideas about care and always her first priority. She apparently gets that same support in her marriage. Of her husband, she says what's best is that "he leaves me alone and I basically know that he believes in me and thinks I can do anything."

THE LEADER: BRIDGING LOVE AND WORK

The Leader is a woman who is focused on love, but not love for the sake of conformity to female stereotypes. For the Leader, love is expansive, it is generative. It can't be contained within a family or a primary relationship. It is love that values relatedness as a life-enhancing force. While the Lover can find fulfillment in the private sphere of home and family, at least for some part of her life, the Leader must go public. She seeks to make bridges between her inner and outer worlds, between her deeper passions and their expression in the external world. Relationship is her medium. Her private experience of caring spills over into an energy for caring on a more public level. As Monica says, "I really think that relationships matter." The passions for loving and working have a thematic and organic connection. In this sense, Monica is typical of other women who choose the relational integrative pattern.

While many women in this category are highly creative in their careers and in the nature of their work, their primary interest, as is Monica's, is in channeling their energy to enhance the well-being of others. Relationship is always foreground, creative energy is focused around it and is honed and developed in response to it. Specific forms of artistic work may be integrated into a woman's life, but they tend to revolve around, and stay in the background of, relationship. Relational contact is both the focus of her work and the context for it. This is not the woman who loves things that she can do alone. She enjoys the collaboration, affiliation, interaction of a strong social network. We call this group of women Leaders because the focus of their energy is moving people to connect, to change.

Some interesting trends in our data expand on these generalizations about the Leader pattern. In a question about satisfaction in relationships, Leaders appear to be happier in their primary relationships than women in all other groups. In general, Lovers and Leaders think of friendship as the most desirable quality of a love relationship, while Innovators and Artists prize passionate feeling and intensity more.

Eighty-four of the women in our study, 38 percent, were Leaders, slightly fewer than were Lovers. As we mentioned earlier, Leaders were the most likely of any of the groups to describe the story of love in their lives as "love fulfilled." They also overwhelmingly said that the choice to have children was most important to their sense of wholeness.

For the Leader, work of her own is necessary to her life satisfaction, but never sufficient. She requires the relational component. Women in this category typically choose to work in service or health professions. The woman who is a writer, lawyer, environmentalist, social activist, politician, whose energy is primarily relational, generally feels that she is working for political and social change. The passion is for nurturing, connection, touching others' lives. Her marriage or personal relationship is often a base from which the Leader can move out into the world to transmit the values, instincts, and specialized kind of knowledge of caring that are her deepest passion.

Responses to our questionnaires seemed to indicate that the Relational Integrative woman is not necessarily married with children; she is not even necessarily involved in a primary relationship. Twenty-two percent of women in the combined relational group are single. Often, the Leader has had a variety of relationships at different times in her life. While the number of lesbians in our sample was limited, in general those lesbian women we did speak with (represented in long questionnaires or interviews, many others probably not self-declared) tended to be in the Leader category. The defining issue in this category is not *how* a woman integrates relationship with creative energy but *that* she integrates it and that relationship is of primary importance, whatever form it takes. A single woman, for instance, may have a strong attachment to a community of friends and do work that expresses her deep concern with the well-being of others.

The kinds of responses we received on long questionnaires from Leaders provide a real flavor of their primary passion for relationship.

Asked what activity makes her feel most alive, one woman says, "Doing intense therapy, dancing, talking with someone who understands me." This woman is a psychotherapist. In her love of dance she demonstrates a pattern typical of the Leader. Desirable creative activity for this woman is often some form of singing, dancing, some active, expressive outlet. Leaders view creativity as a release, a form of having pleasure. They are more likely to think of creativity as "freedom." Innovators, or High Creative women, are more likely to view creativity as a direct form of self-expression, a craft to be pursued in a disciplined way. While creatives value self-expression intensely, they don't always find it pleasurable.

The Leader, when asked what she would sacrifice for creativity, is very circumspect and cautious. Some typical responses might be:

"Time."

"Labor."

"Living within the structure of society."

"Wealth."

Or, simply, "Not much. I would compromise or put things on hold."

Asked what they would sacrifice for love, however, a Leader is emphatic:

"Everything!"

"Security."

"I would not sacrifice healthy love or family for creativity."

"Most things. My freedom, but not my sense of self."

Finally, when asked what she values most in life, this response is typical of the Leader: "Freedom, tolerance, service for others, service for self, outreach, commitment."

From the responses to our questionnaires, we learned that one of the things that makes a Leader feel most alive is conversation with others and what makes her feel most blocked is simple fatigue at the constant focus on other people's needs. For one woman, even her most inward pursuits had to do with the need for connection: "I love to read because that allows me into other people's thoughts."

Rheatha Foster gave up a career as a theater stage manager and actress to become an expressive therapist because, as creative an arena as theater was, her job didn't allow her the sense of relational connection that she craved. She wanted to be more engaged in bringing her creativity to bear in ways that were helpful to other people.

Women in this category feel a strong need to make a difference in the world. They are very much in touch with the pain of others and they want to do something to help. For some this sensitivity arises out of their own personal pain, and for others it arises out of a sense of compassion in the awareness of their own privilege and other people's lack. Their values are frequently but not necessarily deeply spiritual ones. They have a strong sense of purpose. Their lives have often been affected by loss or struggle. They are frequently supported by fathers in their desire for achievement outside the traditional pattern of home and family.

In general there is more a focus on giving love than on being loved. Caring is caring for. These are women who are nurturers, who see the potential for growth and connection in the people around them. Leaders have very intense energy levels, and like Monica, sometimes think sleep is a waste of time. They often have so many relationships and commitments in their lives that their focus is blurred and they spread themselves too thin. They're very vulnerable to "burning out." They're also vulnerable to directing so much of their energy to public work that their close relationships suffer.

Timing and life phase are important elements in this category— some women merge career, family, personal relationship from the beginning, others move out into the public sphere only after children are grown or at least older. Some women start out as Leaders and move gradually away from a focus on relationship to an interest in more artistic or more inward intellectual work. Some experience a kind of personal dialectic from focus on the outer to focus on the inner, going back and forth more sequentially, but never stopping permanently in one or the other mode.

The two integrative categories combined, Leaders and Innovators, were disproportionately represented in the forty-to-forty-nine age group. Lovers tended to be younger, thirty to thirty-nine, or older, fifty to fifty-nine. This pattern suggests that Leaders may start out as Lovers and integrate work in their lives as their children age. Mid-life divorce may be common for Leaders or Innovators as they struggle to move more to a middle ground in the balancing of creative and relational energies.

Like all choices, this Relational Integrative pattern has its darker side. A woman who chooses it may have a hard time having access to more inward, self-directed talents and aptitudes. She may have a hard time claiming or reclaiming parts of herself that are not relationally focused. It was in this category that a very high percentage of women told us they had given up creative pursuits such as dance or writing out of a fear they wouldn't be good enough at them. This is what they told themselves anyway—or was it that the mandate to be relationally focused was stronger?

Leaders are at high risk, like their counterparts in the Lover pattern, of focusing on relationship at the expense of self, of still feeling conflict, like Carol Smith (chapter 3), between wanting to do work of their own and being compelled out of anxiety to care for others. Their choice of career or creative focus can sometimes represent a need to follow a "female," therefore socially acceptable model for achievement. Or sometimes, the choice of a relationally focused career is more determined by the sense that few other options are available to women.

The woman operating in this integrative pattern is subject when it is her sense of passionate conviction that dictates her choices. The inner imperative is that connection is important, that relationship is the primary and most meaningful thing to work at. The woman who becomes object in this pattern focuses on relationship because she believes it's the "female thing to do" and is blocked from accessing other ambitions, other more self-focused creative energies.

The path of the Leader is fraught with complexity. Women who choose it take on a daunting task—to extend themselves to a whole world of people who become the medium for expressing their own unique relational, artistic, and spiritual vision. This is a group of women who have their fingers on the pulse of human growth and development, who in their intense desire to move others, find themselves unalterably changed.

CARING FOR THE WORLD

Donna Hilleboe DeMuth is also a family therapist and increasingly a writer on issues having to do with the dangers of modern life.[3] She and Monica contrast in many ways. Donna is older, a decade or two removed from Monica. She lives and works in a rural setting, Monica in a suburban one. Donna went to college and graduate school and then left the world of work outside the home for thirteen years to raise her children. They're both passionate about family therapy and the importance of relationship, yet the emphasis and nuances of caring are different. Their two stories are variations on a theme.

For Donna, there has been integration but less continuity than for Monica, less coherence between the two opposing forces of her energy. Donna tells us, "The pull between the passion for relationship and the passion for my own creativity has been like the ruling force of my whole life." Yet the way it started out was purely relational. "When I was young I was always in love, I mean *always* in love, but it was always with a person. When I was young I would also go to lectures about what social workers could do and I was just on fire. But I didn't call it a passion then, I think I called it religion or spiritual—it felt like the sort of thing that happened in church and it was very separate from this life of mine in which I was always in love with some guy. The two felt absolutely unconnected. That part [the passion for the intellectual] was very separate, it was the private part of me.

"I do remember feeling, when I was a very young person . . . there are people suffering out there and I can feel it. And I really believe that some of us are vessels in which that kind of existential pain comes through. Ultimately I learned that people who have my kind of skills can help with the healing of the world." But the drive to have children and marriage was absolutely central to Donna. She says, "Actually, never have I had any doubts that raising children was my destiny—it was absolutely central and necessary and it still is and all the times when it was terrible I never questioned that it was mine to do. And the drive for me was not culturally imposed—it was culturally *reinforced*— but as I see now other women my age who are grandmothers who have choices about how much nurturing they do with their children, they really choose it and I do too, I don't say that I love it all the time, but it's my nature. There's a part of me that really blossoms when I'm with young children."

Donna had four children in seven years. During that time, her husband, also a social worker, built a strong and successful career. He was an active leader in his field—and he also did much of the housework. "The division of labor was not typical—his standards of housework are much higher than mine so that it proved to be a practical solution. I did the child rearing and he did a lot more cooking and housework than any man I ever knew in that generation."

Donna felt fulfilled by focusing her energy on marriage and children, but other energies were left untapped. She had been used to being an academic success in her own right—she had studied at a prestigious women's college. She grew up in a family where there were no male children so her father, in particular, had encouraged her to achieve. He had wanted her to become a doctor, and when she declined, he offered to support her husband through medical school instead.

While her dominant energies were relational, the achiever in her went underutilized and invalidated. "I think I underestimated the part of me that was intellectual. I think I saw my role as healer as, 'have a family, raise them right, they'll heal the world. Support my husband.' He was going places and I was going to be the support person and it didn't feel like a sacrifice. But I felt like the part of me that wasn't being used was the searcher, the quester, the rebel. I mean I had a really good education and all of a sudden it was gone. But I must say that during those years I never stopped reading, that was a real passion."

Donna had a degree but no professional life of her own. She followed what went on through her husband's work, had a sense of public connection primarily through him. "The other thing is that I was so tired all the time . . . I mean where was I going to find time and energy to do something with my mind?"

In her marriage she found validation for her femaleness, almost for her role as Smiling Woman. "He validated me in the conventional way that men validate women, by my looks, my sexuality, my attractiveness. He gave me a black—I'm still with this man for this fact—he gave me a black sexy cocktail dress right after our third child was born. I felt like a cleaning woman and there he comes with it. I still have that dress. I can't fit into it of course, but it's a beautiful dress. But he didn't value me at all as an intellectual. He still doesn't. That's not what connects us at all. That part of my life is totally separate from our marriage.

"But it was much more important for me as a young woman to be affirmed sexually than it was to be affirmed intellectually. I already had that. I had a family who really pushed me intellectually and wanted me to achieve. And in a way it's very clear to me that choosing to be valued for my traditional female self was a way of rebelling against my father. But the need to excel didn't go away and part of what I missed when I was raising children was that recognition and validation I'd had as a youngster."

The validation ultimately had to come from a man. One year a Norwegian exchange student lived with Donna and her family and along with the intense intellectual stimulation he provided, he would walk around the house marveling at all that Donna did. "He validated me and he validated my mind," she says. Along with the encouragement of other important male figures in her life, his recognition of her helped her to regain some sense of her own competence and her need to express that.

When Donna did move into the world outside her home and family, she felt an immediate sense of integration between her work raising her children and her professional role. "In raising children I had to learn so many things about *attention*. I don't think there is a skill that I've used as a therapist that I didn't first use as a mother. Because when I started being a therapist no one had to teach me how to do it, I already knew how to do it. A lot of it was from the process of listening to children—hearing what they want to say that they don't tell you directly.

"Part of the satisfaction or the passion or the drive or the love of being a parent or a grandparent is not just the nurturing part, it's the curiosity part and the exploration part. I mean children are fun and children stretch you and lead you. That kind of curiosity about what people are like and what life is like has been an integrating force."

We asked Donna how the move out into the public sphere of work affected her marriage. "The form of our relationship changed in terms of his being dominant or my seeing him as dominant when I started to feel myself as powerful ... what else? And I think that [happened] when I went back to work professionally, which was when our younger child was five, and I started having immediate success. I had a lot of success right away and I was terrified. My expectations were very high about what I should be able to accomplish. I think that was one of the reasons I didn't strike out into the world sooner, so in a way it was a little safe to stay with the kids. You know you can not really feel good about yourself until you have made it in the outside world. So I started making it in the outside world and I started surviving and the kids did not go down the tubes in spite of everyone's predictions about what happened when women went out to work.

"I shifted my passion to building this mental health center and becoming competent and I really learned so much in those years. I took on enormous jobs that I had no qualifications for whatsoever. I was really kind of self-centered at that point and I needed that because I needed to catch up."

Ultimately Donna became interested in family therapy and went to study with Virginia Satir, one of the first female pioneers in the field. In the course of that work, she became interested in issues of nuclear threat and "really allowed my own terror, pain, and panic about the imminent demise of the world to surface in me." It was a time of transformation for Donna, a time of transition in both her professional and personal life. She now had grandchildren and part of what she felt was "Oh my god, what if those children don't get a chance to grow up?" The recognition of the irrationality and violence of the outside world had tapped into her personal sense of vulnerability—she had a sudden encounter with the specter of loss. It was a turning point in her work. "It really changed and deepened my life and created a sense of my being involved in something bigger than me. I had never been able to write professionally until this came along."

But she did begin to write and she banded together with a small group of other professionals to study the impact of the nuclear threat and issues of global survival on families. That work is ongoing, the outcome of her engagement with her own inner distress and her deep passion for relationship and connection. Donna has been intensely engaged with her professional life and her family for years, her energy seeming to have been vast and flowing until she almost drained herself. She has been a sought-after therapist, consultant, developer of projects, but now one senses another type of energy beginning to emerge in her. It is quieter, more inward, more reflective.

"At any rate, I've got a million ideas and projects but I've been doing it more alone in the last six months to a year . . . writing alone, going to meetings alone and I don't know where it's going to take me. I've never wanted it before and now what I want is a lot of time alone and not to have to rush and not to have a program and to take a day and just do what comes."

Perhaps it is a time of taking stock, the sort of psychic break one takes before moving on to a different phase in one's life. Whatever "comes" for Donna is certain to be infused with her deep compassion and caring for relationship, even if its new focus is more directed to the relationship with herself and her own creative needs.

AGENCY AS GENEROSITY—THE POWER TO GIVE

What came through powerfully in our talks with women in this pattern was their generosity of spirit. Perhaps "generosity" is the most accurate definition of the energy of the Leader—generosity being the "will to give"—the uninhibited use of self and one's talents to enhance the well-being of others. This category provides perhaps the clearest, though not the only, model of love as agency.

What most determines agency is the use of power. But if women are to fully experience their power to effect change, they need to have their capacities valued and validated, and they need access to the intellectual and creative skills that make it possible. They need to believe in the importance of their contribution to others' lives, they need to know what they do has meaning and will not just be looked down on as more "women's work."

Women in this category may have conflict if they experience their work as becoming too intellectual, too "unfeminine." They may limit themselves to aspects of creative expression that don't assume power, agency, initiative, knowledge, types of work that don't challenge the status quo of their subservience or lower status. Some women would hesitate to write, that being a more valued and more male domain, some would hesitate to assume they could administrate a program instead of just work as part of it. Some women still assume they can only be nurses, not doctors. Women are good at generosity but often they need to become equally good at assuming the more powerful positions in the public sphere that would enhance their capacity to express it and to influence others to do the same.

It's also true that women who follow this pattern have their work criticized for being *too relational*. As if the passion for connection were a trivial aspect of work in the public world. Donna DeMuth's mentor, Virginia Satir, a pioneer in the family therapy field, whose passion was to enhance communication and connection in families, was never recognized as a leader until after her death. People thought of her as too emotional, too lacking in the distant intellectuality that characterized men in the field.

Many men teach, do therapy, and engage in this same kind of generous outpouring of creative skill in the interests of the well-being of others. But for them it's perceived and valued differently, and for many men this involvement sometimes becomes a subtle way to have power over others.

POINTS OF COMPARISON

Neither Monica nor Donna ever doubted that they would be wives and mothers. In this sense they were products of their generations. They were less likely than women are currently to question the *form* their relational passions would take—they were more like Joan Ellis or Ruth in their sense that family came first, that their first task would be to fit the traditional female role. But certain factors made it more likely that they would ultimately integrate other passions, other energies.

Unlike many women, they were both supported by their families, particularly fathers, in their desire to achieve in the outside world. They both had the benefit of privileged educations. Monica moved from college right into her career, Donna went from college to her marriage and family. But both knew instinctively that other parts of them needed to be expressed and given the encouragement and validation they needed, they were able to think about balancing the two. Both had husbands who supported them—Monica's by believing in her and supporting her autonomy and Donna's by encouraging her to pursue a career, though he did not necessarily support her intellectual interests.

Ironically, both Donna and Monica were encouraged by men— some of Monica's first mentors were male. But the feminist movement was ultimately critical in helping both to pursue greater visibility and power in their work. This provides a clear message for women about the importance of social context in their personal development.

Many women in the Lover category become more integrative as they get older and their family responsibilities change. Many Leaders become more Innovators as their relational connections change. They go more inward, develop other parts of themselves. The patterns of our lives are fluid, energies change, and if she's lucky a woman will allow herself to go off on her own tangents until she refinds her center.

THE MOTHER IS THE CHILD OF THE DAUGHTER

Relational Integrative women like Joan Ellis (chapter 5) who move from the High Relational form to integrate their own work later in life often spend a great deal of their creative and generative energy on their children. Just about the time the child faces decisions about work and career, creativity and relationship, a mother sometimes finds herself at the same developmental point. The meeting at this developmental crossroads for a mother and daughter can result in a kind of unconscious competition. But if the two have a close connection, the child, often the daughter, can have a supportive and synergistic effect on her mother's shift from one life form to another. The mother, in turn, provides support for the daughter's choices. The close connection of a parent-child relationship, when it works in this way, serves as a template for the kind of energy and growth the Leader carries over into her work in the world.

Such is the case with Bobbi Keppel and her daughter Wilma.

When we interviewed these women together, what we found was that the influence of the mother-daughter relationship tends to be reciprocal.

One might say that Wilma and Bobbi have supported and stimulated one another's creativity all along—it's been a defining characteristic of their relationship and a wonderful connection that they share. The warmth of their relationship with one another is something that's apparent immediately. We are talking to Bobbi. She says, "It was very hard for me when they were preschoolers. I didn't feel like I knew what I was doing—I didn't know what I was doing." Wilma smiles devilishly and interrupts the conversation: "That's what children are for—to be sure that their parents don't grow old ignorant."

This conversation is taking place in their friend's borrowed brownstone studio. Wilma and Bobbi are busy making a quilt together for their Aunt Sylvia's eighty-fifth birthday party. There will be a family reunion and this will be the major gift. Our talk is punctuated by Wilma's periodic pressure on the foot pedal of the sewing machine and Bobbi's travels back and forth from the ironing board to her work table.

The slowly evolving quilt hangs on the brick wall behind us, a symbol of intimacy, creativity, love. Bobbi tells us that the quilt is a traditional design, the Ohio Star. It will include a square for every living member of the entire extended family, including the cat. Aunt Sylvia loves nasturtiums, so the colors of the quilt are nasturtium colors. Its border is green, the color of leaves. About one third of the squares that symbolically stand for the many members of this family have been sewn onto the backing. It is an intricate piece of work.

Bobbi has recently discovered a talent for graphic design as well as a passion for quilting. She loves making quilts because of the potential for healing and self-expression she experiences working with fabric. Her quilts are works of art—they are representational symbols in color and design of important transformational experiences in her life.

Bobbi is at a transformational point in her own life and in fact, so is Wilma. Bobbi is sixty and Wilma is thirty. Both women are highly creative. Wilma started to pursue a doctoral degree in the biological sciences. But she also paints, writes, quilts, fixes motors, renovates houses, plays music, and is fascinated by more ideas than most of us could manage to absorb in one lifetime.

Right now she is not involved in a primary relationship though she longs to be. Wilma has so many interests and creative pursuits that she lives her life moving from project to project, doing whatever she feels like doing to make a living. She's about to become involved in a housing cooperative. Or she may buy a house and renovate it. Her interests and skills are so varied that she won't allow herself to be pinned down for very long to one.

Both Bobbi and Wilma tend to fall on the cusp between the Leader and Innovator patterns. But in spite of their many creative pursuits, talking with them one realizes that their dominant focus is relationship—the goal of each of them is to be in a relationship with someone who could embrace and support and share her interests.

When asked what's most important in her life, "Relationship is it," Wilma says. "One of the greatest pleasures in my life is to sit around a table with one to a dozen friends for example and watch the conversation and every now and then stick something in. I love people, they're so wonderful, they are just an everlasting source of enchantment and joy for me."

"Is there anything you long for now?" we ask.

"Relationship—long term and primary."

Bobbi is equally creative and equally focused on relationship. For many years she poured her creativity into raising her family. Then she became a psychotherapist. She was married to a warm and creative man, a scientist, until he died of a brain tumor some years ago. Her creative interests were always a part of, but secondary to her relationships until Bob died.

"I had lots of other creative outlets but they were more compatible with the relationships involved in raising a family."

It's not that her husband wouldn't have been supportive of her creative work. She says, "I think I was a real nurturer in some ways and I was a creative nurturer. So, I wasn't doing art, I mean graphic art, but I am sure that if he had known and I had known that's what I needed to do he would certainly have been supportive of my doing it."

After her husband's death, Bobbi began to discover her talent for graphic art. The balance between art and relationships changed in her life but relationship is still, as it is for Wilma, a primary outlet for her creativity.

"[Relationship] taps a part of creativity that I feel is underused or underutilized at the moment. For me I guess that being creative is a way of looking at things—and it's never going to go away. My lovers tell me I am one of the most creative lovers they have known. Just because I didn't recognize it doesn't mean I didn't have it. I don't have to be in relationship with somebody who quilts or paints or any particular thing, it's just being with somebody who is also creative is very important."

Her work also incorporates this need for creative connections. "I guess what I am creative at putting together is understanding how the parts of people fit together and helping them figure out where something is missing or how to go and do what they need to do or what they want to do. I don't know if I will be an art therapist but I think I will be a therapist who uses art. There are some things you can only express in words and there are some things that are graphic and one picture is worth a thousand words."

The energy Bobbi and her husband poured into supporting and developing their children's creativity comes back to Bobbi now in her relationship with them as adults.

"I feel like my children have taught me an enormous amount and they continue to confront me about my own self-criticism. I think that another thing that has been really important for me is that Wilma has recognized all different ways in which she's creative and we have talked about that or we have reflected back to each other. Because of this I really have come to realize how creative I am."

Relational integrative as they both are, Bobbi and Wilma currently struggle to find a form for relationship that fits. Since her husband died, Bobbi has had several different relationships, but like Wilma would prefer one that was primary and long-term.

Relationship for both is central, but the fit will require a person who can engage with them as an equal partner at the particular level of intensity required by their varied interests and passions. One senses that a traditional marriage, or the more conventional forms of relatedness that tend to confine our thinking, will never satisfy for either of these women. They are each people for whom relationship is a necessary path, but the form and structure of that relationship, one that they create for themselves, will be even more critical still.

In terms of Wilma and Bobbi's relationship with one another, it seems sustaining and enhancing, a true friendship. The key to its success seems to be mutual acceptance and encouragement. Armed with a deep understanding of the need for both connection and creative work, these two women seem to stir one another to a fuller exploration and expression of what is most unique in each.

THE WIDER PERSPECTIVE

Women may encourage in their children what they were unable to actualize themselves. On our questionnaires, we ask women what dreams or visions they had as children. We wanted to know how closely their lives resembled their early, most dominant fantasies. It was fairly consistent that women in the Leader category saw themselves being teachers, nurses, helping in some way even as children.

But there tended to be another interesting range of responses in which the pull of the more creative emerged, and the split between relationship and self-expression became a clear psychic conflict. One woman said her vision was to be a "movie star or a counselor." Later that dream changed to "singer or therapist." This woman became a therapist but her responses also indicate that at some point in her growing up she did in fact sing in concert and she still claims that singing is one of the activities that make her feel most alive.

We ask then, if a woman gave up a dream or a creative pursuit, Why? The answers very often reflect the responses of this same woman—"A lack of self-confidence," "Lack of discipline," "Not good enough to do it," "Not a priority." Women didn't necessarily say that they thought consciously that "women didn't think about doing those things," but the discussions of lack of confidence and discipline, the sense that "it wasn't a priority" that represented the answers of many women, speak to the underlying lack of support and encouragement provided in our society for women to choose other than a purely relational form.

Younger women in our sample, meaning women just graduating from college, tend to see the integrative path differently. They think not so much in terms of integrating love and work or creative interests, but in terms of integrating love for others with love of self. Self-love is synonymous to them with going inward and being in tune with one's deeper interests and feelings.

While one woman said clearly that she would not sacrifice healthy love or family for creative activity, she also talked in depth about the need for self-love. While she highly values relational activities, making love, helping, talking, being connected with friends, and while she chose one of the more typical career paths of the Leader, she also finds time to herself to be critical to her well-being. She says that what connects many of her nonrelational interests is that they are solitary experiences, private. They involve closeness to nature, reading, skiing—activities that are enhancing to the self. She has a sense of private space—having her own room is critical. She clearly senses that connection to others also requires that she be connected to herself. She says, "I feel really free to pursue whatever I want right now and I have done the things I like to do. I'm faithful to my heart."

In younger women, one sees the Relational Integrative path permitting the interests and needs of the self to be in greater balance with the passion for relationship. These women seem to have less conflict about valuing self—time for it, privacy, solitude—they seem to value more the necessity to be self-caring as a part of caring for others. This same woman says, "I think loving yourself is the most important thing in life. It is the groundwork for loving others, creating, feeling centered. I always give myself preference over others—unless it's an emergency."

One can look to the changing social context and the relative greater valuing of self-definition for women in our culture today to explain this trend. The path of the Leader, more than any other, permits a woman to use the resources and creative energy of relationship to affect and influence others, and to bring the energy of connection on many different levels to bear in a world that desperately needs it. And increasingly it permits a woman to embrace the deeper passions that emerge from an understanding and valuing of the self.

CHAPTER EIGHT

Innovators: The Creative Integrative Pattern

"WHEN I LOVE PEOPLE I want to create something with them and when I'm creating with people I'm sharing love with them and I don't use one to replace the other because the great good fortune of my life is that there is not a dearth of either."

These are the words of Elia Wise, a woman who was a TV and film development consultant for more than a decade. She is currently a writer of both screenplays and books. She speaks eloquently about the place of creative energy in her life. "My commitment to making everything artful became central to my life, so that by thirty I was good at it already. My house looked beautiful, my wardrobe looked beautiful, relationships were beautifully responsible. It started as a need to be understood. It was critical for me to have everything that I was inside myself wholly expressed in everything I did in the world, so that then I could be seen and perhaps related to."

Elia's childhood was one of abuse and neglect. Because her one sibling was much older, she felt like she was an only child and she spent much of her time alone. "There was a point in my childhood when there was nothing alive, creative, or constructive happening in my environment and so in order to stay alive, my dialogue became a dialogue with creativity which I saw as my dialogue with the universe. One day I saw something on television, an exotic woman, a snake charmer. So I became madam snake charmer. I would tie together all the silk scarves I could find anywhere and make a long thing that would go all over the house. The way I made a place to be in the house was to have this long thing that trailed all over. That part of me could somehow be places that it wasn't safe to be in the house otherwise.

And then I would play this game that I had no model for. I might have seen a five-second image, or maybe eight seconds of television, but from it I produced an entire universe.

"We had an entry hall to this house that I lived in that had a beveled little glass pane in the front door. When the sun hit it at a certain time of day after school, it would reflect prisms all over. Well, that was a perfect place to be madam snake charmer. Or, one day I asked somebody about Jesus Christ and they told me he rose from the dead. Having had that exposure, I would invent that thing. So for two months, I played graveyard people who would rise from the dead. So whatever I heard, every new idea, was someplace to go."

THE CREATIVE INTEGRATIVE PATTERN:
INNER NECESSITY AND INNOVATION

For the Innovator, creative self-expression is as much a necessity, as intense an energy, as the need for relatedness. In childhood, most of us learn very little about how to bridge our outer and inner worlds, how to keep ourselves company, how to express ourselves in a some-times silent world. The Innovator makes things up. As was true for Elia, every new idea becomes "someplace to go." The Innovator is the woman with a passion for ideas, for music, for abstract forms, for any artistic medium, for a specialized career, for a chance to bring her ideas to bear. Since passion is not only a matter of what one feels, but also a matter of what one thinks and believes as well as the *way* one thinks and feels, the Innovator is highly mentally focused. Her relational life and her mental life are equally powerful forces. She is at her most innovative in finding ways to blend the two.

Innovators were the smallest group in our sample, about 10 percent. They most resembled Leaders in their tendency to describe the story of love in their lives as "love fulfilled." They find relationships with children slightly more satisfying than Artists, and interestingly, they are the group *most* likely to say that relationships with parents are satisfying, in some cases even more so than those with children and friends. Forty-three percent of Innovators in our sample were married. But, emphasizing the importance of creative expression in their lives, 67 percent said that a creative activity is what makes them feel most whole.

If the need to *be in relationship* and to move others to a sense of connection in the larger world is the defining passion of the Leader, the need to *create a medium for connection* is the striking aspect of the

Innovator's experience. The Innovator takes the need for connection to a symbolic level. For the relational woman, contact with others is what satisfies, understanding and implementing knowledge about the ways connection comes about are a creative focus. But for the Innovator, the medium is as important as the connection itself. As Elia says, her creative innovation started "as a need to be understood," and that's how she came to try to express herself in everything she did. For her, the *form* of expressiveness, the beautiful clothes, the artfully designed home, the well-written sentence, were all statements, communications about herself that were integral to her sense that she was connected to other people and to herself. Not just the message but the medium was important.

In their need for an expressive medium, Innovators most resemble Artists. Often their choice of medium *is* artistic. They differ from Artists, however, in several ways. Since relational connection is critical to them, they struggle more than Artists for a balance between their creative expression and relationship. They may tend to sacrifice the extent of their artistic or work involvement, the intensity of their focus, more than the Artist would. They compartmentalize less and integrate more. The Artist's sense of identity is defined almost exclusively by her work. While Artists often have relationship, if they didn't, their work would still serve as a centerpiece of their lives. The Innovator needs both, so struggles more to find ways to make the two work together. While the Artist sets limits that make her art a clear priority, the Innovator will tolerate more interruption, more flexibility in the progress of her work or career. While the Artist's creativity is more exclusively focused within one artistic medium, the Innovator can apply her creativity to many different media. The feature that most characterizes women in both the creative groups is the intensity of their internal lives, the tendency to focus inward rather than outward to locate a sense of themselves.

This pattern most clearly captures the synthesis, the essential sameness of the energies of creation and love. Both have to do with making connections, with giving and taking, with exploration, aliveness, growth.

Most women who pursue this path have been creative all of their lives. As we'll see in the stories of the women that follow, the talent for innovation, putting different forms and ideas together and coming up with something new, often emerged in childhood. The energies that shape a life of creative integration tend to emerge more clearly in childhood than do those of the relational categories. Reflecting back on their childhoods, many of our interviewees could remember that their interests were blocked or not supported, but all have strong memories of heightened sensitivity to color, to music, to the out-of-doors, or, like Elia Wise, to themselves and their own internal process. They remember themselves as children playing or creating—they have memories of either loving times and experiences that were generated while singing, dancing, playing with parents or siblings, or they remember creating fantasy worlds to help them cope with the pain of a lonely childhood. It's as if they have a strong desire to reconnect with that energy of their childhood—it forms a constant in their lives, an intrinsic part of their identity. If they cannot reclaim it or maintain that connection in some way as an adult, they feel frustrated and unhappy.

Writer Norma Marder comments on this essential connection with childhood experienced by the woman who expresses creative energy: "The child stays alive in us," she says.[1]

The presence of artistic talent may shape this energy differently for different women. But the energy itself is creative—the need to express, the need to connect, the need to create forms, products, symbols that convey meaning, caring, passion, power. Raising children is a necessary, but not sufficient form of creativity for most of these women. The impulse goes beyond the biological—it is the need to put something of oneself into the world, to create meaning. Since we're often most in touch with this sense of wonder as children, it's not unusual that childhood becomes the soil from which the seed of creative energy grows.

One might say that from a very early age, these women had a strong sense of self as *separate* from others. In many cases it was resilience and strong will in the face of feeling different that became the thread of continuity from their childhood to their adulthood, because in a woman these qualities are more discouraged than rewarded. Their creative work often became their primary means for forging connections with the outside world, a way of making themselves known.

CHILDHOOD, COHERENCE, CREATIVITY

Linda Russell is a singer and actress with a passion for the historical. When one visits her in her New York City apartment, the experience is like stepping off the teeming life of a modern city street into another world. The apartment is full of antique books and furnishings. She serves us lemonade in big ceramic ale mugs that look like they belong in an Irish pub.

Linda does a one-woman show called "Patchwork: Voices of Nineteenth Century Women," in which she portrays twenty different women talking about the joys and sorrows of their lives, all from actual diaries, letters, and songs. She writes music and she performs. She is best known in concert and on tape for her inspired relationship with the dulcimer. Her music is haunting, but more compelling are the stories she tells in her songs—many of which evolved from childhood memories of life on a Wisconsin farm with a mother who loved to sing.

Linda is married but has no children. She considers love and creativity equally important in her life. In fact, much as Elia Wise was to explain to us, her memories of love as a child were intimately connected with the creative ways in which that love was expressed.

"I would get into the attic and find my dad's love letters to my mom, but they were extremely creative because he would paint, draw cartoons on all the envelopes. Complete cartoons that would have somebody walking along and say, gee, who's that cute girl? And then somebody else responding. My dad was extremely creative in his expressions. So I used to just pore over it. It was just a wonder to me."

One of the cuts on Linda's album describes poignantly the experience of the family riding in the car through the pastoral landscape of Wisconsin and her mother teaching them songs. The times were ones of intimacy, harmony, filled with a sense of the wonder of being part of a secure and loving family. But Linda's sensibilities were unique and specific to herself. "As a child I would never look at what I wanted to be. I was just too scared of growing up to try to figure out, oh, when I grow up I want to do this. I was mostly alone, living in the country alone until my brothers and sisters were born, so I had a lot of my own time, my own imagination to keep me company. I loved tragedy. As a kid I would just sort of dramatize poor little waifs left out in the snow and I would enact all these things. As a kid I was always fascinated more by that kind of play than being a princess or anything rich."

That childhood experience forms a sense of continuity and connection for Linda. She says, "It's through my songs that I am telling about my childhood which I enjoyed very much. I *am* a direct line from my childhood. The things that I loved as a child I am now able to do as an adult. So writing about my childhood is pretty directly communicating who I am. And that's also true on stage, because I have a lot of emotions in me and on stage I can get them all out."

Linda had the good fortune to have parents who were supportive of her developing creativity. Involved in community theater, photography, music, themselves, they encouraged her and sensitively did not push prematurely when Linda's temperamental fearfulness blocked her at first from pursuing her career seriously. But one day, she remembers walking into the living room and announcing, "Mom, Dad, it's time. I'm going to New York." They supported her wholeheartedly.

To Be Seen and Not Heard

Sara Eyestone's childhood was marked by her sense of not fitting in, of being at odds with both her family and her peers. What made her different was her acute visual sensitivity and her innovative ideas, even then, about how things should look.

Sara is a well-known artist whose work is most respected for its bold, passionate, and compelling use of color. In a profile of her written for *Lears* magazine, Ingrid Tomey describes Sara stepping off a plane to meet her in the Dallas airport. "She glided up the ramp like a single, bright sail on a lonely horizon. Color. She wore a cherry red trench coat and yellow shoes and wonderful sunglasses framed in red and black swirls. . . . The riot of color shouldn't have surprised me. 'Color,' she wrote me, after our high school graduation, 'is my absolute pleasure.' 'Contradiction,' I wrote back, 'is the soul of metaphor.' "

Flowers are frequent subjects of Sara's paintings and drawings and she seems to give new meaning and scope to the concept. Her work is vivid and romantic. Sara is an entrepreneur and businesswoman as well as an artist. She has parlayed her considerable artistic talent into a lucrative and successful art business that runs on her massive reserves of energy and ideas. She has achieved the seemingly incompatible goals of being a successful and respected artist and a businesswoman as well.

When she reflects on the sources of her artistic energy, she is down to earth and pragmatic. As she says, "I run out of dog food just like you." But she is clear that her creative energy was ever-present and continuous from childhood.

"As I now understand it, at almost fifty years old, I was born artistic, inventive, and creative. I have a very clear memory of my early life, like a baby dress of white dotted Swiss on maroon that my mother made me when I was about fourteen months old. I've seen it in pictures a number of times.

"A few years ago when I asked my mother why she ever picked

maroon for a baby dress, she asked me how I knew the color since all our old photos were black and white. I said, 'I wore the dress, Mother, I saw it when I was wearing it!' I can remember things like the gold brocade on my grandmother's couch and the pastel flowers and prints on her wallpaper. Those are the kinds of things that make me realize the level of awareness I have.

"From the time I was a child I always felt like I had good ideas, but I was in a situation where at all times children were to be seen and not heard. As loving and devoted as my mother is, her role set the example. Her 'job' was to raise the children, which was her measure of success as a woman. She was no different from a lot of other intelligent women of her generation, trying to do her best—this was how it was done and what you expected of your children, etc. And when you had a child that has her own style or her own slant or a better way to arrange the teacher's bulletin board, it depended on the parent or the teacher whether the child was considered rude or considered brilliant. If anything came back to my mother that wasn't positive, it was traumatic for both of us."

Sara conveys a sense that she suffered from being different, that her difference caused her parents conflict and embarrassment. In spite of the intense sensitivity to color and pattern and the obvious artistic sensibility she demonstrated from an early age, Sara still remembers clearly the primary vision of her childhood: "In my Doris Day vision as a child I planned to be married and have a lot of children and have my husband distinguish me. I never intended to work, I wanted to have a wonderful time with my children and have a romance with this man who would take care of us all."

Sara married and had four children, and later divorced and remarried. But her involvement with art took hold of her life and eventually became its defining force. The first marriage ended when it became obvious to her that it was and always would be devoid of romance and would never be integrated with her work.

In spite of her "differentness" as a child, Sara's ideas about relationship were quite conventional. As we'll see later, it was only as she developed a stronger sense of her own needs and uniqueness that she learned to integrate relationship in a way that supported the creative imperative that had so dominated her childhood.

For most women for whom creative, generative energy is strong, even a lack of family resources and support in childhood is not likely to block the imperative to express themselves. Many Innovators seem to fall into their chosen medium by happenstance, but if one looks more closely, there is always a coherent theme or symbolic meaning to the choice.

An Accepted Voice

Sharon Gainsburg is a sculptor who lives in the same New Jersey community as Sara Eyestone. As an artist she is equally successful. Her pieces, notable for the power that emerges in their fluid, graceful, almost lyrical forms, are commissioned by and placed in private homes and corporations all over the country. The year C. Everett Koop was leaving office, she was commissioned to do a sculpture of an abstract model of DNA as an award for his work in infectious diseases. A copy of it is now given annually to other award recipients in the field.

As well as working in her studio on her own pieces, Sharon maintains an active schedule teaching stone carving to a wide range of interested people in the community. Like Sara she has been married, divorced, and remarried when the form of her first marriage could no longer contain the imperative to create. She has two children. Her childhood could not be considered nonsupportive of her emerging talent, yet it provided little that would even have helped her recognize that she had it.

"As a child I wasn't raised with any artistic training and I started doing sculpture when I was in my twenties as a lark, as a hobby. Did it for ten years as a hobby. I didn't have a formal education as an artist, there was not a lot of art talk as I was growing up. My family was very simple and they really were into survival. Survival meaning day to day, going to work, coming home. My mother was a single parent in the forties, which was very unusual in those days. She didn't have any education, so she really had to fend for herself in this big world. I have a sister who is older, and I had a box of Crayola crayons. There were eight colors in it and to me that's all that existed. When I got sick, I would get cutouts and there weren't any paintings hanging on the wall and there were very few books in the bookcase. We were just into day to day, mundane existence. When I had art at school, I found that I copied well, but I can't really say I was creative, but I liked the process. When I was fifteen I fell in love. My first big love. I fell in love with a boy who was five years older than me and he was very much into the arts; he played jazz piano, he could paint and draw. And he was the one who introduced me to the outside world. He took me to the art museum. He took me to jazz concerts. He loved classical music. He was a combination of a mentor, a father figure, and a lover. I was like a little tiny flower and he just peeled each petal down and when it was open he just showed me the whole world. And it was at that point that I knew that I had to get out of my circumstances and that meant I couldn't become a secretary. . . . There was just this determination to rise above where I was at, and not on an economic level, but on a self-sufficient level. To do better for myself. To educate myself. To learn more. Because I realized there is a whole world out there."

Sharon enrolled herself in a vocational program where she learned to be a medical technician. And then, having broken up with her first boyfriend, she went one day to visit his brother, who was taking a sculpture class and who showed her what he was doing.

"I started looking at that sculpture and I connected with the feelings I would get when I was in the art museum. There's a feeling I had in the art museum, at fifteen I didn't understand it, I just knew it was different from anything else I had ever experienced. And then when I looked at the sculpture, I started to get that same connection. And I knew it was something I wanted to do, but I didn't feel I had any talent. He encouraged me. I took the class, and that's when I got into doing sculpture. But I always saw myself as a hobbyist."

So it was in adolescence for Sharon that the powerful energy of a love for art, along with a strong sense of a need for self-definition and self-sufficiency, began to take hold in her life. But looking back now on her childhood, Sharon thinks she sees the roots of her particular choice of medium.

"I feel very powerful when I'm working. As a child growing up, my sister was five years older than me and my mother and my sister would be negotiating things and deciding things and I was always the baby. And I always felt that opinions never counted. And I think—it just hit me that part of this whole thing, this desire, was so that I would have a voice that would be accepted.

"I needed to make my own statement. And I think the sculpture has done that for me. But I never started out—it's like it wasn't in my conscious mind to do it. It's just that I had to do it—it was a driving force. I didn't understand it, it was there."

THE CHARACTERISTIC INNOVATOR: DETERMINED, STRONG-WILLED, AND SELF-SUFFICIENT

What most characterizes the energy and passion of an Innovator is a strong sense of determination. Being determined is the basis of their capacity to innovate. Reading their responses on questionnaires and interviewing Innovators personally, one experiences a focused sense of drive and determination, almost a willfulness in their sense of purpose and clarity. They *will* say what they have to say and do what they want to do. They also *will* balance their work with love.

They will be self-defining and create the forms they need to operate in. Not least among the driving forces in their lives is the quest to find balance in work and love—it is to be assumed, it is to be expected.

If the Leader or the Lover has enormous amounts of energy for others, the Innovator has enormous amounts of energy for all pursuits that are consistent with her sense of what's important and what she enjoys. The woman in this category is passionate to *know*. She will study and work tirelessly to develop her range of skills and interests. She tries continually to take in the world around her, to learn what she can learn. She may equally have a desire to teach that grows from her own fascination with the world. She thrives on challenge and a sense of mastery. She tends to be a perfectionist in her work and to have a need to see things done "right." This need is consistent with her sense that the medium is the message—what she does is an important expression of herself.

The flavor of this intensity and determination emerged in our questionnaires in responses like this one:

"I am most alive when I have something big that has to be done with a very short time line. I feel most alive when I am pushed to my limits physically and mentally—I like living on the edge. . . . I had a dream of being a doctor and living in Africa like Albert Schweitzer. I wanted to discover cures for rare diseases."

Innovators frequently find outlets for their creativity and intensity in very specialized careers. The editor, the corporate executive, the consultant, the academic, the computer specialist, the scientist, the doctor for whom medicine is more about science than about relationship, the businesswoman, are all Innovators. Women who pursue an interest, experience a need to put their capacities to work in the public sphere and have never considered not doing so, tend to be Innovators. What is critical to them is finding an external structure into which they can pour their inner core energies. Often they're self-employed because they prefer to define their own work structures.

If, for the Leader, relationship is foreground and creativity background, for the Innovator, creativity is foreground and relationship may become a supportive backdrop. Relationship in this pattern takes on two forms—creative work is either shared with the partner or unconditionally supported by him or her. Even those women for whom creative work generates relational conflict feel strongly that they would never agree to give up their work for the sake of the relationship. It's not even conceivable to them that they would be in a relationship where there was a demand that they do this. Self-expression is such a critical part of their sense of themselves that a relationship that dampened or demeaned it could not be considered a loving relationship. The relational medium must be supportive, valuing, and permit time and space for a focus on work. These same relational qualities are critical to Artists.

Even in relationship, the Innovator is insistent on her self-sufficiency. Love relationships tend to be mutually supportive rather than complementary and caretaking. Just as the form of self-expression is critical for her, a choice of partner is as well.

For the Innovator, having children sets the stage for conflict, children generate guilt. More than any other aspect of these women's lives, children require the setting of limits on their creative work and they require the capacity for innovation. Each finds a way to work around and with the problem of integrating children's needs with the demands of their work or art. Most have had to be highly organized, efficient, willing to accept limits. Sally Mann, the photographer whose controversial work portrays her children in various poses, staged and natural, solved the dilemma by making her children her subjects. As one writer says of her, she made her art a kind of "child care."[2]

The Innovator has significantly less difficulty than women in relational categories experiencing herself as subject—she may, however, feel great guilt and question herself because that's the case. Often she has experienced herself as subject from an early age, either because she was encouraged by a parent or because in the absence of parental focus, she had to make up her own life.

The Innovator loves as subject and demands to be respected as such. She has a clearer sense of her own power. Like the women in the Artist pattern, women in this category often say that their sense of themselves as they acted or sang or painted or sculpted or involved themselves with their work was clear—that they never doubted it was right, necessary, central to their identity.

As we've commented, in the data, a high percentage of women choosing the creative patterns say that pursuit of creative activity is what makes them feel most whole, while for relationals, it was choices having to do with relationship that made for a sense of wholeness. Innovators were not likely to give up their creative dream because of practical concerns, while Leaders more consistently would. Most Innovators who said practical considerations would not block them from their dream were not married at the time of the survey. One could speculate that the Innovator cautiously guards her creative dream by making more careful choices about love.

BALANCE VERSUS COMPROMISE:
THE INNOVATOR'S CRITICAL DILEMMA

The integrative path suggests a balancing of relationship with self-expression, generative love with nurturing love. The balance may not involve a traditional family, husband and children, or a primary relationship. As it did for Ann Ehringhaus in chapter 1, it may involve the integration of solitude with involvement with friends and community. For some, it means integrating creative pursuits with the care of aging parents and the demands of maintaining a wide social network. Or balancing creative work with the demands of commitments to church or political causes.

But it's in this category that the need for balance is in greatest danger of slipping over into compromise. Compromise can come to mean sacrifice. While the Innovator, by definition, tends to hold on to her work at all costs, sometimes there are costs. Traditional family structures impose special problems for Innovators and must often be reworked. Connection with partners and children can suffer, friendships may suffer, and sometimes creative work suffers. There is no easy balance, but the creative integrative woman characteristically struggles valiantly to find one.

In her book, *Composing a Life*, Mary Catherine Bateson makes a virtue out of a woman's ability to live with discontinuity, to follow the thread of her own life through the myriad ups and downs of other people's demands and agendas, constantly confronting new situations for which she must devise new ways to play out old roles. She tells us that what women do is improvise and she calls improvisation a mainstay of creative energy, "the creative potential of interrupted and conflicted lives, where energies are not narrowly focused or permanently pointed toward a single ambition."[3]

And yet, we have to question why women's lives tend to have little coherence if not because they still feel compelled to play the role of the Smiling Woman. Why is it a given that women's lives are interrupted ones, if not for their belief that the needs of others always come before their own? Why are men's lives less interrupted by the needs of women than women's lives are by the demands of men? Discontinuity and change may be a genderless common characteristic of a postmodern life, but one has to wonder if men's lives are discontinuous in the same ways and to the same degree as women's. The Innovator is forced to challenge the notion that a woman's energies must be somehow fit around others. She finds ways for her own energy to take priority within the context of her other commitments.

And yet repeatedly, in our interviews and on our questionnaires, women told stories of giving up creative interests for the sake of relationship, if not for "practical" constraints. While a higher percentage of women in relational categories gave up creative interests for love, a number of Innovators did too and we speculate that the reasons for this were different for each group. One woman who is really in transition from the Leader to the Innovator pattern says that as a child, she wanted to be a writer. "I used to write stories and soap operas. I'd fake sick to stay home from school and do this." When asked how the dream changed, she said, "I stopped writing stories." Only now, at age forty-five, has she attempted to reclaim this passion—she has started to write "articles."

One friend who studied violin at the High School for Performing Arts in New York ultimately channeled most of her creative energy into a career as a therapist. She remembers thinking very clearly that to pursue a career in music would be disruptive to her future marriage. How could she practice, travel, do concerts in far-flung places, and still hope to maintain a committed relationship? She feared the intensity of a musical career, the possibility that music would become more a priority than her marriage. She studied music therapy and decided to channel her creativity into other pursuits.

But her husband, who always knew he wanted to be a psychologist, though he is also an artist and sculptor, never questioned the impact of his career choice on his relational life. He never assumed that what he wanted to do would have an impact on his relational life. It never occurred to him to think of interrupting himself or following anything other than a neatly linear career path to his goal. In fact his wife was the primary support for the two of them while he did just that. She went where his academic work and internships took him. Undoubtedly, she experiences her own life as much less coherent and much more discontinuous than he does his.

Writer and former singer Norma Marder gives another perspective on the idea that a woman's greatest creative talent is to improvise in the face of never knowing where or how one may end up. While improvisation may be a great talent, it is by no means necessarily or exclusively a self-enhancing one. What Bateson calls improvisation, Marder calls not taking one's art or life agenda seriously. For her, improvisation had mixed consequences.

In an essay in the *Georgia Review*, "Deceptive Cadences," Marder describes the domestic events that affected her previous career as an avant-garde musician from the beginning: her marriage, having her first child, and helping to care for her father at the end of his life. She both sang and nurtured and while the nurturing cut into the singing career, there were compensations, and satisfactions, although not in those dark nights of dealing with a child hospitalized for surgery.

The turning point for Marder really came when, in order to have financial security, she and her husband moved the family out of New York City, the center of the world for an artist of her variety, to a small city in Illinois. Looking back on it, she knows that it was a failure of her own will that led her to tell herself that she was just "improvising" and not compromising; sacrificing, not balancing.

"I used to say I would never compromise—not as an artist, not as a person—but I have my father's capacity for fooling myself. After the children were born I dressed up compromise and called it improvisation. I joked with women about improvising in life, made art out of it, became a specialist, turned it into music and theater.

"I look back and say how clever I was, how creative: an artist to the core, able to switch from one medium to another.

"I look back and say I didn't take myself as seriously as I thought."[4]

RELATIONSHIP: THE CRITICAL CHOICE

Innovators often have sequential relationships—their energy is more suited to fluid patterns in which they may live separately from partners or change partners when their work demands geographical or other kinds of changes. If she chooses a committed partnership, more than for women whose energies flow into other patterns, the choice of a life partner is crucial. If the passion for work or creation is to be equal in importance to the passion for relationship, one's partner has to accept and support the focus of energy outside the relationship. Loving as subject, the creative woman seeks an equal partner, a companion, a soul-mate, someone who shares her values, interests, and particularly an understanding of the meaning of her work. If the partner demands to be focused on excessively rather than to engage in a relationship of shared energy for life and the place of work within it, the conflict may tip the balance enough to result in different choices and the breakup of the marriage or relationship.

In fact, in our samples, Innovators, along with Lovers, were the most likely to be disappointed with first relationships with lovers or spouses. It's typical that Innovators first marry or become involved in relationships without understanding their own requirements for support. They try at first to fit the conventional female mold and only after some experience with it do they realize that the price is too high a one to pay. Divorce and remarriage are common in this group. When the data indicates that Innovators also feel fulfilled in their love relationships, it may be that they refer to second marriages. Innovators are women who will not compromise their work for the sake of relationship, and they are less willing than women in the relational categories to settle or accommodate when a relationship doesn't permit a focus on their work.

Both Sara Eyestone and Sharon Gainsburg left earlier marriages for precisely this reason. As Sharon describes it:

"I got married two years after I started sculpting. My husband was very supportive when it was a hobby. When my children were old enough to be in school full time, I started doing it more seriously. He was still very supportive, except when I started to get involved in shows that took me away from the house, not for long periods of time. He started to have difficulty. He would be supportive, but when I came back I would be reprimanded. He would be depressed, he would be withdrawn, he would be jealous that I'd come back with all this excitement and enthusiasm and I'd share it with him and he'd listen, but then he'd change the subject. It was double messages all the time. I would be going off somewhere, he'd send me flowers. Then I'd come back and I'd suffer."

Eventually Sharon's husband got involved in doing philanthropic work and made a decision to move to Israel. He expected Sharon to move with him—she wanted him to wait five years while she developed her own work more. But he refused. He went to Israel, but she did not go with him.

Sara Eyestone's story is similar. At a point when Sara was just beginning to become successful and well-known in her various artistic jobs, she was offered a very lucrative full-time position. Her husband, who had been a full-time graduate student up until then, was apparently uncomfortable with the financial power such a job would provide for Sara. He decided at that point to move the family from Phoenix to St. Louis so that he could take a civil service job that had no real appeal to him.

Sara says, "I knew I was so capable. I was juggling my domestic tasks with my husband and children and my work had been supporting all of us for years. Still, in my head, I was the *wife* and he was the husband and he was saying, 'You're not going to take this job, we're not going to stay in Phoenix, it doesn't matter that you love Phoenix. You're not going to wear the pants in this family. Period.' I gave notice, turned down a job that would have given us twice the income he could have hoped to earn and we left town two weeks later."

For months, Sara was depressed and rarely left her new St. Louis apartment. Eventually, her form of improvisation, her innovation, was to look around her and to realize that she was an artist and she wanted to work but this time she would freelance as a professional, so that the kind of dislocation she had experienced could never disrupt her work again. She never again thought of herself as "supplementing" anyone else's income. She had three small children at that point, and after her fourth was born, she left her husband. Gone was the idea that once married her husband would distinguish her. Snatching victory from the jaws of defeat, it was her depression that led her finally to a fuller idea of her own artistic life and talent and a fuller expression of it.

In the stories of many women we spoke with, as well as women in our private practice, it's a common theme that at the point when they begin to come into their own artistically or in terms of their careers, their partners decide to move. This may be coincidental but speaks to one of the major difficulties with the Creative Integrative pattern. We've learned to think of love in this culture as the woman's total devotion to the needs of the other. When the woman herself begins to focus her energies in ways that are generative and not just nurturing, it creates terrible anxiety and raises complex issues in a marriage having to do with who is responsible for meeting whose needs. When the form of the marriage or relationship cannot shift from a tolerance for generative love as opposed to exclusive nurturing love, a creative woman is faced with a choice: In the absence of the possibility for balance, there must be compromise and some compromises deaden the energies necessary and vital to self-expression.

The Innovator and the Artist most challenge the assumptions of archetypal Jungian theory about innate femininity. If we were to take Toni Grant's position seriously (see chapter 2), the Innovator would be cautioned to reclaim and rebalance her feminine side. She would be told, in somewhat pathologizing fashion, that she was being too male and not allowing her softer, more submissive qualities to yield to love. But it's clear that it's the inherent definition of both femininity and love as passive and responsive rather than generative that's at issue here. The Innovator simply needs a love relationship in which her generative energy is valued, not one in which she accommodates by loving in a traditionally "female" way.

Of her new relationship, Sara Eyestone says, "I have a lot of freedom in my marriage. I came to this marriage knowing who I was and I married somebody who was also established. When David Molin met me I was an artist. It wasn't my art he fell in love with. He loves me. He tells me that I'm refreshing to him. I don't ever need to modify my behavior or change. My husband understands and appreciates that I am not able to do what I do in a conventional eight-hour day."

We're meeting with Sara in her studio at 10:30 at night. Her husband calls to touch base, to know that she's OK. She is likely to keep working there until three in the morning but that won't create a problem.

Sharon Gainsburg says of her second marriage, "I married a man who I truly believe knows what it is to love someone. And what loving somebody means is that you do sacrifice. He sees that I need to do what I do. There's a lot of give and take. I was single for five years before I married Frank and I didn't have to sacrifice very much. And I made a choice to be in relationship knowing I would have to make some sacrifices. I think the key is balance—it's the balance you have to come to."

Stage actress Frances Sternhagen, who originated the role of Miss Daisy in New York theater, had been married for many years when she was widowed. When she speaks of her husband, also an actor, she says, "I do know that my relationship with my husband . . . a great deal of the value in that relationship and the depth of that relationship came from the fact that we both shared a love of acting and understood each other.

"My first big love affair with another man before I married was very exciting. But finally one day he came up to me, he was working at a television station and he was really coming up in the world and he said, 'I'm ready to get married and you're the one I want to marry, as you know.' And I just want to know if you're ready too?' And I said, 'What happens to my acting if we get married?' And he said very simply, 'Well, you'll give it up I guess.' And it was like a curtain fell and I thought, oh, well, that's that. And he promptly married somebody else. When I asked the same question of Tom, he said, 'What do you mean, what happens to your career?' He said, 'Of course you'll keep acting.'

"I think that as the marriage progressed, we both accepted the fact that I was an actress . . . I called him at work and I just said I got this offer to go to Lincoln Center and I just don't know whether I should do it. And all he said was, do you want to be an actress or not? There were times when my career was very painful for Tom and when push came to shove and should I take this job or not, he always knew when a job was something I should take."

Norma Marder speaks to both the positive and negative consequences of compromise. She by no means stopped being creative in her new life in Illinois. She channeled her energies in many different capacities in the community and taught herself to write fiction. She writes in her essay, "My attitude toward compromise changed; life was a process of feathering, of accommodating interruptions, of making collages. . . . Problems of . . . constraint and freedom were popping up everywhere."[5] But in giving up her singing career, she gave up her dominant passion.

"But I am eaten away; that which sang is dying, for there is little singing work in this town. A few concerts a year, some touring. I teach literature to old people and serve on committees. I make needlework tapestries in the summers.

"I accept the truth about myself, hard won, that as an artist I've operated within the limits of my responsibilities as well as the limits set by my demons. . . . Part of me is unhappy, part is happy. Sometimes one wins, sometimes the other."[6]

CHILDREN

What is extraordinary about many of the Creative Integrative women we interviewed is that they have more than average numbers of children. One has to assume that they have both more energy than the average person among us and that they have either supportive friends or partners. Many of them raised children at the same time that they were in the most crucial developmental phases of their careers. Frances Sternhagen had six children, Sara Eyestone four, Sharon Gainsburg two, Norma Marder, two. For most, children were less disruptive to work than marriages. Each had extraordinarily creative ways of finding time and energy for both.

One senses that for Innovators, having children is another medium of self-expression, learning, and exploration—they experience themselves as generating something, having access to yet another form of creative energy. The sacrifices each had to make for children, while they were sacrifices, seemed less disruptive because they were more within their own sphere of control. Sara Eyestone carried her children around with her in backpacks and set up a play area for them in her studio. She painted and they hung out with her. Sharon Gainsburg simply stopped work in her studio each day at three o'clock when the children got home from school. She viewed this, again, as a sacrifice, but one she was willing to make. "When I started working more or less full time, then I had my children to deal with because they were interrupting my creative process. And one day I just thought about it and said, the first twenty years were for me, the middle twenty are really for them. I had them, I cannot shortchange them, and then the next twenty years will be for me. So at three o'clock when they came home from school, I would close up things, be with them, and it was OK."

Frances Sternhagen, too, made sacrifices, but somehow the sacrifice made for a child is less deadening and disruptive of a career than the larger compromises that may be required in a relationship.

"Certainly with six children, I had to hold myself back. There were times when I was asked to do something that took me, oh, to California for ten weeks or something like that—I would just turn it down. My priorities were pretty clear. Fortunately, the jobs I was offered were never really exciting enough for me to ache very hard.

"I always knew there was work in New York for me. There were a couple of times when I really thought, oh gosh, I should just be a better mother and stay home and bake cookies, which I've practically never done anyway. I should be doing the normal thing. And my older daughter at the time when I mentioned this, I said, oh, I feel so terrible, I'm away so much in the evenings and I'm not home. I should be a better mother and I should be home. Mandy just said to me, oh, mom, you'd be impossible if you were home all the time. So that kind of clarified it for me."

Frances Sternhagen will admit that her husband shouldered much of the responsibility for the children. When she did consider leaving him at one time, she was clear that with six children, had she left she could not have pursued her career and been a single mother.

For Norma Marder, having children earned her the scorn of others in her profession. She tells the story of going back to the conservatory after having her first child to rematriculate on a scholarship she had won earlier.

" 'I want you to realize something,' Brownlee said, his voice resonant and impersonal. 'You've disgraced yourself by having a child. You've disgraced yourself and wasted our money,' he said coldly. 'You've disgraced the school.'

"Nevertheless, my scholarship was renewed, and I took on the tasks of half-time mother and half-time musician, determined to do each well."[7]

Even the women who have not had children eventually want them. Perhaps there is something about generative energy that is heightened in the presence of children. The differences between the ways Lovers and Leaders compared with Innovators and Artists think about and relate to children and the impact of those differences would be a fascinating question to pursue further.

THE BALANCE SHEET

In expecting and striving for a balance between work and love in their lives, Innovators confront all the conflicts and problems experienced by "superwomen" everywhere. When they do have children, their talent is more for generative love than caretaking. The Innovator may do well at valuing, validating, encouraging, stimulating, playing with children. But a partner may need to be more able to provide some of the day-to-day emotional and physical caretaking. Our culture doesn't provide great support for this pattern. Women are not rewarded for leaving their children to the care of others so that they can go be creative. An Innovator or an Artist may find herself sacrificing her art to nurturing. Her very talent for being innovative and creating workable forms for herself, especially when the voices of society ring in the head with appeals to the Smiling Woman image, can become a source of self-doubt and self-criticism.

On the other hand, the woman who truly pursues an artistic or professional career may be scorned within artistic circles for sacrificing her art for her children, as Norma Marder was. Women in the corporate world often face discrimination in terms of career opportunity when they have children. This is a path in which the split image begins to have a practical and painful reality in its impact, particularly when children are involved. Our social institutions don't support the need for child care or a workplace that can also be a "home place" where work and care for children is integrated.

In her personal relationships, which, again, can often become more a challenge to her creativity than children, a woman may confront struggles with competitiveness, envy, power imbalance. The two biggest barriers to relational life, beyond being with a partner who does not support or encourage a woman's work, are organizing time and the ruinous prevalence of self-doubt.

The single woman in this category runs the risk of isolation. Being so self-defining and self-directed, having so great a need for work of one's own, can make finding compatible friendships and work colleagues difficult. The single Innovator may need to pour more of her energy into finding relationship forms that are satisfying—usually her work creates less conflict.

When a woman can find a good relational match, the benefits of this pattern tend to outweigh the difficulties. When it works well, this pattern permits a woman support and partnership, the capacity to relate to one who values her as an equal and who encourages her creativity and growth. She, more than women in any other category, learns to integrate different types of love and to define the patterns of that loving for herself. She experiences both interdependence and self-sufficiency and she has the satisfaction of making a statement, of truly putting her own stamp on the world around her. She is subject and her level of energy demonstrates how free a woman can be when that subjectivity shapes her life.

THE QUESTION OF MEANING

For the Relational Integrative woman, relationship is a touchstone and meaning occurs in the connections she creates between herself and the people who populate her world. The creative women in our sample found the creative process itself to be a source of meaning and identity in their lives. The experience of producing art or other forms of work had many meanings that each struggled to articulate, but all seemed to agree that it was central to their being and sense of wholeness.

Sharon Gainsburg thinks about her work as a way of learning about herself. She says, "Whatever you do in the studio is just an example of how you handle things out there in the world. To me, the creative process is just a process about learning. Learning about me, learning about me in relationship to emotions, the world. It's a self-discovery. I had this need to create, this passion to create, to learn about myself and to be able to contribute some beauty to the world. And to teach people to see in another way."

Linda Russell talks of the moments in her life that are most gratifying: "feeling that when I sing I sing right out of my power, and I have the power to move people."

Creative Integrative women know the power of subjectivity and agency. They are able to translate their deepest energies and vision into connection with others through the medium of their work. But for all that their work is central to their sense of themselves and to their highly generative natures, love and relatedness remain a foundation, a necessary but not sufficient aspect of their lives. Linda Russell speaks movingly of both the dark and magical sides of love in her life: "The day my husband left me was two days before my fortieth birthday. I called a gathering for my birthday of all my best women friends and my mom and we went to my girlfriend's rooftop apartment. I didn't know when I was calling these women that I was in a state of shock. I had no idea if it was going to be a wake or a party that I was calling them to. And it was so incredible. We told stories, we sang songs, my mom led us in all these songs she had taught me as a kid. So I felt this complete connection to my childhood and my adulthood. All these women had been important in my life. And we went on until two in the morning on that rooftop. Magical things happened that night. Nobody has ever forgotten the tales that were told. It was just an amazing, loving circle. And that was the tremendous healer at the worst moment in my adult life as far as relationship was concerned. I just knew that I was going to be okay. Whatever happened, this showed me that I had love on this earth. I didn't have *that* love, but I had love."

The medium had been song, the powerful bridge between her creative and her loving self. In this story, Linda captures the essence of the Creative Integrative woman's sense of self: one who experiences and expresses loving, passionate connection within the medium of a creative event.

CHAPTER NINE

Visionaries: The Woman of Passionate Conviction

WHEN WE FIRST MEET, Frances Wilson Peabody is eighty-eight years old. She lives in the center of Portland, Maine, in a turn-of-the-century Victorian home that she has painstakingly renovated with minute attention to historical detail.

Frances is a slight, gracious woman who, at eighty-eight, still keeps a busy schedule focused almost entirely around volunteer service. Currently, she is one of the prime movers behind the Maine AIDS Coalition. She does public relations, speaking, and generally lends her knowledge of community organizing to this group that is the major source of support for the growing population of AIDS patients in rural Maine.

Our interview has been difficult to schedule because Frances's calendar is full, as her life has been. She helped to organize the Coalition because her grandson recently died of AIDS. She wanted to do something to help. Her daughter, Barbara Peabody, has inherited her mother's sense of dedication and generosity—she started a national organization for AIDS patients and wrote a book, *The Screaming Room*, that chronicles her son's death. It has become a well-read classic in the growing literature detailing the outrages of living with and dying of AIDS.[1]

Frances's views on politics and on women's lives are both traditional and liberal. Our meeting takes place in the middle of the Anita Hill–Clarence Thomas hearings. Frances says, "I know that they're going to pass Thomas because it's a lot of men judging a man. They're not going to judge him as a woman would judge him. Women know what she's talking about—they know but a lot of them don't want to trust their instincts. They don't want men to think they think that way. Women are so molded by their lives and their peers and their families that they don't even realize they are thinking this way."

Frances believes women are every bit as capable and creative in the world as men. But she also thinks that there are certain "female" tasks, like raising children, that women find more inherently satisfying and enjoyable. She refers to her own life—she had five children, she lost one to crib death and nursed two of the other four back from bouts with polio. Her life has been one of privilege, hardship, service, and loss. She has been sustained by her deep conviction that "One gets a great deal of satisfaction out of feeling that you have helped someone else—what you give comes back ten-fold. My philosophy is that we're here to develop and mature for some reason, and I feel it's much more satisfying to do things for other people."

Frances gave up many years of her life to nurse and retrain her daughter Charlotte who was paralyzed by the polio. Of this time, she says, "Well, it wasn't a sacrifice. I was just awfully glad to have the chance to do it; that's all I wanted—to have the chance to make her better."

EMPOWERED BY BELIEF

There were a number of women we interviewed who might be relational or creative or both, but who seemed remarkable because of the energy of their vision. When we tried to define what "moved" these women, it was clear that they each held in their minds an idea or conviction about what was meaningful and important in their lives and they translated that vision directly into action. They are women who, though our peers, seemed somewhat larger than life. They are quietly heroic women who, if we looked for parallels in history or current culture, would remind us of an Eleanor Roosevelt, a Marian Wright Edelman, a Gloria Steinem. They inspire because they are so dedicated to the vision that drives them. While they could remind us of those more visible women who have moved many, it seemed that they were equally committed in their smaller, more particular ways.

Frances Peabody is one of those women. She is a Leader in that her focus is always on relationship and the care of others. But she is also like the Innovator in her determination and her creative use of self. She has spent her life working for the benefit of other people. Nurturing and generativity are both expressed in Frances's life—the synthesizing factor, the dominant force, is conviction, vision intently focused on the rightness and necessity of a particular way of being. The vision is inspired by hope and thrives on a sense of affirmation and possibility in life.

Conviction is a characteristic of women in each of the patterns, passion demands it. The relational woman passionately believes in relationship, the creative woman is passionate about expressing an inner imperative through a specific medium. But the woman of vision is most driven by the passion of some larger belief, whether it be in social justice or in self-determination. Action flows from that belief. The organizing principle, the through-line of the life, is a deeply felt sense of purpose and mission. Both action and relationship are central to the actualization of that conviction. Visionaries tend to integrate the qualities and energies of the four other forms combined.

When asked about the passions of her life, one woman responded in a way that would be typical of a Visionary:

"One, the earth and treating it with love and respect; two, porpoises and horses; three, restoration for dysfunctional families; four, helping educate and inform impoverished young persons about responsible parenting; five, feeding and clothing our U.S. starving."

These passions aren't just imaginary ideals for this woman—she acts on them. When asked how she nourishes her passions, her response:

"One and four, by volunteering to teach parenting and ways to respect the earth and each other; two, donating and writing Congressmen; three, I created my job (family addictions therapist); five, donating money and doing community education."

Rather than helping individuals, the Visionary sets out to help groups, the country, an organization, the world. Women in this category tend to be social activists, to be service-oriented, to want to "make a difference," to focus on a larger sense of purpose that is of benefit to groups of people beyond themselves.

Many visionaries are entrepreneurs and politicians who believe they accomplish larger social agendas through their management of a service-oriented business or a political career. They combine the self-determination and willfulness of the Creative Integrative woman with the compassion and social skills of the relational.

Frances Peabody's life is rooted in ideas of service and help, and those beliefs were played out both in her personal life and in her public life. When Charlotte contracted polio, Frances had herself trained and spent two years teaching her at home and five years doing physiotherapy with her daily. "I was determined she was going to be able to walk again." Having been completely paralyzed, Charlotte did in fact walk again. As another daughter was to say of her some years later, "Charlotte didn't dare not get well when Mother decided she was going to."

Frances has been a widow for many years; her husband died at fifty-eight. For a time after his death, she took over the management of his business herself, then was to oversee its sale and disposition. When she wasn't managing the business, she was busy with her many other volunteer interests in the community. She is a great lover of history and has been active in the state historical society. She has been on the boards of numerous organizations including landmark commissions, has helped to write books to provide scholarship funds for students at the local conservatory. She says, "I think I have a certain kind of imagination. I am creative in some ways, and I love to do things like that. It's a challenge. I've started one or two programs and organizations that I've worked in and it's been fun to work in them and see them develop and so forth. There are lots of ways to be creative if people would just let their imaginations go and have the courage. You have to have some courage in back of it, energy and perseverance. I must say I've done some things that scared the daylights out of me but they turned out alright."

Frances is preeminently a woman of action—but her action is informed by vision, determination, and a sense of purpose. About her future, she says, "I don't want to hang around beyond the years where I can be useful." Her life has been nothing if not useful. Many have benefited from her active creativity and sense of concern. Typically though, she thinks of herself as the one who's benefited most.

There is no question that economic privilege, education, and an ethic of service instilled by family, social status, and the training of a Seven Sisters' liberal education had an impact on Frances Peabody's sense of conviction and determination. But one can look to women whose early backgrounds were vastly different and see the same sense of determination, the desire to make the world a better place, the desire to make a difference, that typified Peabody's system of personal belief. Vision is a necessary component of a passionate life. We found that even women at the bottom of the economic ladder, displaced homemakers, recovered their lives slowly by virtue of having a vision of what they could do to make their lives better. All had a sense of determination, a system of belief in possibility, hard work, perseverance. In most cases, women who had faced the greatest hardship were the most determined. They had overcome enormous obstacles by sheer force of will.

A DECIDING MOMENT

Paulette Hines grew up in Elizabeth City, North Carolina, today a sleepy rural community that lies just south of Norfolk, Virginia. She was part of a nuclear family of four children and an extended family that she describes as "humongous." Each of her parents had between nine and eleven brothers and sisters, and all of those had children of their own. "Family was very broadly defined. There was a whole network of people including aunts and uncles and teachers who in a small community like that basically treated you as though you were family. Everybody about you was doing the right thing and advancing."

Paulette is a wife and mother but her passion is her work—she is the director of the Office of Prevention Services at a large community mental health center just outside of New York City. She is a leading author and presenter on African American Families and a former president of the State Association of Black Psychologists.[2]

Her sense of mission and purpose are clear and seemingly they always have been: "Well, it's basically taking my knowledge and skills and applying them toward the reduction or elimination of human problems. Trying to address social issues in the community . . . trying to prevent problems before people become debilitated . . . promoting health, promoting wellness, trying to address human suffering or to prevent it basically. I think from the time I was a little kid that was always a concern of mine. . . . I grew up in the fifties and early sixties and I was a child during the time that the civil rights movement was really gearing up and I can remember looking at the television and seeing Martin Luther King really moving the masses and having a sense that I wanted to do something in my life to make a difference in the world. I also come from a long line of Baptist ministers and teachers and nurses and people who were in the helping professions, and one of the things that I was always confronted with, particularly as a black child who did well in school, was that people would ask you, Do you want to be a nurse? Do you want to be a teacher? Do you want to be a secretary? And that angered me because it was so limiting. So I knew that I wanted to do something that was about helping people, but I didn't want to be constrained or pushed into those particular occupations. I think there was always a piece of me that wanted to find a different way to do it and this is where I ended up. I think it was as much determined by what I didn't want to do as what I did want to do."

For Paulette, there was a deciding moment in her life that set the emotional theme, sparked the initial energy that has shaped her vision.

It happened when she was five or six years old. "I remember going downtown to buy a cone of ice cream, and being told that I could not eat it there at the counter [because she was black] and being angry enough about it that I set the ice cream back on the counter and refused to pay for it. I have this sense of being in the drugstore by myself, perhaps whomever I was with was outside, but it's a memory that's always there, sort of a pain and anger about it that I think has driven me in some ways also."

Paulette is one of many women who doesn't necessarily think of herself as creative. But she does acknowledge, "Whatever creative moments I have are probably driven more by tough moments than otherwise. That's one of my ways of dealing with adversity. A lot of people sort of space out and fall back. And one of the things I do is dig in deeper and work harder."

The theme of taking action in the face of adversity or pain is consistent in the stories of both Frances and Paulette. The one thing that Paulette hopes to teach her children, two young boys, is "how to cope with stress and adversity—it concerns me that when that time comes in their lives, whether it has to do with racism or just having to struggle to make ends meet or whatever, that there is something inside that they can pull on that lets them know that you can come out on the other side. That's a major concern."

Paulette's race is both the source of her oppression and her strength. She says, "It's very hard for me to think of myself as just a woman and not a black woman, I can tell you that. It's just the general sense, the lifelong sense is, what color is my reality . . . first and foremost who I am is my race more so than my gender. But I think that the advantage of being a black female that I have to pull on would probably be the legacy of so many strong, creative, and energetic black women who have come before me. Who have given me an example of how to do it and I think inside I carry this notion that I ought to be able to do it or should have to do it or can do it because they did it."

For Frances Peabody the central theme in her life was loss, for Paulette it was social injustice. Both seem to draw on a sense of inner resources, the capacity not just to cope but to overcome, a capacity current theorists might call resilience. But it's a resilience that is composed of a mixture of creativity, action, resourcefulness, and a deep desire to connect with others, to encourage and instill in others the same strengths they find within themselves.

Paulette is another Leader who incorporates qualities of the Innovator. The Visionary stretches the Leader pattern to its most expansive point by taking her determination into the highly public sphere of social activism. Paulette's energy is relational but she is moved most by principle—the conviction that people can be helped and strengthened to overcome the adversity imposed by what we can't control and also by what we can. One might say that her vision is fueled by a compassionate anger at the injustices that we suffer at one another's hands.

CHANGING THE WORLD

That same desire to make the world a better place that characterizes Frances Peabody's and Paulette Hines's personal vision describes the energy behind Sheila Wilensky-Lanford's highly successful children's bookstore. The founder of Oz Books in Southwest Harbor, Maine, says, "I am a child of the sixties, and I wanted to change the world."

A former social studies teacher, Sheila particularly sought to change the way history was taught by providing young people with quality books that would expand their world view. One has a tough time finding the Care Bears in Oz because they aren't there. Instead, there are classics and books that promote gender equality and racial justice. People notice the difference. When she opened Oz, a local newspaper described Sheila as "a woman with a mission."[3]

Sometimes Sheila's mission has felt compromised by necessity. Being an entrepreneur also means dealing pragmatically with money. "I have a real hard time ethically sometimes deciding whether to have some books that I know are popular and I know will sell well." But Sheila *has* actualized her dream *and* she is financially successful, although people told her it couldn't be done in a town with a population of five thousand. Today, ten years after its inception, Oz not only retails books, but sponsors a series of talks by guest authors and public workshops for adults.

It was the power of her vision that got Sheila started in business. "Everybody said it couldn't go here, in this town." First she sought financing through the male banker at the local bank. " 'This is not the kind of business that would fly in this town,' he said. Then I went to a local person, a woman, who was manager of another small bank. I had the business plan and all the paperwork that I was supposed to present, according to the books, but I think what sold the idea was my saying, 'This is something that I really believe in.' She must have had intuition too because she said, 'I think it's a great idea,' and she gave me the money."

Sheila believes in taking action.

"Trying is dying. It's like when you say you are going to try to do this, it's like death. You're not doing it. You just do it."

The story of Sheila's transition to being an entrepreneur chronicles her development from Lover to the Innovator pattern.

There was a preface to Sheila's bookstore venture. She started her adult life in the deep shadow of the Smiling Woman. Initially, she didn't think she had to make her life happen for herself. Like the artist and entrepreneur Sara Eyestone, who thought her first husband would "distinguish her," Sheila married her husband because he seemed to possess all of the qualities that she wanted in herself. Like so many women who confuse "He's everything I want" with "He's everything I *want to be*," Sheila says, "I married him to guide me. And to be vicariously what I wasn't that I wanted to be. Henry was a brilliant man. And that's one of the reasons I married him. He was a brilliant handsome WASP and I am Jewish, and I always wanted to be smarter. I didn't care about being pretty . . . I always, even as a teenager, at that time when most girls wanted to be popular, I wanted to be smart and I didn't feel like I was very smart. And so I vicariously married this man who was all of this. Even though he said to me when we got married we would never be rich. He would never make a lot of money, he came from a very intellectual WASPy family but he did not want to compete out in the world. So he never met my expectations. I said oh God this guy is so brilliant, he's going to write a book or invent something . . . and he'll become famous and we'll make a lot of money. And we were sort of trying to be hippies back then and as the years went on I didn't want to be a hippie anymore."

Sheila wanted him to be more ambitious. Perhaps if he had been, she might have had an easier time molding her life around his agenda, deferring to him. But the combination of his lack of ambition and her own strong ambition led her to rebel.

Sheila was emerging from the High Relational pattern. Having children might have forced her back into that mold. But it didn't.

Although having children did activate her "genetic Jewish guilt," she fortunately knew that pouring all of her energy into mothering would not fit for her. "I had to do something out of the house or feel totally like nothing. I was not a big cookie baker.

"Wonderful times with my kids were not the mainstay of my good feelings. On a big scale, it was always more my work. Having my kids certainly has been very important and I'm glad I had them, but it was not enough."

So when her daughter Brook was four and a half and her son

Ethan, eighteen months, Sheila made her trip to the bank to get financing for Oz.

VISION AND THE COURAGE TO CHOOSE

Shortly after starting the store, when it had begun to be successful and Sheila had realized that she was going to have to make her life happen for herself, she became pregnant with a third child. She recognized that having this child would make the emerging shape of her life a more difficult fit. "I didn't want to give up my business. I didn't want to have a third child." She was at a crossroads.

After a lot of agonizing she decided to have an abortion. Having the abortion was "very very traumatic for me. I already had two children and it was much more traumatic for me than for any friend I have known personally that's gone through the same thing. And I thought of that kind of as a rebirth. If I was going to kill this protoplasm, then I was really going to have to put some energy into myself."

Later she read *In a Different Voice* by the noted psychologist Carol Gilligan, who, in Sheila's words "found that abortion has either made women step backward or really go through this creative thing."

How did Henry react to Sheila's increasing focus on her own agenda? Before he married her, Henry had been a filmmaker, done all kinds of interesting things. Although he was very supportive of Sheila starting the store, and mentored her in some ways, he then, as she sees it, became competitive with her. She feels that he always thought he was right, because he knew he was very very smart, a scientist, a logical thinker.

"He always knew the right way. Whenever I left the dishes for him to wash, the glasses had to go on the right side . . . he was trained as a scientist through and through, so it was a major event. He always talked about the store as if it were both of ours. And I really didn't like that. The store was not his thing. He did all his big stuff before he knew me. He made some suggestions once in a while, but it was basically mine, like my baby. I'll take people's recommendations, but it's my thing."

The enormity of the decision to choose her own life rather than that of the fetus, invest energy in her own dreams rather than pushing Henry to make her dreams happen for her, was profound. Not only did Henry talk about the store as if it belonged to both of them, but Sheila herself reacted to the dramatic shift in herself as if suffering an internal backlash.

"I won't say I was crazy or near a breakdown or anything after the abortion, but I was not in good shape. I was petrified to even drive my car by myself into town." The growth of confidence in her, the difference in her levels of anxiety before Oz and after it have been remarkable to Sheila. "Now, I think, I am like a totally different person. I'll go anywhere."

Sheila describes her mother as very traditional and says that for years she blamed her mother for her fear. Now she feels more forgiving. She also worries about her daughter hanging onto her own strength when she gets involved with boys although, "she is much stronger than I was.

"As Gilligan says, there is something that happens there, to girls between eleven and sixteen. I see it in my daughter. She has a very strong presence and confidence in herself about most things, but a couple of years ago she started crying and she said she was afraid she would involuntarily start to like boys, rock music, and clothes and she didn't want to. She said this when she was about ten. She hasn't talked to me about how she feels about boys but I think she is starting to get interested in them. That's all fine with me, as long as she keeps her strength too."

The form of her marriage fit worse and worse for Sheila the more successful she became on her own. Having married Henry to "guide her," she had become the guide. She was divorced in March 1992.

VISION AND MONEY: THE ECONOMIC IMPERATIVE

The woman whose vision leads her into her own business, like other career women, may be either an Innovator or Artist, depending on how single-mindedly she pursues her goal. Unlike most other career women, or painters, or composers, or writers, however, women entrepreneurs really are in charge of their own lives and finances. Women like Sara Eyestone who are both artist *and* entrepreneur are unusual. Even the highly successful corporate lawyer, editor, physician, or broker takes orders from someone else. The entrepreneur gives them. She takes full responsibility for making her vision real.

Sheila and Frances are both models of women who take action. They visualize the incarnation of their dream and then take the necessary risks to make the dream come true. They also have the ability to break the process into the component steps. They know how to do things, have the ability to network. If the essence of creativity is connection, they have the ability to make bridges between events, people, or situations so that they see opportunities where others would see obstacles. And they seize opportunities because they are not afraid to promote their ideas, let others know what they want.

Many of us, as women, have no hesitance in promoting a cause. We work, like Frances Peabody, for the AIDS Coalition, for the hospital, we run the church's fund drive, totally unashamed about baldly demanding money from the powerful and rich. Some of us can even do it for women's issues, like lobbying politicians to legislate insurance coverage for mammography, or marching as pro-choice advocates for reproductive freedom. But when it comes to marketing our own seminars, charging what we're worth, convincing the bank to loan us money for a mortgage or a business, we have trouble.

The artistic woman may have trouble taking her work seriously. Women are, after all, not meant to create symbols or produce culture. But an entrepreneur has to stride down still more sacrosanct male corridors, those of power and finance. Women traditionally have not had access to those corridors.

Consequently many of us are uncomfortable with the issue of earning, charging, collecting money. One therapist remembers, as a new private practitioner, having trouble taking the check directly from the client's hand. Initially, she kept a "fee jar" so the client could drop the money in without her having to take it directly.

The artist and musician have to value their time and ultimately put a price on their work. The entrepreneur has to be able to take large financial risks and be confident that she has something to offer that will bring a monetary return. She has to have the ability to "pitch the idea" to financial backers in a convincing way. And she needs some stereotypically male attributes like aggressiveness and raw nerve to carry her ideas through.

The businesswoman may have visionary ideas, but she also has the pragmatism and skills to make them work. The Visionary is not just a woman who thinks about change, she also makes it happen.

PRAISE GOD AND PASS THE AMMUNITION: SOCIETY AND THE VISIONARY WOMAN

American society has always valued the entrepreneur. But she wasn't supposed to wear a skirt. And our society has counted on the good deeds of the social activist but she hasn't fared much better than the entrepreneur in the popular imagination. When we think of society's images of female Visionaries of any variety, those pictures reflect great ambivalence toward women who are active rather than passive. Social activism conjures up images of the ridiculed, like the hatchet-bearing activists of the Women's Christian Temperance Union. Some members of the WCTU concentrated on prayer. Others seemed to believe that the Lord helps those who help themselves, and took matters into their own hands. "As early as 1853, Mrs. Margaret Freeland of Syracuse, New York, marched alone into her alcoholic husband's favorite saloon and smashed it to splinters with a club. Other women, primarily in the Midwest, began to follow her example, banding together in search-and-destroy missions, wielding hatchets, clubs, and rocks."[4]

A related cause was that of the suffragettes, and again cartoons depicted the stern-faced, oxford-wearing, school-marm visage of the woman crusading for the vote. Even today, when women push for equal rights, they are frequently characterized by the media, and worse still, characterize themselves in terms such as "angry feminists," or "shrill and strident," or one of those "man-hating [i.e., lesbian] feminists." Today it is Jill Ireland, president of NOW, who invites mixed reviews.

Images of entrepreneurs reflect no less ambivalence. From Diamond Lil, and other famous madams of the brothels in history, to the ostentatiously successful women proprietors of the speakeasies of prohibition days, to Leona Helmsley or Ivana Trump, society has tolerated women so long as they serve the interests of men. They might well serve men by providing liquor, sex, or decoration. Madonna, whose new book *Sex* immediately sold hundreds of thousands of copies, is one of the most successful female entrepreneurs of our time. But, in company with Leona and other businesswomen, society views her with profound ambivalence, fascinated by her, but often contemptuous of her at the same time.

Career women fare little better, even in the nineties. During the recent historic presidential campaign, local newspaper headlines read, "Hillary Clinton Shows a More Wifely Demeanor" . . . voters began viewing Mrs. Clinton as a hardheaded careerist who dominated her mate.[5]

The activist, dry and humorless, sexless, frigid. The businesswoman, raucous and flamboyant, promiscuous and dangerous, Madonna/Whore. Attitudes toward Visionaries capture the split image of woman in yet another kind of split, one that directly depicts men's ambivalence about women's sexuality and their power.

Visionaries are women of mission and purpose, resilience, courage, energy, and perseverance. Whether fighting at the barricades for social change, or fighting for an independent vision as entrepreneurs, the core quality of these women is the courage to go public with their own dream in the face of great risk.

PART THREE

PASSION AND PROCESS

CHAPTER TEN

The Early Death of Love, or, I Used to Play the Violin

WOMEN'S LIVES ARE ALWAYS IN PROCESS, always changing. Ideally, as they have for the women we describe in part 2, our passions find expression in some balance between relationship and creativity, and this balance may be different at different points in our lives. Part of psychological growth involves continually readjusting our lives in ways that give us the best access to the truth in our hearts over time. We make choices, we change, we let go of fear, objectivity, and we move into true ownership of ourselves.

But often it happens that women don't find a form that fits, a structure that suits. So many of the women we talked to did not feel a passionate connection to their own lives, were not the authors of their own stories. Their feelings were deadened, diverted, detoured, or denied. Or sometimes their most passionate feelings and interests simply went unrecognized. They experienced vague sadness, or regret about choices not made, a vagueness about what their deepest energies were. When a woman's access to her deep passions is blocked, she fails to be subject, she fails to experience a sense of agency in her life. The result may be sickness, depression, unhappiness, or addiction.

If one important question is "What moves us?" another is "What blocks us?" How and why are our most passionate feelings and interests obscured, so that many of us have trouble being subject? Beyond the insidious effects of the cultural story of love, the answers to this question lie in the ways the past creates the present, the ways that we lose contact with what moved us in our childhood. Our adult lives often become full of distraction from our deepest feelings and needs.

In part 2, we talked about many aspects of our data that explored the ways that the past creates the present by asking women to remember what moved them passionately as children, adolescents and young adults, and where that energy operates now in their lives. We asked what images they held of a future when they lived in the past and whether those imaginative fantasies form any part of their real lives in the present. We looked at the ways that first love becomes transmuted, truncated, or transformed.

REMEMBERING FIRST LOVE

The sources of our passions can be located in our past. "First love" refers not only to our earliest and often most passionate love relationships, but it refers also to those activities and pursuits that gave us joy, made us feel happy, engaged us wholly. Childhood is a well of feeling, imagination, and creative power. It is also a time when our feelings and creativity may be systematically bred out of us in families and schools that demand conformity rather than uniqueness, function rather than feeling.

We first asked someone for a story of lost love in a professional workshop. A woman in her mid-fifties walked slowly to the front of the room and took a seat facing the one hundred or more therapists in the room. Her name was Barbara.

We ask, "What was the love you lost?"

"My first love; I guess I was about twelve or thirteen and I fell madly in love with a young man a couple of years older than I was. And my father very much disapproved of this young man and did everything he could to discourage that and eventually did. And I still think about him."

"Can you think of a specific way that he discouraged you?"

"Oh yes. He did something very dramatic. I can still feel this experience. My father told me to get into the car, he wanted to take me for a drive. And I can still feel the texture of the seat and the smell of that car. We lived in a small farming community in the Midwest and we drove around to the little church. And when we got by the church he said to me, 'I hate to tell you this but there is a possibility that I am the father of this boy.'"

There is a gasp from the workshop audience, an audible "ohhhh."

"And I was just devastated. I was seventeen at that point."

"Who did you share that with? Who did you talk to to help you heal that?"

"Nobody, till years later. I carried that for, I don't know, thirty years."

"Did you and the boy ever talk?"

"No."

"So you held that a secret?"

"Yes."

"Can you make a connection, Barbara, between that first love, that was so abbreviated, does it connect with later loves for you?"

"I don't know. The man I chose is an alcoholic."

"Do you remember how you felt about yourself when you were in love?"

"There was shame."

"You're still sad about this . . . talking about this."

"Yes, yes. Two years ago, my father told me he made the story up."

There is another gasp from the workshop audience and then silence. The enormity of the power of the parent to cut short this love is palpable in the room.

"Is there another passion in your life, other than people? Is there anything else that so fully engages you that you would consider it a passion?"

"I think that's why I came to this workshop . . . to find out."

"Were there any passions you had as a child?"

"I was the good little girl."

"You had a passion to be good?"

"Very much so, yes."

"If you had all the talent, and all the money, and all the time, what might you have been? Anything?"

"Uuummmm. Oh, I wanted to write a book, I wanted to write a song, I wanted to paint."

"You wanted to write a song; you wanted to paint. Did you ever write anything?"

"No."

"Did you ever do a song?"

"No."

"Did you ever have an art lesson?"

"No."

"Have you taken a class?"

"No."

"Do you sing?"

"No."

"Do you ever sing?"

"To myself."

"What do you sing?"

"Oh, I don't know, popular songs."

"Tell us a song."

"Are you going to make me sing a song?"

There is laughter from the audience.

"Tell us a song. We're not going to make you do anything."

"Tell you a song. OK. 'Smoke Gets in Your Eyes.' "

"That's a passionate song. Who can sing?"

Three or four women come up from the audience and softly sing, "Smoke Gets in Your Eyes." Barbara joins in. Many of the women have tears in their eyes.

> *They asked me how I knew,*
> *my true love was true*
> *I of course replied,*
> *something deep inside*
> *cannot be denied.*[1]

Then everyone joins in; Barbara is sitting crying quietly.

There is probably not one of us who hasn't had the experience of singing some song to ourselves that absolutely captures the emotion that we may be unaware of feeling. There is probably not one of us who doesn't feel some nostalgia for the intensity of first love, a longing to feel again the deep connection to ourselves that passion provides. The women who responded to our surveys all had vivid memories of first love. Their responses captured both the essential irrationality of early passion and the humor of the human condition. Some could inspire a Norman Rockwell painting and others a Euripidean tragedy.

QUESTION: Do you remember your first love? What happened?

"Yes. Jimmy Taub kissed me in the coatroom—-third grade."

"Yes. My parents wouldn't allow me to see him because his father was a painting contractor."

"Yes, he sang to me—'Jingle Bells' in Greek."

"Yes. He was killed in a plane crash."

"Max Sokolsky. We read mystical stuff, smoked a lot of pot together, and spoke in very short sentences. We talked about getting married. I eventually panicked about being stifled. I put more and more energy into doing photography. I think when photography became more central in my life than Max, the relationship ended."

"Yes. Boy twenty-three, me fifteen. Fell in love, he was worried, didn't tell me, disappeared. Broke my heart but it was wonderful while it lasted."

"Yes, very intense, lost myself in the person, scared of being re-jected, ran at first sign might be rejected."

"There were crushes in junior and senior high school, but the first person I think I loved was an instructor in nursing school. We went to the gay bars together and talked a lot. There was not a physical/sexual relationship—she said she wished I was ten years older, but she wasn't willing to risk legal problems because I was under legal age. We re-mained friends for many years."

Many first love memories are not of romantic love at all but of maternal or parental love. In the same workshop where Barbara sang, Elena, a Russian American, told the audience:

"The first time that I remember love is as a child; the first thing I can remember of feeling love, I was a preschooler. My parents came here from Russia when I was three and a half or four and I was playing with some American children who did not want to play with me and I was crying. I came up the steps, and my mother took me in her arms and told me she loved me."

Another memory of parental love:

"I was about three lying on my mother's lap—she had an itchy wool skirt and a soft blue sweater and she was just talking to me and stroking my head."

Some first loves are not for people at all:

"I reached for the violin at age three, loved violins and lullabies."

"Narcotics—they worked emotionally as a 'mother nurturer' for many years until I couldn't get high enough anymore."

What most characterizes an important emotional experience in childhood is a heightened sensory awareness and a later recall of sensory detail. This acute sensitivity to the moment typifies those experiences when we are most fully alive. "I can still feel the ex-perience; the texture of the seat; the smell of the car," Barbara has said.

Sensory recall is frequently described as a characteristic of the condition of Flow that we first talked about when describing Julie Flanders's experience of acting. It is the joy of fully using our abilities. One can experience this kind of joy when one hits a tennis ball cleanly and solidly, is absorbed in playing an evenly matched game of chess, or is polishing a sentence or painting a painting.

One can also experience this kind of joy when in love. When our attention is totally engaged and we can temporarily silence the chatter in our heads of continual self-scrutiny, we are completely present and, on some level, the memory of that Flow experience remains with us, is always there.[2]

When we reclaim the memory of the images, it is with all our senses and those sensory images always take us back to some really critical emotional experience. First loves are critical emotional experiences. They may be intense, comic, or tragic.

But they inevitably prefigure some larger pattern of passion, attention, longing, that will recur in our lives.

Stories of lost love and stories of lost creativity are eerily similar. Disconnection from creative energy is at some level the same as disconnection from "first love."

Back in the workshop, we ask if Barbara's story has stirred any other feelings about lost passion.

Leslie, a social worker, tells us, "While they were talking I was thinking about growing up, coming from a mixed up family in many ways; it was very reinforcing to be the caretaker, to be the oldest daughter; while my mother was ill and was in the hospital for a couple of years while I was growing up, I was the homemaker, and got a lot of praise and reward for that and I didn't know what my passions were because I thought I liked to take care of everybody. And now as an adult, I'm married and I have children, and now I'm at a point and my children are grown, and we're a couple again. And I have time to explore things, but I don't know what the hell to do, except to nurture, and garden and bake, and nurture and grow things . . . but people things mostly. . . ."

"What did you like to do as a kid?"

"When I was a young teenager, I started to do some sculpture in a high school class and thought it was fun. My parents said, 'You don't have time for this; this is foolishness; this is not going to get you anywhere in life; what are you wasting your time with this for?' 'Clay is going to dry your hands out,' my mother told me [laughter from audience]. Clay will dry your hands out; so I put the clay away."

Some of us put away our clay, others of us lose our voices. One woman wrote us at length about just such a loss:

"I remember singing lustily in first grade. My teacher, Miss Galloway . . . I still remember her name, her pin curls flattened by the side of her head, the seams in her stockings, the click of her low pumps as she walked down the linoleum aisles bending her head ever so slightly to hear each child sing. 'Who?' she questioned. 'Who is spoiling this song by singing flat?'

"She stopped by my desk. Shame. Humiliation. Disgraced in first grade. For twenty years, I made my lips move, mouthing the words to a song silently, never raising my voice. I never any longer sang at the top of my lungs."

SHAME MURDERS LOVE

The factors that block feeling and relational passion are the same as those that block creative expression. Sometimes when one is blocked, the energy is detoured into the other; love becomes art, or creativity is channeled into love. But more often, the blockage of deep passion in one area simultaneously blocks passion in others.

It's not news that early experiences have a profound and long reaching effect on us. Much attention has focused recently on the lasting scars left by trauma such as sexual abuse. But the smaller traumas, the "little murders of the soul," are also critical in determining our life's course. Creativity and love can heal the scars of deeper abuse but if they themselves are stifled, if they dry up at the source, we are left with a severed connection to ourselves. Shame is one of the earliest and most major blocks to passion. Leslie was shamed by being told that she was wasting her time with clay and Miss Galloway inadvertently shamed the singer from ever again voicing her song.

Bobbi is the sixty-year-old quilter first mentioned in the chapter on Leaders. She had avoided her love for art for almost forty years because she was so consistently shamed as a child. She says, "My mother's favorite expression was 'Barbara, you ought to be ashamed of yourself.' That and, 'Now, Barbara, you know that is not how you feel.'"

Often children are shamed not only for activities and actions but for their feelings. Shaming of feelings is profoundly connected with discouragement of artistic, creative impulse because those impulses are all about being expressive. Women talk about this fear of self-expression differently, but always powerfully. These are statements of women in our therapy practice:

"If I allow my creative energy to flow, I fear I'm going to be rejected."

"If I allow my creative, real self to emerge, somebody will smash it."

"If I allow myself to be alive, I'll be a target for criticism, annihilation even."

One woman in our survey tells us, "There are times when fear and shame keep me from being passionate. I'm afraid of being alone with it, I am afraid of being judged by others (that they will judge me to be silly, off-track). Also, I'm afraid that if I really let it loose that I will be disappointed that my passion doesn't have all the power and magic that I imagine it to have when it's locked inside me."

These responses are all a commentary on the anticipation of being shamed. To be "annihilated" is to be told that one's "statement," one's feeling or self has no value and is in fact somehow disgusting or displeasing. The connection between shame and fear becomes an intimate one—for a woman, to express self at all, in other than "the body as a work of art" mode or the "art of intimacy" mode can literally feel like risking psychological death.

Shame undermines creativity and it undermines love. Not only creative expression, but the passionate expression of love, requires freedom from the constraints of cultural and family expectations and mores. The "real self" can include a whole range of emotions that women edit and suppress because they're not "ladylike," such as anger, sexuality, sensuality, dislike, displeasure, selfishness, nonloving feelings, envy, jealousy, or even intensely loving feelings.

We experience these emotions as the "dark" sides of our personalities, or the "shadow," in Jungian terms, and we disown them because we judge them as shameful. Or, like Samantha in chapter 2, we assume intense feeling is "immature," sentimental, melodramatic. How often were we told as children not to wear our hearts on our sleeves or not to act like Sarah Bernhardt. Chances are that for most of us our "real selves" are much more wild, passionate, fiery, and intense, angry, vulnerable, frightened, than we ever let on. We constrict ourselves sexually and in the depth of our emotional expressiveness with our children, our friends, our partners. We become fearful of knowing the full range of our feelings ourselves. We know too much how to appropriately manage our emotions, too little about how to let them have their way with us in their fullness. If one is to learn all the forms of self-control necessary to make civilized life possible, one ought at least to know fully the intensity of what is being controlled.

THE PRISON OF GOODNESS

The cultural love story is at the root of much of the shaming and fear we experience at the thought of expressing our real selves and of speaking fully and intensely about our love or our hate. Often our wildness, our subjectivity as women, is devalued precisely for its emotional power because we live in a society that devalues, fears, and pathologizes feeling. The parents who shame us are themselves products of a culture that castigates women's emotions, all emotion.

But for women, the impulse to self-expression in love or work challenges the major rules of womanhood—be attractive, be a lady, be unselfish, make relationships work, and be competent without complaint. As we've seen, it challenges the status of woman as object, the one in which she remains passive and pleasing rather than active and forthcoming.

As poet and author Adrienne Rich has commented, "It is only the woman who refuses to obey, who has said no, who is not a hack, who is creative."[3]

But this is the message of Kathy Bradford's painting, *Good Girl, Bad Girl*. We're shamed for any deviation from typical female roles, and we're typically not expected to exercise the freedom from conformity to social expectations that would be considered acceptable or at least tolerated for a male. And while we are expected to be emotional experts and to be impeccably responsible for the feelings and needs of the others in our lives, we're continually given the message that we're "bad" at love. In short, our attempts to be "good" women may constrict our creativity as well as our openness to deep and emotionally gratifying relationship.

The need to please others often dominates our emotional lives. For many women, the greatest obstacle to creative work has been the fear of losing relational connection and the sense that they are "bad" women if they focus on self rather than other.

As Paula Bennett says in her book on female creativity, *My Life a Loaded Gun*:

> The fact is that one cannot embed one's life in relationships, subordinate "achievement to care" and spend one's primary energy making others happy without paying a price. . . . That price comes . . . from the creative part of the self. . . . Anger's overwhelming importance for female creativity becomes clear . . . for there will be no way for [a woman] to reconcile the energies that make her creative—her imagination, her turbulence, her unkindness, with the qualities she must possess in order to be loved.[4]

Bennett makes the point that a woman's desire for love and social acceptability may be the very force that blocks passion, that alienates her from those deeper feelings that allow her to do work of her own. Paradoxically it is this "embeddedness" in relationship, so advocated by the relational theories of the Stone Center, that can not only support, but also constrain a woman from the autonomy and sense of subjectivity necessary to creative work.

Nancy West is a successful social worker. At the time of our interview she had settled squarely into a struggle over whether and how to retire from social work and pursue her current passion for quilting. The path to her embracing her more creative energies had been a long and arduous one. She had been through a marriage, a divorce, a remarriage, raised four children and had gone back to school for both undergraduate and graduate degrees. Her biggest obstacle to change? The need to please. "I think it's been so deeply ingrained to please others and to do what we are expected to do that to please myself is still a very difficult thing for me. My first husband was the product of a very very patriarchal father, and a very docile mother, and when we were married he said, 'I am the head of the household. You are responsible for the children and the house and I am responsible for earning the living and so forth.' And of course what happened was that as my own self began to emerge, as I began to realize that I did have some ability, that role was more and more uncomfortable for me." Right now Nancy can contemplate a change because, she says, "I have met, fulfilled the need to give unselfishly." Yet when we ask what the constraints might be in her making a change she says, "Guilt. How could I possibly do something for myself? How can I feel good about doing something for myself?" Guilt we tell her. Change just one letter and you have "quilt." A simple shift in language can prefigure a major change in Nancy's sense of herself, a shift from being the object of social constraint to being empowered, being subject.

If Nancy's stance with regard to the female narrative is to fear not being pleasing, Pat Taylor's is the fear of being too unladylike and out of control, a version of the same fear. In college Pat studied and loved theater and went on to get a master's degree in fine arts. But the life-style was too intense, she found herself caught up with "partying, drug use, living the 'night life' of the theater." She had several relationships with men that confused and frightened her. After a period of ill health and general emotional trauma, she went to graduate school for a degree in education and decided that the way to stay balanced was to have a structured, predictable, and one might say, highly female, job. Ten years later found her married, a professional and competent teacher, but feeling lethargic, a lack of direction, a sense that something was missing in her life. She didn't know whether she wanted a child or a career, just "a job" or work that would really engage her fully. She didn't know what engaged her fully. Until somebody reminded her that she had loved theater, that she had been highly trained to work in it, and that she had simply walked away from the major interest of her life to become a caretaker and a "good girl."

Why did she walk away? "I was afraid of being out of control. The life-style seemed so wild to me, I didn't know how I would ever have a regular life. I feared the drugs and the drinking. And also, I thought that I wasn't really that good at it. I mean I thought that in order to stay in the field I had to be somebody really 'impressive.' Yet now it occurs to me that there are a lot of just plain old people who work in the field and not every one of them has to be 'impressive.' And I suppose it must be possible to lead a fairly regular life because a lot of people do it."

When someone asks Pat what stops her from having a child, she says, "Fear. What will it be like, will I be OK as a mother, can I handle it?" Fear stopped her for years from marrying. Pat has difficulty letting herself engage with both the processes of creating and loving, because she fears not being "good" enough, fears being too much herself and not enough what people expect her to be. Because she has never learned that emotions are the source of her strength, not the manifestation of her vulnerability, she fears she doesn't have the capacity to handle her own feelings. In being blocked, she experiences herself as deadened and asleep.

What Pat avoids in her sleep is the risk of feeling shame, the judgment she will heap on herself for being a woman of agency, of full power and passion, the lesson she has learned from many years of living in a shaming world.

ABANDONED DREAMS

As we've indicated throughout this chapter, women's stories speak to the reality that shame and the cultural love story are major blocks to our claiming of our generative power. In our interviews we asked specific questions about what dreams and passions women had abandoned, what constraints had stopped them from acting on a creative interest or a love. First we explored childhood wishes and then we went on to ask about what had changed. Almost every woman who fantasized about being "famous" or engaged in some very active, forceful, and creative venture eventually went on to become a "helper" or to channel the creative impulses into relationship. We noticed that many responses strongly reflected the impact of the split image. A woman might want to be something active that would give her power in the world, but be a wife or a "female" female at the same time.

QUESTION: As a child, did you have a vision or a dream of something you would do or be? What was it? How did the dream change over time? When did it change? What is it now?

"I wanted (fantasy level) to be one, a priest; two, a singer; three, a pianist; four, a dancer and skater; five, a radical activist. Also a bride and/or Miss America. Now I want to be a lively, creative social worker/ therapist who uses creative/expressive therapies, also I've joined a new church where all believers are considered priests and liturgists, where I am free to be a woman and contribute to worship with others in both an intellectual and sensual way."

"Movie star or counselor. Then changed to singer or counselor, then to working with people/social work, and eventually back to therapy."

"Considered being a nun until I read several books about their self-abuse. Started helping kids in school as a kid myself so became a teacher, then a therapist."

"A writer. I used to write stories and soap operas. I'd fake sick to stay home from school to do this. I stopped writing stories. Wrote some poetry in my early twenties and then academic things for school. Only now—I mean real recently am I trying to write an article."

"I had many visions: a ballet dancer, a missionary doctor, helping or enriching the lives of those 'without.' Changed primarily because of lack of money as a child. Today it is to be a serene, wise, loving mother, wife, and community member."

"Helper, Dancer, Nurse. I have always been a helper—lost dream of dancer through no training or support, now combined in my dance therapy work."

"My real dream emerged with my sobriety twenty-four years ago. Dream: to be as great, influential, helpful as Marty Mann. It has changed by becoming more realistic but I've made my mark."

Another set of responses to a slightly different version of the same question that focused on how the dream or passion had changed:

"To be beautiful and loved. It changed in early twenties when I experienced self-hatred. I now experience myself as beautiful in aspects and loved unconditionally by source, not humans."

"A vet—I dreamed I would spend my life caring for animals. I also dreamed I would be the swan that came from the ugly duckling. It changed the summer before my sophomore year in high school. I went to a journalism workshop and found my calling."

"No, I had no heroes. I was busy taking care of everyone. I want to: one, return to Hawaii to visit; two, have a retreat center for relationship healing; three, visit the Holy Land and pyramids and wine country in Italy."

"I thought I would grow up to be good and loving. I idolized healers, or holy women. I thought I would work in a slum somewhere as a doctor or something spreading love and light. I also wanted to save the chimpanzees and learn to talk with dolphins and live on an island with lots of children. The dream began to change in adolescence, when I was using [drugs] so much and falling behind in school. When I realized how hard it was to become a doctor and thought I was too stupid. When I started getting kicked out of schools and became overwhelmed by depression. When I was eons away from my values and didn't know what happened. When I 'realized' I wasn't special. When

I constantly failed. I don't know what it is now. I want to understand God and feel more part of the 'grace.' I want to learn how to be more loving. I don't want to hurt people. I want to feel connected and proud of being human."

When we asked women what constraints got in the way of their pursuing their original passions, their comments were remarkably consistent and similar. They speak of poor body image, a sense of not being good enough, lack of time, lack of opportunity, and deferring of their own passions for someone else's. Shame about their bodies was as powerful a factor in detouring dreams as shame about one's capacities or wishes for a life of active "doing" in the world.

What constraints blocked you from pursuing your dream?
"Lack of self-confidence, discipline, time, not good enough to do it, not a priority."
"Coming from a very sheltered home."
"Only my own unwillingness to make the time."
"Money—lack of it for early instruction. Health—development of nerve impingement. Family—incredible accumulation of responsibilities. Reality—feeling I'd never be 'good enough.'"
"I usually got in my way by getting fearful, insecure, full of self-doubt and self-deprecation."
"For a long time I haven't wanted to continue with dance because I felt too fat and out of shape. I'm slowly resolving this and want to take more classes soon. I used to do a lot of writing and wanted to write a novel and short stories but in college I realized the world of publishing is very competitive and male-dominated and I didn't want to deal with that. I also didn't believe enough in myself to ignore criticism and just write the way I wanted."
"Marriage to my first husband! Eventually I exited from that relationship but lost a love before that happened."
"My career, the other person's career, the potential for rejection. [Creative dream]: I don't think I'm very smart, and I work so hard I have little energy left for creativity—what a damn crazy shame."
"Self-contempt—pushing others away, isolating, raging, judging, seeking perfection."
"Being discouraged by others."

DEFERRED DREAMS

What happens when dreams die or when passions are abandoned? What happens when the impulse to be an active force in shaping one's own life becomes derailed into focusing on others?

One outcome is the dark descent into addiction, depression, or illness. Strong feeling unexpressed can as easily become destructive as it can become a source of creativity. Even if the only outlet for the feeling is a journal entry, with the act of writing the feeling down, a woman stands a much greater chance of staying balanced in the face of strong feeling than she does if she lets it go unexpressed entirely. Misdirected and unexpressed feeling can result in chaos, emotional instability, and "obsessions." Passion turns from a creative to a destructive force when a woman feels she has to disown herself and displaces her own power onto or into some focus outside of herself. In other words, like Sara Eyestone, she looks for a man or a partner or a cause to "distinguish" her while she remains in the background and escapes the fear of distinguishing or listening to herself.

Passion or Obsession?

Many women develop a "passion" for another person or for some work or goal. Often, they're pursuing what's unattainable—themselves—their own subjectivity and power, through something or someone outside themselves. They experience wanting love, attention, fame, recognition, power, and they become so fixated on that person or activity that finally they lose all control of themselves. They seek in another what is unattainable outside themselves—self-acceptance, freedom from shame and freedom from the sense of being passive and powerless to create their own life. Often they look to alcohol, a drug, food, to provide them with a sense of control, relief, power.

As Linda Leonard says in *Witness to the Fire*:

> The relationship between addiction and creativity, as I see it, is not causal. Rather, there is a parallel process occurring in the psyche of the addict and the creative person. Both descend into chaos, into the unknown underworld of the unconscious. Both are fascinated by what they find there. Both encounter death, pain, suffering. But the addict is pulled down, often without choice, and is held hostage by addiction; the creative person *chooses* to go down into that unknown realm, even though the choice may feel destined. . . . Some creative artists descend with the help of drugs or alcohol and continue to create. Some find they must give up their addictions in order to create. And others continue their addictions to the early loss of their creativity and/or their lives. But once in the realm of the underworld mysteries, they must eventually choose to find form and meaning from the chaos and to return to life and society.[5]

Obsession is misdirected passion, passion for what one might possess or gain control over rather than passion for what one might generate or express. The clearest sign that one is obsessed rather than passionate is that the person or the goal one pursues is ultimately unattainable. The obsession represents one's attempt to deny this reality. While passion results in an affirmation of self, obsession may be rooted in an avoidance of self, perhaps rooted in the death of an unvoiced dream. Compulsion, fear, insecurity, anxiety, depression result when our deepest impulses to love and to express ourselves are blocked. Women in our surveys talked most often about the obsession with food, which is really a symbol for the obsession with the body as a work of art—the sense that they were controlled by the need to be externally pleasing rather than internally true to their own needs and feelings.

Obsession, depression, and addiction result from self-alienation, from a silencing of the self, from a belief that the other is full of value while the self is worthless. One seeks the love or approval of the other to give oneself value. Obsession and addiction are attempted solutions to shame, to a lack of connection with the self, depression is a reaction to it.

Sculptor Sharon Gainsburg says, "To me obsession is when you're willing to sacrifice everything for a person, a cause, an ideology. At fifteen I was obsessive. I was willing to give up everything for this guy. And I have learned that when you give over a part of yourself you lose yourself—you don't know who you are anymore."

So, then, obsession is essentially doing damage to yourself? we ask.

"Yes, I think to be obsessive at times is OK. I can become obsessive about a particular thing at a particular time as long as that obsession doesn't take over my life. I can become obsessive about a piece that I'm working on. But I can't let it totally destroy me. It's like I have to find that balance again."

FINDING AN ENVOY

The most common detour from passion happens when a woman appoints a child or a partner to be her envoy into the world of subjectivity. Sadly women find, though, that even when a child or a spouse achieves her dream, she's still left empty and unfulfilled. The more lucky among us take this recognition as an opportunity for transformation and continue past the detour back on the path to our own work.

Sarah Minton, for instance, had passionately loved the violin from the time she was five or six. "I can look back and I can remember in kindergarten, I was five and a half and had taken what was my first, second, or third piano lesson and a book was put in front of me, the old-fashioned kind. Well I went home and I did it. I got so excited over that black print on that white page. I can remember and almost refeel the thrill that went through my body at five and a half when I experienced two notes at the same time. And I look back because now I know what the music was, it was a third, you know intervals, thirds. Certain tones have a harmonic relationship. And I thought it's very much like relationships in people. Some relationships are so harmonious because even though they are two different people they relate to each other in such a way that it moves you from one event to another. Well I can remember at five and a half having that feeling when I played two little notes that were different from each other and sounded so wonderful and led to two other notes. It was a resolution."

Sarah pursued her music after she married, although her first husband did not encourage her. She followed him to live on a coastal island because it was his dream to live on an isolated farm.

Then her first husband became physically abusive. A divorce and a bitter custody suit followed. After her divorce, she commuted five hundred miles to Manhattan every two weeks to study with a master violinist. She felt most alive and committed when she could play music. A second marriage was more fulfilling, but this time she set her violin career aside for relationship. She and her second husband had, between them, six boys.

Sarah didn't end her career altogether, but she converted the energy of performing into teaching and mothering. She told herself it was all the same. All six children, all boys, played instruments. There were two violinists, one also a pianist and one also a vocalist, a trumpeter, a viola player, and a cellist. Sarah's second husband jokingly called it "Not quite the sound of music."

Two of her sons had particular talent. They both played piano and violin, sang, and acted. Both ultimately turned down chances to study professionally, to marry young. Sarah was profoundly upset, infuriated and bewildered because both sons chose relationship over the demands of a creative talent before they really knew what options they had or what the implications of their choices would be. Years later Sarah could see that their choice to put relationship first was a repeat of her own.

Sarah had detoured her own dreams into aspirations for her children and students. She now had no envoy and was faced with the task of reclaiming her own creative life for herself.

THE ABSENCE OF LOVE

The cultural love story defines love as a one way street—it's a story all about what women do for and give to others, never one about what they are given. We know that the experience of many women is in fact dominated by physical and sexual abuse, shaming, devaluing, and attempts to suppress their power. For all that we've spoken of women and their love for others, an important question to pose is what do women get *from* others. Beyond the practical concerns with time and money, many women told us that they simply weren't encouraged in their creative interests.

Certainly there are women who experience relationship as highly nurturing and supportive. Yet for many of the women we surveyed, both parents and partners actively discouraged any departure from the female role. The families of some women had no "love stories" that they could remember. Relationships with parents and partners were among the most disappointing experiences of love. One woman says, "Romantic love in my life has been disappointing—I have never felt loved, merely useful." Asked about the love stories in her family she says, "No stories of love other than love for children."

How does one express love or creativity if one has never felt it, if one has never been on the receiving end of empathy, validation, encouragement? The only antidote to shame is sharing, the mutual empathy and affirmation that come from a deep recognition and compassion for the vulnerability and strength of the other. Some women rarely experience this anywhere but in their contact with other women friends. Because they are not used to expecting it, they often choose partners or relationships that drain rather than support their power to be passionate and generative.

One woman in therapy struggled with ambivalence about staying in a marriage that had become conflicted and seemingly unworkable as she made her way through a graduate program that she loved. As she achieved more success, she became more depressed. She felt certain that the marriage could not survive her being a successful person in her own right rather than just the "wife" who focused exclusively on the needs of her partner. She continually felt guilty for wanting more, for wanting work of her own. Her husband was to admit that he felt more comfortable when he had been the only focus of her attention. Yet he would also claim that he loved her deeply. This woman struggled continually to understand that the "love" she thought she was sacrificing for her work was not a love that really supported her growth.

Ironically, a woman herself may be the last to realize that she suffers from a lack of love in her life—it's a hard reality to face because she inevitably feels that it's because of some failing in her that others treat her poorly. Writer Grace Paley says that the most important thing a creative woman needs to attend to is having a supportive partner who respects her work.

But women also need to attend to being loved, that is supported, valued, affirmed in their own dreams, not only desired and considered beautiful sex objects and useful caretakers. This may be the most critical rewriting of the love story that needs to occur in the psyches of women themselves—that we see ourselves as deserving of and then expect the same love and care that we so freely bestow on others.

RECLAIMING PASSION

To reclaim passion is to remember, as Barbara did her first love, to browse through the photo album of one's past, to resee and refeel the experiences of early love and early creativity that forged the internal connections that define who we are today. One woman says, "I've rediscovered the simple joys of my childhood and discovered how they can help me stay sane in my adulthood."

What she says is that she's reclaimed the power of her childhood and sees it newly, without the lens of shame to block its brightness. We need to know all of who we are, all of what we feel and we need to see and tell the story to ourselves without the constraints of shame, fear, and lovelessness to cloud our vision. Sometimes refeeling will be painful, like a descent to some underworld of buried secrets. We need to nurture, repair, reconstruct what has been painful and capture the enormous power of what has given us pleasure and joy.

At other times, refeeling will catch us by surprise. A time of normal passage to some new life stage, an unexpected experience or awareness of ourselves will stop us short, remind us of some vital connection and we'll know that we need to reorganize, regroup ourselves, change. Those moments are ones of transformation, of reawakening. We're faced with choice, with the choice to stay asleep to ourselves or to reclaim our passion and move to some new level of power.

CHAPTER ELEVEN

Choice Points and Transformations

THE PROCESS OF EMERGING INTO SUBJECTIVITY, of claiming our passions and shaping our lives in response to them, is a process of change. Even more than change, it is a process of transformation, a shifting of awareness at the deepest level in our experience of ourselves. Transformations come about as part of an ongoing dialogue between the self and the world outside the self in which each radically affects and influences the other.

In the course of this dialogue that is our daily lives, we experience moments of "vision" and connection in which something new is revealed. We realize some core truth about ourselves or about the world and we're unable any longer to think, talk, feel, act the way we used to. We have an experience in which the world splits open and life is irrevocably changed. For some the event might be meeting a person with whom one feels an instant flash of recognition, an immediate flare of passion. It may be a relationship with a teacher, a counselor, someone who helps show us something of ourselves, a new way to be. It may be a love, not necessarily a lasting or a romantic one, but one who adds some new dimension of meaning and depth to our experience. It may be an experience with work or social action or some new experience of one's capabilities. Transformation can even be stirred by a place, some landscape that catches our awareness and holds us in a grip that is mysterious but somehow dominates our senses from then on. We may have more than one such experience in our lives, even a series of them. Some may be major turning points, others may be quiet moments of awareness. These moments are characterized by heightened emotion and sensory awareness, and they have a "time out of time" quality to them.

Transformations are moments of grace—they remind us of the energy and passion of the universe working in us, through us. They sometimes seem mundane, but more often, they seem and are experienced as deeply spiritual, as if some larger energy were guiding our growth. They are points of meaning, of contact and connection with something larger than ourselves.

DEFINING MOMENTS

Women frequently talk about transformative events in their lives as defining moments in their growth. Such a moment becomes a marker and the sense a woman has is, "Before this moment, I was one person and afterwards, I was someone else. My life was never quite the same." In our interviewing, we began to ask about "moments" and heard some vivid descriptions of them.

Judy Gomez: "I can't say that I had an active sense that something was missing but I began to feel I didn't have a direction, a center. We went to Monhegan that first summer and the woman who had brought us to Monhegan had a friend visiting her who was an artist and was doing a watercolor workshop and despite myself I said I was going to take it and that was it, it changed my life. I was totally grasped and engaged in the painting.

"Then there was a man on the island who is now eighty-three years old who is a fiber artist. I went into his studio and made a small piece there, a kind of Monhegan abstract and it was the combination of these two things—I knew that my life had changed.

"It was a rather dramatic change. Suddenly I was doing my job, I was being super mom, I was being Professor Gomez, I was doing all my things but I just couldn't wait to get home to work with wool. I couldn't wait for the weekends to be able to paint, I couldn't wait to get back to Monhegan again to really do that. I couldn't wait to do that, I knew that was what I really wanted to do, I knew it immediately. I just knew it, it was an absolute certainty."

Georgeanne Kuhl: "We [she and her husband-to-be, Condon Kuhl] were on a sailboat together and we sailed all afternoon and I had burned up to a crisp but we didn't pay any attention to time and we were just having this long, long conversation. A good friend of ours is an elderly man who sails a lot and he was sitting by the side of the lake where we were sailing and he said, I thought something was going on in that sailboat, you guys were talking so intensely. And it wasn't that we actually made an official decision, OK this is it. There was something about it that once we came in on the shore, that was it. We moved in together. And it wasn't like OK today is the day, let's gather things together, we're going to move in—it was just an understanding. And it was interesting and we both knew that that was exactly the day that it happened—our friend also sensed it."

Nancy West: "I had stopped smoking and I thought, I've gotta have something that's new and different to take the edge off this withdrawal from smoking. So I got myself involved in a very small, intimate quilting class. Three of us with a wonderful teacher and suddenly here was this wonderful world of color and texture and potential for creativity. This class has stimulated all kinds of things in me. Part of the process that came out of this was a friend saying to me, let's go do a quilt show for the senior center. And it was absolutely magical what happened. This drab, horrible senior center with all these tables and chairs was transformed into *Brigadoon* because it went up in a mist and it was beautiful, and then it came down and we were bumpkins again. But during this process we planned for six months and that was a very new thing for me, to plan in a very logical, systematic way. I had never done anything like that. So when this thing was over, I said to my friend, Karen, you know what happened to me? That quilt show allowed me to become that wonderfully spontaneous, joyful creative uninhibited child. The joy I felt in helping this thing happen ... if I could go through life doing something that would give me that sense of childish joy and fulfillment, what a wonderful way to live. So OK. There is the goal ... What is there in life that is going to do that for me? I don't know what it is but I've got a taste of something. . . .

"A long time ago, say twenty years ago, on a beach in Mexico, I was walking along, it was a gray overcast day, I was all by myself. I was there camping with my family but I had gone off for a walk by myself. And I had one of those very very deep spiritual experiences that is sort of unexplained but has never left me of suddenly an awareness of the whole sky and the broad arcing spectrum of that sky with no beginning and no end and I had this sense of being part of the whole ... a part of the universe. I was part of the continuum of all the generations past and all the generations into the future, and suddenly dying wasn't frightening anymore because it was an ongoingness and I am part of that ongoingness.

"I feel this with quilting. I don't with knitting or any of the other but I do with quilting. I feel this tremendous sense of connection with other women. And it's a very deep spiritual, soulful feeling and that was present in that quilt show."

The essence of a transformational experience is *recognition and reconnection, a stab in the heart.* One has some instantaneous sense of "rightness," some recall that the feeling one experiences in the present is part of the essence of self, that it is true, that the feeling can't any longer be denied and must be more accessed and integrated in daily life. Some people actually experience a physical sensation in the heart—one feels a fluttery kind of excitement, a radiating warmth, not unlike a feeling of being in love. When these types of reactions occur, our whole body tells us that we need to pay attention because something important is happening.

These moments occurred for each of these three women at times in their lives when they were ready to encounter some new aspect of themselves, when their life was changing its balance, when they were ready to accept and embrace the emergence of passion. Each describes a sense of feeling unsettled, of something being not quite right, of having a vague sense of there being more to come. But none could really articulate what that "something" was until the moment happened and the passion flared. These recognitions help one to define a new vision and a new way of living but they also confront one with choices, sometimes difficult ones.

Transformations often happen when we step outside the normal boundaries of our lives. We take a class, we travel to a new place, we meet a new person, we are led to see or understand something in a new way. They often strike when we're at some developmental point of readiness, much the same as a flower begins mysteriously to bud only when it's the "right time" in its growth cycle.

Some transformations come about through necessity. We go to college, have children, turn forty. A spouse dies, divorces, we face the challenges of some new life phase. Others are situational. When artist Sara Eyestone moved out of Phoenix to St. Louis with her husband, she was forced to think about her life and her work in a new way. Once she tapped into all the feeling, passion, rage, pain that resulted from not being subject enough in her own life, she began to have a new vision. She made changes in the structure of her life that allowed her creative and relational needs to flow together in a new configuration. She found a better fit.

Nancy West began to envision her life differently because she was burned out with being too good to others. Being a social worker was beginning to lose its meaning and aliveness for her. It was her very dissatisfaction that set the stage for transformation—for her recognition of the real intensity of her creative passions.

Recovery from addiction is a transformation, a true "righting" of one's life so that authentic feelings rather than altered ones become the basis of one's choices.

And finally, love is a transformation—the sudden synergy of the energies of two people that brings them both to a new level of awareness and openness. Love happens, it chooses us. It can be both the vehicle and the outcome of transformation, but it never leaves us unchanged. Of all the forms of transformation it can be the most painful and the most powerful—it is the spark of connection that stirs passion. Of her meeting with her husband, one woman says,

"The love I found when I first met my husband four years ago touched me through my soul. It was love rediscovered. I had the feeling we'd been together before and now it's a love that continues to grow. We trust each other, like each other, are best friends and partners. Every day we grow closer together."

THE DARK HEART

Some transformations take us deep into an awareness of parts of ourselves that are wells of pain, fear, conflict, shame, and despair. We find ourselves in situations that seem to stir darker energies—rage, envy, self-destructiveness, obsession. We violate our own values, we behave in ways that seem inconsistent with our understanding of ourselves. We are not loving, we hate, we abuse ourselves, others, we contact the "shadow"—the part of ourselves we would disown or deny if its power didn't shake us to the core.

Or we may confront some part of us that seems like a void, an empty space—a place where we experience our own nothingness, a deadness that always threatens to overwhelm us if we let it. We confront the ways that we block and hurt ourselves, the ways that we fail to allow love and creative energy to flow through us, the ways in which we're limited and far less than perfect beings.

This is the kind of transformative experience that is a trial by fire, a "dark night of the soul." It's characterized by depression and despair. It's a period of radical disorganization, of the loss of our sense of identity, often a loss of energy, vitality, passion, even interest in living at all. Transformation means that we discover that this dark part of ourselves is part of our wholeness—we learn to integrate and accept it with compassion. Ultimately, through it we discover our strength, our resilience, our true capacity for creativity and for joy.

Often, this type of experience just "happens" to us in the same way love just "happens." We never know what hurt will trigger a transformation by way of pain. It can be the death of a love relationship, an affront to our sense of ourselves in our work, a failure to achieve something we've wanted, an accident in which we're injured, or injure another, a serious illness in which we face the fact that we're mortal.

When we have one of the inevitable experiences of pain or tragedy that occur to all of us in life, it's the process of healing and recovery that is transformational. We move to a deeper level of understanding and integration. Wounding and loss transform us if we let them, if we don't, they send us deeper into a rigidity and despair that blocks change because we become defensive and we shut down.

We permit transformation when we allow ourselves to grieve, mourn, and rage. These emotional states permit us intimate connection with the passion of pain. Creativity can be a vehicle for handling this passion, a way out of and beyond it. Creative action is critical to healing—its energy is life-giving, it returns us to joy. We heal so that we can be open to the whole range of our passions again, and so that we can know that pain is only part of the story of our experience.

Khristine Hopkins is an artist and photographer who was sexually abused as a child by her father. Recently, Khristine had an exhibit of her photographs recommended for a national tour by the New England Foundation for the Arts. Of the exhibit Khristine says: "It's an exhibition of eighteen photographs—small visual metaphors. It's a result of a year and a half's work with women in a therapy group for adult survivors of sexual abuse, of which I was a member. I initially made the photograph of my son and another of myself as part of my own healing process. These two pictures really gave me a lot of relief. The first picture I did was the picture of Mac. He was probably three and a half at the time, and I would look at him and he was so small, so innocent, so beautiful. He posed in the living room window and he was holding a stuffed lamb looking directly at me and it was the feeling that he was so vulnerable. This is your child and there are these boundaries; it is just incredible to me that people can cross these boundaries to harm a child in order to fulfill their own needs. I was definitely dealing with my issues through the camera. Then I did a self-portrait and worked on my feelings about my father."

Khristine talks about healing as the ongoing process of "working with," or dealing with the aftermath of the trauma created for her by her father's abuse. While her art is a valuable outcome of that healing work, it's also a vehicle for doing the work—and one that provides symbolic forms of healing, sharing, and awareness for others at the same time.

At one point in this healing process, Khristine had a transformative moment. She calls it an epiphany. It occurred very unexpectedly during a trip to France with her husband and a friend as she toured Chartres Cathedral.

"I was in Chartres Cathedral and I was overwhelmed by the beauty of it, the spiritual feeling of it, it was just an incredible experience. I grew up Catholic but I left the Church when I was eleven so I wasn't able to have any of that visual beauty that goes with belonging to a church . . . that sense of beauty and light, the music, the candles . . . so when I left there I sort of crashed. . . . We were driving through the French countryside and I felt like every driver on the road was trying to kill me . . . which was probably true! I felt very, very vulnerable. I got back to the place where we were staying and I climbed into bed and pulled the covers over my head and couldn't get up for a while."

The experience remained inexplicable to Khristine until months later she found herself attending, unexpectedly but regularly, the local Unitarian Church where she and her husband had been married. It was then that she realized what had happened for her at the cathedral in France.

"I suddenly realized that I was sitting in this church and there were hymns and beauty and music and light and I realized that what the experience in the cathedral had been about was this sense of loss, this tremendous sense of loss. I could not have that beauty because I couldn't believe in what the church represented."

The deeper part of the story for Khristine was that the father who had abused her died when she was eleven, and it was the events surrounding his death that made Khristine reject the church. Not only did this abusive parent die, trauma enough in itself, but Khristine watched as his mother essentially bribed the church to bury him in the Catholic cemetery, even though he was divorced and this was against church policy. Khristine also knew that he was hardly in the "state of grace" that would make it spiritually "right" that he be buried in consecrated ground.

But in leaving the church out of protest against the violation of values and the lack of recognition of her father's, her grandmother's, and the church's behavior this event represented, Khristine had also lost something that was deeply symbolic and meaningful to her. She had lost access to a place of safety, aesthetic beauty, and spiritual comfort.

A sense of loss is a theme that is pervasive in her life. She says that the most painful aspect of love for her right now in her life is "the feeling of loss . . . I think the feeling of loss is always there. I feel losses all the time. I think we make relationships mundane—the way you deal with the pain and fear of losing the person is to make it mundane."

Khristine's fear and pain live in her sitting side by side with her love for her family and her work. These two aspects of her life aren't separate, they are in dialogue with one another and they affect one another in an ongoing process of change. There was a very clear outcome to Khristine's transformative moment in the cathedral. Her initial confusion in fact led her to clarity.

"I realized that I could have it [the beauty of the church] in a new place that was open to what I believed in. It's opened me up and I can actually photograph in there . . . I found just being there was so comforting and soothing that I asked the minister if I could just come in and do interiors . . . do photography in there when there was no one around . . . to get the natural light. And it was just amazing."

Khristine lives a process of reclaiming and reconnecting with herself at newer and more conscious levels. The process is one that requires creativity, courage, and an openness to love in the face of pain and fear.

Sculptor Sharon Gainsburg would call the pain and fear, the dark-hearted elements of life, "the crack in the marble." For her, creative process is always a metaphor for the process of change:

"Whatever you do here in the studio is just an example of how you handle things out there in the world. I have a process. I usually sit for about ten minutes and I meditate, pray, however you want to call it. I just get in touch with the moment. . . . And then that process is over and I start to work. And if I find that it's not coming forth, then I will think about that and alter my idea. But I realize that whatever I do, if I make a line here and it doesn't work, then I dig a little deeper. And what I sacrifice for that is size. But I'm going to get what I want, it just might not be as big as I want. So I always know that I will end up with something, but it might not always be what I started out with. And if I'm willing to be flexible, just like in life, if you're willing to be flexible, then it works. But if you keep your parameter so rigid, then what you end up with is something that is not, for me, flowing, it's not expressive, it's very static. As you can see, my forms are not static. I don't do cubes and blocks. So, it's that flexibility, an openness. And it's a faith, a learned faith. To have faith in myself, faith in the process. That I will get to the next step, it might not be today, tomorrow, but I must leave it. And when I leave it, I can't berate myself that I failed today. That's what I've learned from the creative process. And that's what I teach my students. You know, this isn't working, let's try something else. No [they say], I wanted this or a piece fell off. Oh, a piece fell off, what am I going to do? The stone cracked. And I look at them and I say, you know, in life, when things don't work out the way we want, we have to come up with a better idea. And this piece falling off is going to force you to think about something broader or deeper and then your piece is going to be better. It's going to be different, it's going to be smaller, but it's going to be better. And I relate everything I do in there to what happens in love."

This process of working with the self, of working with the "cracks in the marble" with "learning to bear" the shocks and pains of life, the soul pains, is part of a creative process in which we become more solidly subject over time. We come to own and to create ourselves. Once we understand the processes of subjectivity, we come to understand that transformation is ongoing, in small daily ways, in larger, more noticeable moments, and that what we are is change and choice, pain and joy, continual movement, an ongoing becoming of ourselves. The ground of our growth is relationship and love, the energy that keeps us moving is creativity. The merging of the two is passion. We grow better when we listen to our hearts. The shapes of our lives change with the deepening understanding of ourselves.

TRANSFORMATION AND CHOICE

As Sharon Gainsburg implies, allowing a transformation to have its way with us requires trust, a belief in process, a willingness to live through the darker moments of our experience with the awareness that we will emerge at some new level of integration and power. We need to be willing to confront the rejected parts of ourselves if we want full access to our own energy.

For many women, transformations are not solely an outcome of the encounter with the self nor are they effected only by the relational dialogue between self and other. The majority of women in the world are deeply affected by their encounters with a culture and society that inherently limit choices, options, access to resources, and the ideas we have about ourselves. The types of traumatic change triggered by rape, violence, battering, sexual abuse, an unwanted pregnancy, poverty, classism, racism, sexism, ageism, and the general devaluing of women's experience are not necessary nor are they uncontrollable trauma. They are politically determined. They are the effects of the ongoing objectification of women that is still dominant in our current lives and still a mainstay of the power imbalance inherent in a patriarchal culture.

What is controllable is a woman's response to them—if we react to trauma as victims only, then we remain objects. If we access our rage and our sense of determination that safety and equality are basic rights of all of us, then we make very different choices. We take action, and that action frequently benefits those beyond ourselves.

For a man, transformational events might occur in the context of testing one's sense of mastery in work or accomplishment. But for a woman, transformation is much more likely to be triggered by a relational experience. Difficulties or shifts in contact with lovers, spouses, friends, children, all radically affect a woman's sense of herself and can set the stage for emotional change. On the other hand, a settled and secure relationship is often what permits a woman to be open to spiritual or creative transformation. Debbie Wells speaks to this "relationship first" experience for women in a way that most of us could relate to.

"For me it was necessary to be involved in a relationship that was ongoing and semipermanent in order for me to free myself up enough to do this other stuff. Once I had the marriage thing taken care of I was free to look at other possibilities and I felt secure enough to try them. I believe it was some kind of preconditioned message because my parents told me that marriage was my goal."

THE QUALITIES OF THE PASSIONATE LIFE

Whether the transformative moments we experience represent developmental leaps in our own growth or whether they are imposed on us by outside forces, the critical question is, what qualities most influence how we make use of the knowledge we gain about ourselves? What does it take to shape a life creatively, to find a form that fits? What makes the processes of love and creative expression the same—what qualities do they hold in common?

There is only one word in the language that can adequately describe the experience of the artist facing a blank page, easel, a new piece of music, an untouched piece of stone or wood. The same word describes what happens to the person in love—with another person, a child, a goal, an activity—who realizes the real depth of energy and commitment and openness that love will demand. The same word describes the performer about to sing, the musician about to play, the athlete about to jump, the therapist or doctor who sets out to help. And the same word describes any of us who set out on some new life task or phase, whether it be a career, a relationship, becoming a parent, facing our own death.

The word is fear. Some say terror, others say dread. But the basic emotion is fear. Fear at facing life full in the face—fear of being called on to act and to risk, to put one's self on the line. Fear of what is not and cannot be known—the outcome.

Unquestionably there is also excitement, anticipation, hope, confidence. But the starting platform of any change or new venture is basically fear—the not knowing if one is adequate to the task, the awareness of vulnerability, and the potential for being hurt and for failing.

When we live our lives as objects, we stay rooted to the familiar and the conventional and we become slaves to fear. We don't take risks. When we are passionate and fully subjects of our own lives, it's not that we don't have fear but what we have more of is courage. We become willing to say yes to whatever may come next. Courage doesn't exist without fear. Frances Peabody says "There are lots of ways to be creative if people would just let their imaginations go and have the courage. I must say that I've done a couple of things that scared the daylights out of me but they turned out alright. I was really scared but you go ahead and hope that you're doing the right thing—it does take courage and it does take energy, perseverance." Or as the quote from Roxana Robinson in chapter 6 puts it, "there is no bravery in a landscape without danger."

A great many of the qualities critical to living life with passion follow from courage. Rollo May, who wrote eloquently on both love and creativity, says of it, "The word *courage* comes from the same stem as the French word *coeur*, meaning 'heart.' Thus, just as one's heart, by pumping blood to one's arms, legs and brain, enables all the other physical organs to function, so courage makes possible all the psychological virtues."[1]

What follows from courage is honesty, the willingness to encounter the self, a sense of intentionality, an ability to trust the process.

The courage to trust process means believing in magic, having a vision and following it, letting the imagination play, letting go of the controls all the time realizing that the final responsibility for the outcome of the creation rests with yourself. It means exercising the discipline it takes to learn skills and to shape at the same time one is wild and lustful and exuberantly out of control. It means having the capacity to dream and to be practical and pragmatic at the same time. It means having some basic trust in the importance of aliveness.

During a recent visit to Haystack Mountain School of Crafts, a renowned summer colony for the study of the fine arts, we noticed a "manifesto" tacked to a post in the metal shop. It is by the artist, Michell Cassou: "After all, we cannot know what we are going to express. What is really creative is bound to be a surprise because it is something we couldn't have thought of. This is the thing that we resist the most. We want to know where we are going, why we are doing it, and what it is going to give to us. We want to know it all. To be creative means becoming more familiar with being a little lost. If we are always full of what we want to do, there is no room for the new."[2]

The courage to act in the face of our fear leads to compassion for others. In another random quote found in the "Sunbeams" section of the magazine *The Sun*, Barbara Garrison says, "Fear grows out of the things we think; it lives in our minds. Compassion grows out of the things we are, and lives in our hearts."[3]

To "say yes" to the creative process in our lives is an act of affirmation and power—it means that we embrace what we can't really know but what feels intuitively correct for us. We make decisions, we make choices based on inner knowledge, not outer expedience or external control. The passive person conforms to what is expected, the passionate person decides, exerts will. Life flows from those decisions. The passionate person has a sense of agency—she makes life happen, she allows her inner process to define the shape of her life. The passive person settles in and lets life happen to her without regard for her own needs and rhythms.

This same kind of courage that is critical to creative and psychological process is as critical to love. There is no love without openness and vulnerability, without a "letting go" into the unknown dimensions of ourselves and the other person. In some sense we are what we love, because the will to love is typically triggered by some deep recognition of the parts of ourselves in the other that we hope to integrate in ourselves. The will to love is often not a rational process—it involves knowledge of the heart more often than knowledge of the mind. Most of the women we interviewed spoke of the complete irrationality of love. Unless it is an abusive or self-defeating kind of obsessive love, it is often the irrationality and unexplainable quality of love that makes it most passionate, most intense, and most fulfilling.

Willard Gaylin, in his book, *Rediscovering Love*, comments:

> Loving demands, beyond trust and commitment, an abandonment of self, an abdication of autonomy, a painful fusion with another vulnerable person or many other persons. Such heroic requirements cannot be motivated by logic and sensibility alone but must be driven by the romantic elements of our nature. Mature love will always straddle the romantic and realistic realms of the human imagination.[4]

The qualities that make it possible for us to shape our lives, to integrate love and creativity, are paradoxes—vulnerability and courage, choosing and letting go, wildness and discipline, imagination and action, solitude and connection, work and play, joy and pain, darkness and lightheartedness. The still point of the process is action, choice, the manifestation of transformation.

CHOICE—THE POINT OF ACTION

Before Judy Gomez experienced her moment of creative transformation on Monhegan Island, there had been other unsettling recognitions. Two years after she had divorced her husband, she unexpectedly found herself in love with a woman. "I mean I was clearly a lesbian my entire life but I just didn't realize it. We fell in lust, then we fell in love. I fought it for three or four years. I didn't fight the falling in love, I mean I didn't fight the sexual aspect of it. I knew that this was me and this was what I wanted. But it was very frightening with three little kids to conceive of. I would say to Leslie, you know I love you but my kids need a father."

This is the kind of relational transformation that characterizes women's lives. A shifting sense of self often occurs in the context of some relational change. But when changes in awareness like this "happen," one is faced with the need to make choices and to act. Literary agent Lilli Cohen, whose relationship is described more fully in chapter 13, says of her own life, "I knew that my first marriage wasn't working . . . it was a choice to leave it. Not an easy choice, but nevertheless a choice, and I guess when I was about twenty-four years old my eyes started opening a little bit and I just started listening to what I needed to do for myself. I moved out of New York for the first time in my life and I met my now husband when I was in California so I think that was a real choice period in my life having a lot to do actually with the times and the women's movement and having things open up for me in a different way that I never even thought were mine to have. Now I feel everything is a choice—a choice that I'm making or a choice not to make. That's where part of the creativity comes in—by choosing."

As women resolve some of the relational questions in their lives, as they resolve their conflicts about love, they are likely to go on to be more focused on creativity and on choices that determine careers, self-expression, and their place in the larger world. If the relational choices they make block them from doing this, they tend to focus on changing relationship first and then changing their forms for creative expression.

Such transformations are very related to life phase, or they happen, as they did for Lilli Cohen, at specific times in the life cycle. When love and creative work are both congruent, a woman feels most whole.

CHANGING FORMS

Women often shift from one dominant life form to another. A Lover may become more integrative, a Leader may move more into the creative, Innovator pattern. Sometimes High Relationals discover that their focus on relationship was a function of socialization, and like Kathy Bradford, they shift to a High Creative pattern. Moments of transformation, of recognition and reclamation, are integral to the process.

What steps characterize a shift to a new form? Transformation is both event and process. The *event* of recognition occurs first, then acceptance follows. One embraces some no longer deniable truth about the way one feels. One learns to accept one's own process, one's own needs and feelings. The critical aspect of transformation as process is time, taking one's time. Transformation is not efficient, it does not follow neatly linear steps to a preset goal. It is an emotional process. In our highly achievement-oriented, product-oriented culture, we have little sense that our emotional awareness is important enough to take time with. But ultimately change is the one thing that can't be rushed.

Judy Gomez needed time to integrate her awareness that she loved a woman, she needed time to envision how her future might look with that reality embraced. Lilli Cohen needed time to understand what form fit her better than her first marriage, she needed time to make a better choice. Neither love nor creativity can be framed by a calendar or a clock. When one lets go and accepts the recognitions about self that transformations bring, one does it at one's own pace.

Recognition presupposes that what one experiences is not obsession but truly is passion. Obsession is defined by pain and positive changes don't lead to pain, though they may be painful. The process of making a decision may be painful because it involves loss, the letting go of one part of one's life in order to more fully access another.

Once there is recognition and acceptance, an emotional resolution, one moves into the action phase of transformation and the primary characteristic in this phase is will and commitment. Until one makes an active commitment to self, to following through, nothing happens—recognitions go unheeded. Unacknowledged recognitions come back to haunt. If one doesn't pay attention in the present, the awareness will emerge again at some point in the future, often in a more painful, unavoidable way.

Transformations become painful when we don't act on the basis of what we know to be true; when we don't acknowledge abuse; when we want to follow an important impulse and don't; when we ignore evidence about the fact that a relationship or a career or a physical setting isn't a good fit; when we ignore something we truly love; when we don't let go of what is truly negative for us; when we don't pay attention to the intensity of the energy leading us in one direction or another. These kinds of avoidances only block the flow of change temporarily until another, often more harsh situation reminds us that we need to do something new.

Change to a new life form, commitment to action, may involve major adjustments—divorces, career changes, life-style changes, moves to new places—it may involve reeducation, a whole new phase of learning about the thing one has a passion for. The transitional period may be difficult, but it is often one of intensity and engagement and a heightened experience of being fully alive.

Since most of us need money to meet our practical needs, the process of fully embracing a new passion may involve a long period of planning and financial adjustment, a series of gradual steps that will allow increasing involvement with what we love to do and less involvement with what we have to do.

One friend, mentioned earlier, worked as a psychotherapist for many years until a lifelong love of botany and naturalist studies became more and more an undeniable passion. She began the process of transforming her life slowly, at first taking courses, reading, spending every spare hour outdoors. Gradually she began to develop ideas about how to turn her passion into a career. She explored many different possibilities, none of them particularly lucrative ones. She continued her old line of work at a less intense pace while she explored the new one. The more involved she became with botany, the more irrelevant material concerns seemed to become. Her motivations changed, the quality of her time changed, she found herself enjoying each day of her life more intensely. She described herself as fully engaged. "Once in a while I would emerge from the field or the woods and notice a shopping mall and think, Oh, clothes. But they seemed so irrelevant—I mean what did I really need many for?"

At this phase in a transformational process one may set goals and timetables, but they always remain flexible, in the same way that Sharon Gainsburg describes flexibility as important to the outcome of a piece of sculpture.

Condon Kuhl, the man in the boat with Georgeanne who was mentioned earlier in this chapter, is an artist. He and Georgeanne moved from Iowa to a rural Northeastern town because that had been their dream. He talked with us about the concepts of commitment and setting goals. In describing their process of decision-making and setting the change in motion he says, "We didn't say, this is what has to happen, we're going to make it do this. We said, these are the forces we've set in motion, our goal is to get to here. We had a five-year plan, a ten-year plan. I think goals are very important. I think they make things happen. Without them you can sit and dream about something and it's always out here in this unrelated land where there is no real route so you have no means of reaching it. If you set goals, if you make commitments. . . . When we set the goal we had no idea how we were going to do it. But we were in the right place when certain things came about to take advantage of them. And if we hadn't had that goal, and hadn't had a basic commitment, we'd have let those go by because we didn't have anything in place.

"The goal was to get here. We didn't know how. We didn't have the details. We didn't have the road map yet. In fact, it never came, it's still emerging. If we had had to have it all laid out with the end in sight, have all the facts and figures in mind, we wouldn't have done it because the problems would have been so overwhelming."

Condon and Georgeanne's process is a positive model because they were both people who wanted to access more of their creative energy, to reserve more of their time for their art and they wanted to be in a different, more nurturing environment. But they also needed to keep making a living. Their goals were based in a realistic view of what was needed to get them where they wanted to be. They did things in stages. They accepted limitations, they were open to opportunities that fit with their vision.

The real mark of a transformation is that one's priorities change, one thinks differently, so one acts differently.

Whatever one loses in the process is usually replaced by a deep sense of satisfaction and involvement that can't be bought in the currency of money.

PASSION IN THE BALANCE

While the transformational process sometimes involves pain, the deepest pain is to not be fully engaged with one's own life. To lack spirit, energy, enthusiasm, dedication, whether it be in relationship or in work. The surest route to frustration, alienation, heart sickness is to fail to love what one does and those one relates to; to lack interest, excitement, joy, appreciation; to fail to be wholehearted and in being halfhearted, to fail to give generously back, to share one's passion with others.

In a strikingly sad comment from one of the women in our survey responding to a question about the story of love in her life, we read, "The story of love in my life is that of a deep, committed, devoted love that fell apart while we were tending to other responsibilities."

The pain of this story is no doubt very understated. It speaks to the ways that passion can be sacrificed, ignored, and lost. This woman might say, "There were too many other things to be done, there just was never time." But the loss of connection, of the sense of deep devotion, is a poignant one, the result of a loss of focus, of not taking passion seriously. It's a loss of enormous magnitude, one that can't always be recovered, and it reminds us that passion needs to be carefully guarded and valued if our lives are to be full.

CHAPTER TWELVE

In Her Own Good Time

This is how I think about time. Life is very short and you never know when it is going to end and we are not young anymore. So every minute is incredibly precious and I want to live each second as if it is the ultimate minute of my life, because we are at a very vulnerable age and you just never know.

JUDY GOMEZ, AGE FORTY-NINE

I tell myself that I don't have time for love. I'm so busy with my commitments to school and vocation and feel I'm behind in my career and so I'd better not get waylaid by falling in love now.

CONNIE BARNES, AGE THIRTY

IF A WOMAN WANTS to live the passionate life, she must understand and value her own time. Some women feel they don't have enough time because they are living life so fully that they can barely squeeze their multiple passions into their days. Other women feel they have too little time, and none of it to themselves, because they can barely fit themselves into their lives. The difference between these two groups is only partially a difference in external circumstances. Primarily, each group thinks about time and values themselves differently.

Many women view having time as an organizational problem rather than one that has to do with ways of thinking and ways of valuing. We think that we need to use time better rather than value time differently. But if we pose the wrong problem, we come up with the wrong solution. The problem lies in our failure to value time and ourselves. The solution lies in understanding and accepting the rhythms of our own time.

When one recognizes the significance and value of time and its critical relationship to passion, priorities become more clear. Donna DeMuth no longer squanders energy on new relationships, no matter how interesting, if there is not a mutual commitment to continuity. Her friendship time is too valuable. She says, "I don't make any new friends unless they are going to come visit me in the nursing home."

Donna is not going to "waste time" at age sixty-five forming new friendships. Judy Gomez changed her entire life structure when she recognized the value of time.

Sometimes a woman doesn't learn to value time until circumstances force her to think about it. Jenny Francis says she never realized how important her own time could be until she was in recovery from alcoholism. Other women need a separation or divorce to realize that their own time can be valuable.

Recently, a man whose wife had just left him said bewilderedly, "I can't understand it; we've been separated two weeks and in that time, she has resumed buying music, taken up exercise again, gone to the theater. Those were all things I thought she had lost interest in because they had disappeared from her life." His wife's leaving him was triggered by his affair, an affair he said he pursued because passion had left his marriage.

As women, most of us wouldn't be at all bewildered by his situation. We can easily imagine that, once they were married, his wife felt she didn't have "time for herself." What we often don't know is how the loss of time for ourselves may result in a loss of passion.

The diagnosis of a terminal illness may force one to recognize the value of time. Or we may simply appreciate the difference between the quality of time that we experience during a break in routine such as travel, and the quality of time in everyday life, and return from a trip vowing to value our time more.

Why should it take an extraordinary circumstance to make women consider this issue? Just as our ways of thinking about love are affected, our ways of thinking about time are conditioned by the cultural narrative that dictates what activities are important and whose time is more valuable. But when a woman recognizes the critical importance of her own time in the face of either tragedy or exceptional joy, ordering priorities often flows easily and she may choose to rearrange her entire life.

THE QUALITY OF TIME

For Judy Gomez, experiencing the contrasting quality of time in different places and within different life arrangements was central to a choice to rearrange the form of her life. At some point after she and her new partner had chosen to live together, they began to leave New York for Monhegan Island, where she had originally had her "transforming moment," for the summers. Four years later they left New York altogether and supplemented their time in Monhegan by buying a house together in Santa Fe, New Mexico for the winters. Judy fully retired from academic life to pursue art, and Leslie discovered her passion for doing adult literacy work and left teaching children.

Monhegan, like Ocracoke, is an island. Ocracoke's shore is dune soft, Monhegan's is granite hard, its headland rising one hundred fifty feet above the sea, twelve miles off the New England coast. The Native Americans called it *Monahigan*, "the island of the sea." Until recently this island with its six hundred species of wildflowers, its spruce forests, and its two hundred resident artists, writers, and musicians, was lit only by kerosene lights and the locals hung a sign in a store window saying, "If you cannot live without your newspaper, ferries depart daily for the mainland."[1]

We have talked quite a lot about women and islands, not coincidentally. As Anne Morrow Lindbergh wrote in *Gift from the Sea*, "Existence in the present gives island living an extreme vividness and purity. One lives like a child or a saint in the immediacy of here and now. Every day, every act, is an island, washed by time and space, and has an island's completion."[2]

As Leslie told us, "Going to Monhegan initially was like going to adult summer camp. You become fast furious friends; there are no superficial relationships because you don't have time. You don't have years to develop this 'Well, I'll see you in May for dinner' type routine. . . . And what we really wanted was a life that incorporated more of that with some reality."

Judy adds, "There was such a gap between the quality of our relationships, the quality of our time. In Monhegan every minute was precious, walking, watching the sunset. On Monhegan the big moment of the day is sunset. There's no superficiality about your time with people. Every single person in Monhegan is creatively involved in either writing or painting or their work or something. There's such a gap between Monhegan life and New York life that we just couldn't stand it any more."

The heightened awareness of time that Judy and Leslie experience on Monhegan can also be described as a kind of "time out of time" or a suspension of time. It's similar to the time sense of the person in the throes of early love or the throes of creative work. Time seems expanded or contracted—moments seem like hours, hours seem like moments. Certain stretches of time may go by totally unnoticed, one forgets to sleep, disregards the normal routines of a day, and exists in a state of "Flow" in which passionate focus structures time rather than time structuring consciousness and behavior. When passion isn't "flowing," neither does time—it seems an obstacle, becomes an excuse to avoid ourselves and generally becomes a great source of frustration. Time becomes something to be juggled, something to be fought against. A woman says to herself, "I would write poetry if only I had time, I would make love but there just isn't time." Time becomes the enemy, the external controller to which we give over power to alienate us from ourselves.

Living each moment as fully as if it is the ultimate moment is an ideal that many of us dream about. Frequently, women and men both say that only on vacations do they feel fully alive. It is the rare person who hasn't returned from some vacation feeling a renewed connection to themselves through art or music or reading the book they've been hoarding all year. On vacation one rediscovers time to find the serenity in solitude, the glory in nature, and one wonders why time in "real life" can't have more the quality of vacation time.

We talk about spare time, stolen time, free time, time well spent, leisure time, wasted time, quality time, vacation time, extra time, not enough time. We say time is precious, for all time, time is short, it was such a waste of time, time flies, time and eternity, we had a good time, take your time, time stood still, where does the time go? How much time do you have? Our language itself points to our American preoccupation with the idea of time. Linguistic differences convey different attitudes. Not all cultures have similar words to represent time. For example, as Lippard says in her work on art and prehistory, "Among the Hopi there are no words for past or future; and interestingly also, process is as important as product."[3]

No matter the language, people have always sought to understand and describe time. They have spoken in terms of clock time, sacred time, mythical time, real time, ceremonial time, dream time. They have described the shape of time as linear, circular, or spiral. Ancient cultures have represented their understanding of time in symbol, such as "The zodiac snake, the Mexican serpent with a head at both ends of its body. The ancient Chinese understood that circular and linear time were not incompatible and reconciled them by having two time mandalas—one round and one square."[4]

We measure time by both calendars and clocks but each measures something different. Our earliest attempts to mark and measure time date back to solar calendars such as the Anasazi one in Chaco Canyon, New Mexico, rediscovered in 1977. The time marked by this calendar was not linear. The development of the linear time that a clock measures today, Lucy Lippard reminds us, ". . . developed over the millennia with patriarchy and industry."[5] Christian, Darwinian, and clerical time were equally linear. Interestingly the circular calendar of the Anasazi and the emphasis on nonlinear process in the Hopi may have had their roots in what were essentially matrilineal societies.

Contemporary artists symbolize time differently yet. The artist Charles Ross has created "calendrical solar burns (*Sunlight Convergence/Solar Burn: The Year Shape*), executed beneath a large lens on his New York studio roof. Each day the passing sun burns a curve—'the day's signature'—into a wooden panel. . . . When the burns are placed end to end, following their actual curvature, they form a double spiral—an ancient year-symbol that reverses its direction from winter to summer and is a migration symbol among Southwest Indians—time and space unified." Ross proposes art as a point of contact with the universe energy matrix.[6]

THINKING ABOUT TIME

What is time anyway that naming it, describing it, understanding it, and controlling it has been a central obsession of *man*kind? All great spiritual traditions teach a way of understanding and valuing time. Roman Catholicism, for example, has historically been future oriented. Eastern mystical traditions have always been concerned with the "now."

Philosophers have always struggled with questions about time. Is it objective, comprised of matter? Is it subjective, a category of mind? Philosophers such as Kant as early as the 1700s recognized that time and space were not objectively real, and out there, but concepts, categories we impose on our existence to order it, to make thought possible.[7] Heidegger devoted his entire life to his fascination with Time and Being.[8]

But to the ordinary person time has always seemed absolute. "The idea that a universal time can be used indiscriminately by all, irrespective of whether they are . . . a person at rest at home, the driver of an automobile, or a passenger aboard an airplane—is so deeply ingrained in most people that they do not even conceive of alternatives."[9]

Thanks to physicists like Einstein and Stephen Hawking, we now know that time is not absolute. There is no such thing as "true time." Time is relative, and apparent time differs to different observers. What is more, time and space are related and affected by what happens in them.[10]

And of course the subjective experience of time is qualitatively different from all attempts to objectify it as the following passage by author John Hanson Mitchell testifies:

More and more now I find myself thinking there about time, how it drifts in from the future, how it brushes past us briefly in the present, and then drifts off again to become the past, and how none of these stages, neither past, nor present, nor future, are really knowable. Presented with this dilemma, I have come in recent years to accept the primitive concept of ceremonial time, in which past, present, and future can be perceived in a single moment, generally during some dance or sacred ritual.[11]

Or, we would add, during moments of passionate encounter with another or with the self.

Conventional turns of phrase like time flies, time well-spent, wasted time, represent the state of our own postmodern thinking about time as absolute, quantifiable, and a valuable commodity which some possess more of than others. Waste, efficiency, enough time, not enough time, all are ideas tied to the concept of quantity. Our language represents a view of time as *material*. "Taking time" means stealing. What are we taking time from? Who is the keeper of the time? Do we imagine that time is other than a construct, think of it as a real object, a real commodity in the marketplace? We talk about the value of time as if some time is more valuable than other time. We speak in terms of "what my time is worth."

Our assigning monetary value to time and much of our rush and hurry seem to be related to the pragmatic and functional emphasis of American culture. We live in linear time and are frantic to amass enough, and do everything fast enough. The images of our heritage remind us of this driving push to the finish line. The "Gold Rush," the great American land grab of the homesteading era, the drive to lay the railroad track coast to coast. Today, youngsters in elementary school are already selecting course work for junior high school based on their "career goals."

The emphasis on the goal, the finished product rather than the process, seems to speed up our subjective experience of time, and speed and efficiency become the measure of value.[12] We are infuriated at delay. Drivers in vehicles waiting in line to exit Manhattan via the Holland or Lincoln tunnels have been known to smash their cars into the vehicle ahead of them, provoked by their impatience with waiting.

Since we think of time as a quantifiable commodity we try to become ever more efficient. But we are not necessarily more fulfilled. Many of us ask where we are rushing to. And what do we have when we get there?

The most common sexual dysfunction in America today, lack of desire, reflects our emphasis on efficient time. We are efficient at reaching orgasm but we have no time for love. Rollo May writes:

> There is a fundamental relationship between eros, time, and imagination. Eros takes time: time for the significance of the event to sink in, time for the imagination to work, and if not "time to think," at least time to experience and to anticipate. This is why someone in love wants to be alone, wandering here and there by himself, not concentrating or trying to work; he is giving eros time to do its work. This significance of time is one of the characteristics which distinguishes eros from sex ... time for the integrating process to take place.[13]

We need meander time, time to wander, luxuriate, spiral around, be playful. It is this time expanded, time to luxuriate in, time for playfulness that is necessary for either love or creativity to unfold. Oddly enough, focusing on the now or "meandering" can both expand one's sense of time.

In the nineties many of us are asking ourselves questions about time, and studies increasingly reflect a trend for Americans to value time over money. Our broker says, "Since the economic downturn of 1987, I have decided to spend more time home with my kids." "Downshifting" has become a buzzword of the current decade.[14]

The changing attitudes toward time of those who do "downshift" reflect dissatisfaction with the result of our material attitudes. According to John Robinson, an authority on time, "there is ample evidence that people feel starved for time. We are at a point when the value of time to most Americans is reaching parity with the value of money."[15]

A friend who had left her first passion, music, for twenty years has resumed violin study and performance. Following a week-long music workshop she says, "It is clear to me that I have more energy for this than for anything in my life, and it's clear that this road leads to nowhere. It is sometimes easier not to be involved at all, otherwise there is just this ache in you." The ache is for the reconnection to her first passion, but the value of passion does not always translate into monetary value. If she honors what she has learned about her reconnection to her first passion, she will not have the time to make the money she does now in her psychotherapy practice. Her conflict may lead her to "downshift" or not, but it is clear that if she stays connected to music again, she will soon be at a choice point like the one Judy experienced when she gave up psychology for art. The conflict may make her think about her time differently.

THE IMPORTANCE OF THE MOMENT

Along with the trend toward "downshifting," there is an ever growing movement in the West to adopt more Eastern or spiritual views of time. Along with this spiritual movement goes an emphasis on process, not product, a deemphasis on getting to the goal line.

Most of the great mystical traditions represent time as literally stopped when one is totally focused on the present, as one is in meditation. When we are totally focused in the "now," time "stands still," we forget to watch the clock.

Krishnamurti, the religious philosopher, questions whether time would exist at all as memory if it were possible to give total attention to the moment.[16]

Trungpa Rinpoche, the Tibetan Buddhist master, speaks of the release of energy when one is in the present moment. Mindfulness produces joy, or aliveness, a kind of freedom.[17]

Sonia Johnson, the radical feminist author, writes, ". . . when we give up even a bit of what we want for some 'good' in a nonexistent future, we are cutting our Selves off from the moment, off from life, out of creativity and power . . . in our atomic universe, *now* is what time is. In nonlinear time it is a limitless possibility—to *be*. To be whatever is possible for us at this moment, to create and experience our Selves joyously, richly, fully, and magnificently, right *now*."[18]

Some of the most joyous women we interviewed have this sense of being focused in the present. We asked Mary Nolan what she has learned about time living on Ocracoke island. She has essentially learned Anne Morrow Lindbergh's "island lesson." Mary says, "I have learned the concept of mindfulness here on Ocracoke. And for me it makes time stand still. It slows time down. As I age, when I'm not practicing mindfulness, time is speeded up. When I allow myself to be totally here and now, time stands still. And this is the place where I have learned this." When Mary returns from her morning walk and says, "I saw a white egret perched in a cedar tree, like a candle flame," she has taken time to notice, be mindful.

The composer Lynn Wilson described a month-long Tibetan Buddhist retreat as time to be with herself. "Meditation," she said, "is a dialogue with myself similar to the sustained dialogue I have with myself when I compose. It is almost a sexual relationship with myself, like the sublimated joy that one experiences with creativity when your complete energy is focused on working through a particular creative problem."

Meditation is a form of "doing nothing." To meditate without a "gaining idea" means to meditate without a goal. Being without a goal is not the same as purposeless. "You mean you sat and did nothing for a month?" friends ask. "That would drive me crazy." To sit for a month would seem like incredible luxury to most of us, a time out of space, out of daily life that would be almost impossible for most women in relationship to manage.

But virtually all of the women we talked with who had the sense of living life passionately knew the value of their own time, and the value of solitude.

FEMININE AND MASCULINE TIME

Historically, many thinkers have conceptualized kinds of time as either masculine or feminine. Time is clearly not a gendered phenomenon in and of itself. Just like our stories about love, our perceptions of time are attributions that are impacted by cultural stories, myths, and constraints. Gendered ideas about time probably have much more to do with the ways that power and responsibility are constructed, rather than with inherent or innate differences in biological rhythms.

Masculine time has been conceived of as linear; feminine time has been more often conceived of as cyclical, circular, or spiral. The claim is that masculine time leads us to focus on product; feminine time makes room for process. Therefore it is feminine time that is creative time. Not coincidentally men who are artistic, creative, are often thought of as having accessed their more feminine sides.

Carol Ochs, a writer on women's spirituality, emphasizes that women's experience in creating, mothering, and letting go teaches us respect for process. Cyclical time, or what is thought of as "female" time, is also spiral time. Matthew Fox writes, "The ivy and the grapevine, both spiral, are symbols of rebirth and resurrection among the Celts. . . . The spiral is also the basic shape that the nucleic acids take in the DNA molecule, the basis of life." (See endnote for full reference.)[19]

Ruth, in chapter 5, who studies Chinese literature and the early goddess religions, says: "The reason women think in cycles where there are no beginnings and ends is nature is in cycles, moons wax and wane, the seasons cycle, and menstruation is clearly the same. It comes, goes, and returns and we know it is coming, and will go and return. It is beyond our conscious will and is a force that cannot be controlled by our mind. This monthly reality influences us deeply. It *is* magic. Cycles are eccentric—a little earlier, a little later, very late, cold snowy springs. I think of time as slightly irregular circles, as more a Slinky toy with God in the center seeing all at once. In other words history repeats itself but not exactly and maybe mankind moves around time rather than through time."

Author Susan Griffin also sees feminine time as cyclical, in tune with nature. Cycles ebb and flow like tides. Men, according to Griffin, have a more linear view of time, fight time, rather than accepting that natural process is cyclical.

"The race car driver is fearless. He speeds past death. In his speed is endless virility. Time is his executor." [20] Women's feminist spiritual communities, some of them adherents of witchcraft and "goddess religion," almost always have, as part of their ritual, the drawing of a sacred circle.

And finally, Abraham Heschel, writing on time and space, asserts,

> To enhance our power in the world of space is our main objective. Yet to have more does not mean to be more. The power we attain in the world of space terminates abruptly at the borderline of time. But time is the heart of existence.
>
> There is a realm of time where the goal is not to have but to be, not to own but to give, not to control but to share, not to subdue but to be in accord. Life goes wrong when the control of space, the acquisition of things of space, becomes our sole concern. [21]

It seems specious to argue that certain ways of thinking are inherently male or female simply because they either mirror other processes within the natural world or they don't. We all make efforts to "control" time and we equally all stand in awe of its power over us at different points in our experience. Our constructions of time are more likely to evolve from the roles we're required to play so that time is not either linear or circular, male or female, it is whatever we define it to be.

COMMON CONUNDRUMS IN WOMEN'S THINKING ABOUT TIME

Anne Morrow Lindbergh wrote, "Island living has been a lens through which to examine my own life in the North. I must keep my lens when I go back . . . I must remember to see with island eyes." [22]

Once we learn the value and significance of our own time, why is it so hard for us to get it? When we talk about "stealing time for ourselves," who is it we think owns time? Clearly, if this is the language we use, we think time belongs to someone besides ourselves.

In our surveys, when we asked, "Is taking time for yourself a conflict for you?" women's answers suggested their confusion about who owns time. One woman writes, "Yes, when my husband is writing, I have less time because I run and do our private practice plus my forty hour a week job at the hospital." Another writes, "Yes, sometimes I feel guilty. Most of the time I get shortchanged, but recently I find myself doing more for myself. Alien at first, but I talked myself into it . . . I deserve it, it's my turn. . . ."

Another says, "It is very hard for me. I tend to give more of myself to my friends than I do to myself." And another, "Sometimes . . . usually my husband 'clears the way' and makes me free, and encourages me to take time for myself. I usually prefer 'doing for others.' I'm more at ease."

A husband's writing is "more important" so his time is more valuable. She "gives" her time so that he can have his.

Another is "shortchanged" and has to take turns with time.

Still another has a husband who "gives her the gift of time" implying that it is *his* to give. If we view time as a material commodity, it is no wonder that we would believe that men control the access to that resource as they control access to so many others.

We were also struck by the readiness of women to blame themselves for not having enough time. When we asked women who felt they didn't have enough time for themselves to tell us why, over a third felt they didn't set priorities. Women tended to blame themselves for not setting priorities without realizing that the image in our mind's eye of a Smiling Woman makes setting priorities an irrelevant idea.

The 1992 film on the All American Girls' Baseball League of the forties, *A League of Their Own*, illustrates the assumption that the Smiling Woman doesn't set her own priorities when a man's priorities conflict with hers. Dottie, a great baseball player, is set to play in the World Series. Then her husband unexpectedly returns from the war. Wordlessly, without question or negotiation, she hangs up her catcher's mitt the week before the Series and gets into the car with him to return home. The scene shows her smiling straight into the camera. Her sister protests, "But you love baseball." But Dottie assumes her time is her husband's so that what she loves is not a priority.

Maybe it's true that women don't set priorities. Certainly many of us tolerate interruptions. Some of us don't mind those interruptions. Rosemary Tuck says women have evolved split brains anyhow, that we've learned to do many things at once, to be reading a book while listening for the need to intervene with the children at the same time that we're conscious of something cooking in the oven and the call we're waiting for from the washing machine repair person. But this capacity to split our focus isn't fine for others of us, it creates frustration and robs us of the attention we need for our own priorities.

GENDER DIFFERENCES IN THE ORGANIZATION OF TIME

Women's interrupted lives are a function of their socially constructed responsibilities. Two Norwegian psychologists have examined the social construction of care and domestic work in marital relationships. They say that two principles govern women's time, the principle of "rests with" and the principle of the "running wheel."[23]

"Rests with" means that the responsibility "rests with" the woman for everything the man doesn't explicitly agree to do. Her participation never has to be explicitly specified because it is assumed that she picks up all of the pieces all of the time.[24]

A second principle, "the running wheel," conditions a woman to continuously carry her child's state of mind in her mind. She adjusts her own timetable to that of her child, as if she has a wheel in her head that simulates the cyclical organization of events. By the principle of "the running wheel," she can preplan and adjust to any state of affairs. As Hanne Haavind and Agnes Andenes state, "In every moment of the day and the night, whatever activity you are carrying out, whether you are together with your child or not, the wheel is always there to be checked and controlled for what has to be done and what has to be paid attention to, to secure the necessary quality of the child's actual condition." Therefore, women who delegate care to their husbands still hold the "running wheel" in their heads as the final responsibility "rests with" them.

As women, we intuitively know what these concepts of "resting with" and "running wheel" mean. For example, a woman in one of our seminars describes herself as a third-generation feminist. She then says that she has delegated responsibility to her husband to pick the children up from school and take them to the dentist. And then she says, "I have to go call him to make sure he didn't forget."

We know that she still feels that the responsibility she has supposedly delegated rests with her.

Masculine time is organized, in contrast, by the combined principles of "time as gift" and "time as investment." In other words, time belongs to the man and he is free to give it or invest it. According to Haavind and Andenes men and women both take refuge in the ideas of essential differences to protect this unequal arrangement of responsibilities by attributing it to women's internal capacities for nurturing.[25] In other words, the argument that women are biologically programmed to naturally nurture obscures the social story about responsibility.

We were not surprised to find out how often women's creativity is fit in around the needs of the "running wheel," that the quilt is "something that can be picked up at will," that crafts are easier to integrate than performance art. Our results confirmed the tendency of married women to turn more to kinds of creativity that do not disrupt others' schedules. It is also no wonder that many of us go to bed at night with the wheel running in our heads, unable to take the time to concentrate on love.

Although both men and women complain of feeling rushed and pressured, women actually do have less free time than men. A UNESCO study shows that, worldwide, mothers that work outside the home have less than two-thirds the free time enjoyed by their husbands. They have less leisure than either women who stay at home full time or working men.[26]

Professor John Robinson, cited above, validates the subjective experience of most women when he says, "Women with jobs and with children have the least amount of leisure. Having a husband does not result in more leisure for women with children. Being married reduces the free time of a woman by an hour a week; being single increases her free time by four hours." [27]

If there are actual differences in the amount of "free" time men and women have access to, there are also marked differences in the way each gender thinks about time. A simple phrase like "time together" means something entirely different for a woman than for a man.

In a scene from the film *Tin Men*, Danny DeVito's wife grumbles, "We hardly ever do things together . . . if we went on a picnic it would be fun."

Danny says, "I don't understand about a picnic; you go somewhere and put a thing on the ground and eat. Ants get in the food. It's better sitting in front of the TV."

Time "together" for women also often means talking time. Lillian Rubin asserts in *Intimate Strangers* that physical proximity is enough intimacy for many men, while women want to talk about feelings, actually interact.[28]

Examples of this difference are common. For instance, a friend and her husband were spending the night with us en route to their vacation rental. They arrived late afternoon with their infant and were to leave by noon the next day. At 10 P.M., Luis, whom we knew only slightly, asked if we minded his turning on the television. We said no, but his wife was highly irritated.

We asked them how they thought about time. To Sarah, every minute with friends should be "quality time" which to her meant conversation. To Luis, "hanging out time" in which he could just do his normal thing, watch Friday night TV, was not only OK, but a sign that he felt very close to us. For him it *was* "quality time."

Of course, gender generalizations don't always hold up. It is usually more interesting and more important to ask individuals, women and men, about their subjective experience of time. Time is the currency often most valued in relationships. Differences in the ways people think about it frequently trigger arguments that are really arguments about who is more important or more valuable.

GETTING THE TIME—INTERACTIONAL DIMENSIONS

When we do make our differences and our thought processes explicit, we can make changes. In our relationships we cocreate rules about time and we often base those rules on an assumption that the man's time, or simply the other person's time, is more valuable.

Samantha, the Navy wife, is still negotiating different rules about time with Mike. When he was away on deployment for six months she really saw how much more of her time was her own.

First she said, "I'm beginning to look at how I'm living with him gone. Like eating. It's going to be an important issue what time we eat dinner. Jill and I just, if we're hungry when she gets home from school, we eat dinner and then later we have a snack, or if she's not hungry and I'm not hungry we wait, or she eats and I don't or whatever. Mike likes to sit down to dinner and have us all together, which I think is a great thing too, but it's going to be a big change."

Another recognition had to do with interruptions. "When I pick up a book I'm in another world. This is my world and I do not want to be interrupted. Now Jill this summer has really come far in respecting that. But Mike hasn't. If I sit down with a book I'll read the same sentence over and over because he keeps talking. It's not even exactly an interruption, He's watching TV . . . Oh did you see that? Oh I forgot to tell you . . ."

In Samantha's family, an evening ritual involved everyone sitting in the same room together focused on his or her reading or needlework or individual interest. No interruptions were permitted. Samantha liked her family rules about time better than her current ones. "It felt great. To know that this was my time and that I would not be interrupted.

"With Mike, it's more like, Now I want family time, I'm ready for family time so all you guys drop everything. Why does he make all the decisions about when?"

By the time Mike came back from deployment, Samantha had decided to change the rules about time. She wrote a "position paper" consisting of twenty-eight statements, such as:

- I want the hours of 8–9 A.M. free of interruption for personal exercise time (5 days a week).
- I want the approximate hours of 11 A.M.–3 P.M. free for personal time (5 days a week).
- Exceptions: Lunch out or together at home 2 times a week.
- I will not run errands at night or in evening. My working hours are:
  6:30–8 A.M.
  9:00–11 A.M.
  3:00–8 P.M., weekdays

Mike agreed to cooperate although he made some small modifications in the schedule. What's more, he felt more entitled to take some of his own time without needing to provoke an argument and he and Samantha moved one step closer to marriage as a partnership satisfying to both of them. But negotiations for change can only be made on the basis of a woman knowing that she is entitled to her own time. It wasn't up to Mike to "give" Samantha the time.

GETTING THE TIME—INTERNAL DIMENSIONS

It's not enough to feel entitled to time and know how to negotiate it in relationship. Using time well, living life fully, requires a conscious examination of our own process. We need to know how we think about time, what kinds of time requirements we need for different purposes, what constitutes quality or Flow time for us, what makes up renewal time. Then, and only then, can we organize our time so that we can follow Barry Stevens's advice, "Don't push the river; it flows by itself."[29]

Our time will feel like it flows easily if we are in tune with our own rhythms. When our rhythms conflict with someone else's, we at least need to know what we need for ourselves before we begin to compromise and adapt.

We asked Joan Ellis about her experience of time, noting that she and Corson viewed time differently, that she had used time differently from him, including making her decisions about how it should be spent, with whom, when, and in what periods of her life. It was not surprising that she had thought about time a great deal. In fact, her differences with Corson about time led them to the choice point in their marriage.

That point came in 1978. Corson's company had become successful enough that he could indulge all his travel whims. The children had also left. Joan and Corson saw that sudden free time differently.

"I suddenly realized that Corson thought he was going to die by the time he was sixty and I thought I was going to die when I was eighty. As I look back, he was operating on a timetable of having about ten years left to live and I was operating on a time table that said I had about thirty years left to live. And if you believe that, if that is your operative presumption, you plan very differently and you see very differently. And he's still doing that. He's going full tilt knowing that he's going to die, and he's going to pack it all in and see everything he can and do everything he can."

During that time, indeed, Corson took one trip after another in a search for new experiences and exposure to different parts of the world. But Joan was spending part of each week in Manhattan, trying to write her first book. Conflict was inevitable as Corson really wanted Joan along as a travel companion and Joan was welcoming "free" time for the first time. They separated amicably after a couple of years of marital therapy that clarified their separate paths.

Now Joan lives alone in her redesigned space that is open and uncluttered, like a metaphor for her love of open uncluttered time.

"For me, time means empty chunks on the calendar and when it's empty, I can sink into the kind of way of life that I love, which is being here. Which is, I look at the calendar this morning and I think, God, it's a great week, and a great week means there's nothing on it. Which means I can get up and I can roll up and back and forth to my computer and write my movie reviews . . . and there's a mixture of writing, desk work, indoor work, outdoor work."

Acknowledging that she doesn't totally compartmentalize so that nothing intrudes on her writing time she says, "I haven't got a perfect writing schedule yet. I mean, not one where I don't let anything intrude, because it does. If the sun broke out right now I'd probably run for the tractor just because I love the feeling of sun on my back and being out there, or getting the wood in, whatever. But that hasn't worn off of me yet [the newness of living alone], and the exhilaration of knowing that nobody is trying to stop me from doing that is still so red hot that I just kind of wonder when it's going to go away and it doesn't. And that's not to say that this isn't all shot through with a lot of communication with some very good old friends."

Interestingly most of the friends don't live near Joan and she finds that very helpful in terms of time.

"They're very good old friendships from way way back. And if they were living here, I think they could become the kind of friendship where you had to remember each other's birthday, whereas now, they are wonderful friendships where you pick up the phone and you are right away into some marvelous conversation. It's a real connectedness, and I think sometimes, when people are living with each other, you get off on too much little stuff, surface stuff. So I really treasure those friendships."

But Joan can enjoy little stuff in other ways. "I love superficial time and playing time. As long as it isn't dinner party stuff."

THE PASSIONATE PROCESS

Because women's stories have been told largely by men we have learned a false reverence for linear process. And it's true that linear process has its place. The march straight toward the goal reaches the goal. A respect for linear time with no detours is necessary for meeting deadlines. But deadlines are often directly opposed to lifelines, because they quite literally deaden the creativity that will not be hurried, that takes its own time. Connecting to our passions, respecting our own creative rhythms, these are our lifelines.

The passionate process, creative and/or loving, differs for different women and can change at different points in their lives. Respect for the diversity of process is as critical to passion as respect for the diversity of forms that express women's energy. Sometimes a woman assumes that her own process isn't alright because it doesn't fit some preconceived idea of what process *should be*.

Joan thinks in terms of not having yet managed not to let anything intrude on her writing time, but our perspective would be to see what we call her "meander time," her time to putter in her environment and spontaneously follow a different impulse as *part of her writing process*. Meander time is spiral time. It is a coil, a corkscrew, a helix. It scrolls and winds, and circles downward and upward, inward and outward. It's what writer Barbara Euland calls "moodling."[30]

Linear time is efficient, spiral time, inefficient. Therefore we think of linear time as "saving time." But efficiency for Joan might be the thief of time because if she efficiently did things in tight linear order, she would violate her own creative process.

Her process might even involve taking a nap in the middle of writing.

But to get that spiral time, Joan first has to get the unpleasant work out of the way. "I tend to get up and get the tedious work out of the way because I really operate best if I've got a completely clean slate with my mind. I get there by having a clean desk and a clean calendar.

"I'll try not to go out to my tractor until I've got all the grunt work done too, because if it's hanging over my head, I'm not going to think half as happily out there as I do if it's done. The tractor is connected to my creative process. I think wildly on the tractor. I always come in with something. I usually go out with something in one state in my mind and come in with it in a different state."

Monica McGoldrick is equally aware of her own process, her own time. She says, "I hate wasted time," and we already know that she thinks of sleep as "pretty much wasted time." As we saw, Monica has multiple projects, multiple energies, and she had her first child at forty-one, adding an enormous expenditure of energy. Music is one of the ways she reconnects to herself.

She particularly loves many operas and requiems, acknowledging the Irish fascination with death that seems to infuse some of her love of music. When we asked her how she makes time to listen to music she said she had never thought about it but then said, "Well like now, today, on my way over here I listened to *The Pearlfishers*, which is one of my favorite operas. I love Scott Joplin, so I mostly write to Scott Joplin. What I'll do is I'll have something and I'll listen to it over and over and over and then eventually it wears thin for a time and I leave it and then I come back to it later. Sophocles [her husband] is the same on this, not wanting to waste time listening to any music he doesn't absolutely love. He once made himself a tape, which was my kind of tape, of the aria from *La Wally* by Maria Callas repeated sixteen times so that you wouldn't have to keep playing it again."

When Monica reflects on the ways she has changed over the years she says, "I dare more to say what I think; I dare more not to waste my time."

Lynn Wilson, the composer we met in chapter 6, makes her time with herself central and organizes the rest of her day around that. She knows that the dialogue she has with herself is necessary to her dialogue with others.

Lynn protects her morning time for composing, turning on the tape deck and interrupting herself for nothing. When her composing is going well, she is in the Flow, time is standing still and she may compose past the time she has set aside. She emerges then from her studio to take relational time, starved for companionship and the sound of other voices, but the parade may have passed by, the party over. She willingly pays the price of the foregone party. Is she sorry that her relationship with herself is so primary? "I long, yes, for a primary relationship with someone else." But does she long for it enough to be "waylaid by love"? No. She feels she probably wouldn't fall in love with someone for whose sake she would compromise her composing.

A Necessary Order

Betty Mount is forty-eight. She has been partially disabled from a swimming accident for many years. Her priority is keeping herself as mobile and independent as she can, although she acknowledges and accepts interdependence.

We wondered whether, under the circumstances, she felt she had organized her time or that her time had organized her.

"You have to be organized in a situation like mine. I live alone and I have to do things at a certain time, when I'm able. For example, in the morning I'm stiff and have to do exercises. So everything is done in order, a very precise order. Therefore you can't do a lot of the things you might want to like say 'Ah, I don't want to cook dinner now,' but you have to get dinner now, because you have to eat now and you have to stay on a schedule physically, that's very important. A nap is necessary. I can't afford to gain weight, I have to do my exercises because then I wouldn't be able to get in and out of my wheelchair."

Betty used to organize her time around others rather than around herself. "We had three children in three years. Then you get up at five or six o'clock in the morning. Your life suddenly becomes one long day in the kitchen. Now, at my age and time in life, I have to come first because the most important thing for me to do is take care of myself so that nobody else has to."

For at least sixteen years, Sara Eyestone had at least one pre-schooler, and she would not have been able to paint if she believed, as so many women do, "I haven't got the time and space."

She had to claim the time and she adapted the space.

As she says, "And so I was going to wait to paint to have all my babies and then wait until they were raised, I mean what are we talking about? So my thought was, to try as best I could to do it all." She had a playpen at the end of her painting table with little easels in her studio and art supplies for the children. "I have a lot of order. I scheduled my babies for feedings every four hours around the clock; one ate at ten, two, and six; one ate at six, ten, two, etc. I have order in my studio; I keep my paints in color families. . . . They're not in alphabetical order but all the yellows are together and all the purples are together and that makes it more efficient, and the same thing is true at my house. Every telephone has a dozen pencils and a stack of tablets so that I don't have to take a phone call or somebody else takes a message and has to run around looking for a whatever. I wasn't born efficient. I learned that if I'm not I can't get as much done. I used to go to bed right after the ten o'clock feeding, sleep until two, but at two I'd get up. So from two until six in the morning I had total uninterrupted time."

And like Monica McGoldrick there is no wasted or meander time.

"Everybody's different but I talk to so many women who are artists who say, you know, of course I have a child and I can't do anything until they're da da da da . . . and I think, Why don't you try it?"

Some of us can work in "snatches," even four-hour ones, on the run, in airports, and hotel rooms; others of us literally require huge uninterrupted blocks of time. One novelist decides on a stopping time when she sits down to work and she stops at that time no matter how the work is going. She feels that the structure forces her to be more productive with the time she has available.

Some of us require the nap, the break, the change of scene. Others go straight to the finish line, and hate any distraction that takes them off course. And as our lives and energies change our process may change, so we must remain awake to our own changing rhythms.

THE TIME OF YOUR LIFE

Different shapes of a life present different obstacles and opportunities for women to honor their own process and maximize their own quality time. There are also differences within forms, differing styles of organizing or thinking about time within a particular form. Lovers and Artists are likely to think about time very differently and set different priorities. Women in the integrative groups *are* integrative precisely because they organize and prioritize time differently from women in the other two categories. Monica fits work in around family and in some cycles fits family in around work; Sara fits family in around work. Joan needs a lot of inefficient or meander time. Samantha, a Lover, has very little "time of her own," but as she negotiates a little more, she finds that a little bit goes a long way toward making her life form a better fit for her energies.

We must own our own time if we are to be subject, if we are to seize power and brave passion. What seems to be important is to understand our own relationship to time, to know our own rhythms and styles, to develop flexibility about rearranging our priorities. It's important that we become increasingly clear, each time we are faced with choices, about what the priority is at that moment.

Living in our own good time is a complex balancing act. If we are too efficient, always looking to the future, to the next thing to be done, the book to be read after we do the housework or the article of someone else's to be proofread after we read the book, then our own time is always beyond our reach. Yet if we are too singular about our own needs, time either for love or self-expression, we live in danger of ignoring the energies that others' agendas can lend to ours, the synergy that explodes when energy meets energy and results in passionate encounters.

CHAPTER THIRTEEN

The Passionate Relationship: Creating New Forms

MARY CASEY HAS BEEN DIVORCED and a single mother for over a year. With four children, two of them preschoolers, it hasn't been realistic for her to find full-time work. Child support and welfare payments combined don't cover her expenses. She wants to take classes to make it possible for her to eventually go back to work. At the point when she was about to be evicted from her apartment for nonpayment of her rent, she saw an ad in the paper placed by a single father looking for a roommate to help defray his household expenses. Even though he had advertised for another male, she went to meet him and they talked. They worked out an agreement that is a fit for all of them: Mary and her children now live in a comfortable home that is affordable on her small income, and the single father is able to save money so that he can eventually provide better for himself and his son. While they are not family, they once in a while provide some of the support a family might for one another. For now, they have all found a form that fits their immediate needs.

FORM AND BELIEF

Mary's primary concern, her primary passion has been to ensure the welfare and survival of herself and her children. Having found a form and a living situation that takes this into account, she's much more likely to be able to think creatively about herself and the kind of work she may eventually want to do, and to find a form for those passions as well. For Mary, the threat of eviction forced a change—she needed to think more creatively about her situation because the "old idea" no longer worked. Luckily, neither she nor the single father were constrained by rigid ideas about what could or couldn't work, and they decided to try something new.

The shapes our lives take on and the kinds of relationships and living situations we establish work better if, beyond survival, they permit us access to and full expression of our passionate selves. They work best when they permit a resolution of the splits and divisions of self that are generated by our beliefs about love.

For a woman, the greatest block to achieving a form that satisfies is the assumption that she is solely defined by her need for relatedness and that it is only in relationship that she can fulfill her "basic" female nature. We block our own thinking about possible forms for our lives by assuming that only relationships of a certain nature can satisfy. In fact, our very socialization has set us up for disappointment relationally, because our expectations of relationship generally far exceed their real capacity to provide us with outlets for all of our complex needs and energies.

One woman who has returned to music as a serious pursuit questions how viable her marriage is because she can't share her passion for music with her husband. She worries that this passion for music is a more intense part of her life than her connection with him. Or, does she really worry because she is discovering a sense of herself and her own power outside of relationship, and her belief that this is somehow not "female" constricts and frightens her?

Chronic dissatisfaction with relationship can often be a signal for a woman that she is looking too much to relationship and not enough to herself and her own creative interests to provide her with a sense of herself. Dissatisfaction can also be a signal that the form of one's relationships doesn't fit. When one contemplates a change of form or a choice of form, it's important to question how much is enough? Do we expect to feel passionate intensity as much in our relationships as in our work, how do we balance the flow of energies, which is more important? Could we ever allow ourselves to accept that at certain times, under certain circumstances, a creative or work interest might engage us more than a relationship? That connection to ourselves may be more compelling than our connection to someone else? And do we understand that the passionate dialogue with our own inner life can infuse the dialogue with the other, so that passion synergistically increases passion?

These are threatening questions for most of us—they raise fears of loneliness and lovelessness that generally don't become realities. But when we choose forms for our lives, we need to decide how much of our energy we want to channel toward others and how much to reserve for ourselves. Our *beliefs* about what is acceptable and not acceptable, enough and not enough, become the major shapers.

Anne-Marie Dunatov, in an article for *American Health*, reports on research that shows that couples who choose not to have children, for instance, are often happier than ones who do. Their major problem is facing the scorn and disapproval of friends and family. She counsels "childless by choice" women to have a way of managing disapproval because of the strong and pervasive belief in our society that a woman isn't "whole" or "normal" unless she raises children.[1]

Decisions about work and career often have as much impact as relational ones. Certain kinds of careers will be more demanding of time and energy, some will be more or less intellectually challenging or stimulating than others. Some will provide more emotional satisfaction than monetary reward. Questioning our beliefs about "how much is enough" plays an important part in the struggle for balance between emotional fulfillment and economic power.

FORMS THAT FIT

Forms have to fit our energies, our preferences, our deep longings. They have to be flexible enough to change as we change, to develop as we acquire new information about ourselves. They must provide safety and challenge enough to support the courage required to keep them alive.

In relationships, we have a broad choice of forms: heterosexual, lesbian, children, no children, single by choice, single by circumstance. Our friendships may be close, intense ones where we see or spend time with one another daily, or they may be more distant, geographically limited ones where we have intense visits or times of contact only once or twice a year. We may have strong male friendships, only female friendships. We may have a great deal of contact with our families or very little. We may have a network of friends that becomes a "family of choice."

Within those relational forms, we have many other choices to make and patterns to shape. We need to pay attention to the rhythms of our own time, our aesthetic sensibilities, our preference for environment. We have to find a balance between work and play, our own needs, the needs of children and partners, togetherness, separateness, deciding what, at any given time, is foreground in importance and what is background.

We need to choose the work that we love and create a life- and work-style that will provide us access to it. Do we want to work for ourselves, for someone else, make money doing what we love, or simply do something to make money so that we're free to do what we love? What will the major source of satisfaction in our lives be and how will we keep it alive? Most important is that we find a form that allows us to experience ourselves as both relational and creative in the balance that is most consistent with the themes and impulses of our life over time.

Forms that fit have two other characteristics that are critical: One is a relational balance of power and entitlement and the other is the absence of destructive competitiveness.

Power is often claimed in relationship to another and power is intimately connected with our assumptions about gender. Different forms of relationship are vulnerable to different kinds of power struggles and conceal different imbalances of power. The rightful use of power is to negotiate the fitting form for you in relationship to the other. When one doesn't do that negotiating, the consequences can be destructive. Author Katherine Mansfield writes in a letter to a friend:

> Jack can never realize what I have to do. He helps me all he can but he can't help me really and the result is I spend all my energy, every bit, in keeping going, I have none left for work. All my work is behindhand and I can't do it. I simply stare at the sky. I am too tired even to think. What makes me tired? Getting up, seeing about everything, arranging everything, *sparing him*, [emphasis ours] and so on.[2]

The necessity to spare her husband is an assumption on her part about entitlement. Jack is *entitled* to be spared. Why? Does he have the economic power? Is his work, his inner life intrinsically more important than hers? Or does he have more power in her eyes simply by virtue of his being the male while she is the female Smiling Woman?

How does his importance and entitlement get conveyed? Is it blatant or subtle? In Ravenna Helson's research on creative women in marriage, she finds: "91 percent (of women) report subtle forms of condescension—signals that speak volumes." For instance, "I would get terribly angry when we were discussing something important and he would continue eating or taking notes for school or doing some silly task around the house. He was, in fact, telling me that his particular activity was more important than what I had to say."[3]

As we look at the kinds of relationship forms women have chosen and can choose to create, we need to keep in mind how the form we choose reflects an acceptable answer to the question, whose work is more important?

What about competition as a struggle for power? Competition needn't be destructive. Our adrenaline can flow in the race, our best efforts can be challenged by our rival. Competition and envy can enrich us with new knowledge if we see them as clues to what we long to be. But if competition slaps us down, shuts us up, if, " 'It is like we're rivals or competitors somehow if I try to express myself,' then competitiveness destroys connection, both to the other and to the self."[4]

A relational form, to be enhancing, cannot permit an imbalance of power that obscures a woman's work by false attribution or benign neglect.[5]

And finally, the form of relatedness, whether a woman lives alone, with her children, her sister, her partner, or with friends, must provide for a reasonable distribution of domestic responsibilities. We know that an overload of domesticity can be a killing field for creative work and in some cases, for the self. Sylvia Plath's experience and her ultimate suicide is a dramatic example: "the smog of cooking, the smog of hell floated in her head. The smile of the icebox annihilated. There was a stink of fat and baby crap; viciousness in the kitchen! And the blood jet poetry (for which there was never time and self except in that still blue hour before the baby's cry) there was no stopping it."[6]

Plath's story, more than most, depicts the potential consequences when a woman chooses a form for her life that is not a fit, when power imbalances, competition, and the overwhelming tedium of domestic life are not negotiated and changed.

Shaping a life requires a constant vigilance. The moment we begin to sacrifice too much of one thing that's important for another, our bodies, our psyches, and our souls will suffer. We won't necessarily always be happy, but when a form doesn't fit, we will begin to feel a deadness settle in. Embracing our passions doesn't always guarantee happiness, but it does guarantee aliveness.

MAKING RELATIONAL FORMS WORK: COUPLES AND LIFE PARTNERS

If women are to change the shape of their lives, their relationships of necessity will change as well. If we are to define love, power, and entitlement differently, we will need different visions for connecting with our partners. The process of that connecting will become a creative venture in itself.

Old rituals and structures will no longer work. All the evidence is that they don't now. Our concepts of family and couplehood will become much more individualized and authentic—for each of us relationship will respond to our own unique needs rather than forcing our individual needs into a preconceived mold. Ideas about gender difference will fade as a social preoccupation. Men's work and women's work will no longer be relevant ideas. Passion, feeling, skill, and interest, along with a concept of shared responsibility, will determine who does what. Women won't view themselves as less important or their agendas as less relevant than a man's. They won't assume that they are sole owners of a biological intuition that makes them more significant to children. A full life is the birthright of all of us and with this goal clearly in mind, couples will make that possible for one another. Lovers, Leaders, Innovators, Artists—all require different relational forms. In our interviewing, we deliberately talked with a number of couples to understand more clearly what types of patterns lend themselves to successful couple relationships. We were interested in how women balanced their energies and what perspectives their partners had on the question of form. Definite patterns seem to develop in these relationships. Couples, either consciously or spontaneously, evolve predictable dynamics for their partnerships that enhance the well-being of both. Those patterns emerge from the temperaments and the dominant energies of each partner. In a relationship that's a good fit, those patterns serve the needs of the couple, the couple doesn't adopt rigid roles that are defined by social expectations.

Georgeanne and Condon: The Collaborative Couple Relationship

Georgeanne and Condon Kuhl (see chapter 11) are both artists who recently relocated to a coastal community to pursue their art and to be in the environment they love. Condon is a jewelry craftsman and Georgeanne a watercolorist and papermaker, but the two have merged work and relationship and they now frequently collaborate artistically, creating pieces that reflect the different skills of each. They both left behind stable and financially secure jobs in academia and administration in the midwest. Theirs was a very conscious decision to find a form that better fit their inner leanings. Fortunately, they shared those leanings and both were willing to sacrifice all that it required to make such a major change in their lives. Both were previously married. It might have been the fact that they shared a common dream and passion with one another that cemented this second marriage for each of them.

We've talked to both Condon and Georgeanne, so we have gained a unique dual perspective on the meaning and "style" of the relationship and the ways that it works for them both.

For Georgeanne it seems that what works best in the relationship with Condon is the sense of integration she feels between her emotional life and her artistic life. She says, "There is a sort of totally integrated love for my husband that is about work and ourselves and our garden and all those things together. I think that love is very much expressed in my work. Even more recently it has been in terms of the collaborative work that my husband and I have been doing together—it is sort of like we have been bouncing ideas off each other for years and just last year we decided this is kind of silly that we are doing this separate work—there is no reason we can't be doing work together and it has been incredible.

"The compatibility was already there, so we'll sit down and actually do the drawing together and have a think-tank session where we will have a theme that we're working on. It keeps growing, it seems to be just a natural process. We will decide the parts of the piece, most of them have been like wall reliefs or sculptures in the round, and where we will each do the components and we'll be responsible for a certain part of the component and then we'll put them all together. So we each have our own part that we create on our own, but then it all comes together."

Condon is less fluent than Georgeanne when he talks about the ways that love and work come together for him. While he clearly feels as intensely about the relationship as Georgeanne does, he seems less direct about expressing it. Of their relationship and his feelings for Georgeanne he says, "It's settled down into just a varying pattern. It's all still there . . . at the beginning you give all your energy over to it. It doesn't just die. But what it [change] means is that we're expanding, we're putting our energy into other things we need to do. When you're putting your energy into your work there's a whole different mechanism."

Perhaps that mechanism is not really so different for Condon than for Georgeanne. Condon does say he "loves" his work, though the impulse to define it this way is ours and not his. He would call his creative energy "an incredibly strong force, and I think that is one of the things that Georgeanne and I have brought together to both ours [work] because we understand that. She's not in one field and I'm in another. We've come together. And I guess in a way, it lets us work together, because that could also be a conflict. We could be in competition with each other."

Georgeanne and Condon have a style of relationship that we call *collaborative*. While collaboration obviously means they work together on a common task, that they are in essence artistic and business partners, it suggests a more fundamental joining of underlying values and relational styles. Both "love" the same things, their energies are similar, their values lie in enjoyment of the environment, enjoyment of their artistic passions, in together wanting a certain life-style that is less structured and materialistic, more creative and autonomous. Each had a dream of living by the sea. But relationship is also critically important to each of them, so in this sense, because they need to merge their love for creative work with their relational lives, they might both be described as Creative Integrative, as Innovators.

The collaborative relational style is often a good fit for the Innovator. What Condon comments on is that they each "understand" the importance and meaning of their creative work. Sharing this value base, they're more easily able to merge their separate work interests in a way that is supportive of the needs of both. Georgeanne talks about the rewards of collaboration—Condon is more likely to talk about the potential problems.

This kind of balance in styles, preoccupations, and skills is typical of the collaborative couple. He says, "I don't think that the issues involved have been worked out enough. It's still very much an evolving kind of thing. When you're working on a piece [yourself], it's all your piece. The high is much more intense. When you're sharing it with someone else, you pull back on it some. We're going to hit details in each one where my solution would be different than her solution. I have technical skills that she doesn't have and she has technical skills that I don't have. So it's going to be a problem bringing them together in a way that makes a piece work. That's mechanical, you know that. There are a lot of things to deal with."

The struggles of collaboration don't seem far different from the challenges of creating a workable life together. Both Condon and Georgeanne are more than pleased and fulfilled by the way their life change has progressed. Their similarities are obvious, their differences more subtle, or at least their way of articulating themselves differs subtly. When asked what the passions of her life were, Georgeanne responded immediately, "Condon my husband is a passion and work is a passion and the garden and the children and the grandchildren." When asked the same question, Condon responded, hesitantly, "Art."

What makes him feel most focused in the present? "The art, totally, totally focused. And it's not divorced from the love or anything else. It's all total here because we're both driven. It's as important to both of us—it *is* the relationship."

When they needed to divide the space in the house into separate work areas, it was Georgeanne who relinquished most of her studio to a showroom in the summer months. It was Georgeanne who talked about the difficulty of juggling being an artist and a mother. While Condon feels that neither one of them claims or receives more from the relationship than the other, that it's mutual, one wonders if Georgeanne, because she is the woman, doesn't naturally give just a bit more, accommodate just a bit more.

Condon and Georgeanne work hard at maintaining some separateness in the midst of much time spent together working and living under the same roof. She meditates and gardens, keeps a journal, maintains contact with friends back home. She teaches art classes, an activity she also loves. Theirs is a collaboration that seems to work—it has helped to actualize both their dreams, it expresses both their most defining energies in a way that most of us would envy. The heart of the collaboration rests in what is shared, in mutuality of passion and perhaps, most important, mutual understanding of the importance of those passions and the intention to support the other in expressing them.

Judy and Leslie: The Supportive Couple Relationship

Collaboration is one form of relatedness that allows for the emergence of passion. But two people may not necessarily share the same work or even the same interests. Another form of mutually enhancing relationship is the *supportive* style. A collaborative relationship is typically always supportive, but a supportive relationship is not necessarily collaborative, except in the sense that two partners must collaborate in creating a supportive structure for one another.

Judy Gomez is the fiber artist, previously a college professor, whose transformational experience described in chapter 11 had to do with her discovery of both her creative passion and her sexual preference. Judy is clearly an Innovator whose fifteen-year relationship with Leslie is supportive of their two very different sets of interests and creative pursuits. Judy talks at length about the ways her relationship with Leslie provides for a much deeper sense of connection with herself.

"From the time we were together, I could just be myself. There was never in our relationship, there never has been, a question of me having to live up to anything other than what I want for my life—and that's working out a relationship with each other.

"In the marriage, I was living in the shadow of this man's image of who I should be. I don't think I ever once in those thirteen years asked myself what I wanted from my life or what was important to me."

It was not that Judy's husband was not supportive of her. He encouraged her to go into academia where she became a professor at the same time that she was raising three young children and pregnant with the fourth. Judy credits her husband with "giving her confidence in herself as a woman."

"You know he loved me to death, there was a certain fulfillment in being loved and adored. But I think I was more in love with the idea of family and kids than I was in love with him." The process Judy describes is subtle. While she accessed certain parts of herself in the marriage, deeper truths about her own needs went unrecognized. She was not truly subject in her marriage—she depended on her husband and on external definitions of femaleness to create her sense of identity. She made no choices clearly arising from her own knowledge of her passions. As this became more clear to her, she left the marriage. Two years later, she met Leslie.

When she and Leslie met, Judy felt an immediate connection with some other part of herself that had gone unnoticed. She describes her relationship, or rather herself in her relationship with Leslie, as 100 percent different, though she hesitates to ascribe the difference only to the fact that it is a lesbian rather than a heterosexual relationship. She says, maybe it's a function of age, of its being a second relationship. Undoubtedly it has much to do with her experiencing a much clearer and deeper connection to herself. "It's 100 percent different. We have more fun. We enjoy ourselves more. We give each other more freedom, we nurture each other more. I mean there's no competition, we don't compete."

Leslie agrees with this assessment: "I don't think that competition is only a function of heterosexual relationships, but between us there is no competition so that contributes a lot to the relationship."

When asked who was more important in her marriage, Judy responds immediately, her husband. "Everything was centered around him." With Leslie: "I would say it's equal. We just sort of work things through, there is a very natural and joyful flow."

Judy and Leslie live in Santa Fe, New Mexico. Like Condon and Georgeanne, they made a decision to move to a new place to have a better quality of life, to follow their inner leanings more.

It's tempting to think that their relationship is so qualitatively different because the stresses now are much more minimal. But then one remembers that Leslie helped Judy raise her four children, and that for many of the early years of their relationship, the stresses and pressures were actually more profound than they might have been for two heterosexuals.

Currently, Leslie, a former teacher, does literacy work, Judy does art and teaches college courses part-time. Together they have developed a spiritual practice that involves teaching and working with groups in the community. They love to ski, to sit in their hot tub and look out into the mountains. Leslie studies Spanish and both take banjo lessons. The two share a common vision if not the same work. Their mutual goal: "In a very ongoing way to be continuously in touch with who we are and what we want and how we can express that and how we can make our lives useful and meaningful. We feel we have a great gift living in a place like Santa Fe, which is extraordinarily beautiful and nurturing to every creative need we could ever have. So the spiritual dimension and the work of bringing it and offering it to others is a way to return to others what we feel we've received."

Leslie is the more relational of the two, Judy at this point more an Innovator, except when she's with her grandchildren, whom she describes as her greatest true passion. Leslie and Judy's support of one another emotionally and creatively is obvious simply in their way of being together, it simply is assumed. Each has become expert at knowing what the other needs and how best to encourage her to have it. Their relationship "fits" for them extraordinarily well and they have an ongoing commitment to be watchful and to make choices that maintain their joint vision of how they want to be together.

Notice that Judy and Leslie have made it a point to share some common loves—spiritual work, skiing, recreation, that bring them together on a regular basis. In supportive relationships, connection is as much a priority as the individual interests of each partner. Couples who adopt this style tend to be particularly skilled at building shared interests and activity so that separate work or artistic passions don't take them off in totally separate directions.

Supportive relationships may work best for women in the integrative categories, Leaders and Innovators. They're characterized by unqualified mutual support of each partner's interests and creative agendas. One partner always assumes that the other's work and needs are equally important and will make every effort to help create the conditions that allow for the other to pursue them.

Lilli Cohen and David:
The Parallel Couple Relationship

Lilli Cohen is the literary agent who spoke so powerfully to the issue of making choices in chapter 11. Lilli has a different version of a supportive style relationship. An Innovator, she and her artist husband live in a fast-paced urban center where ambition and a focus on work and career are the norm. Their relationship is a blend of styles—it is supportive but its structure is *parallel*. The two do very different and very separate work. They are a "dual career couple," and while devoted to one another, work is a dominant focus for each that is more foreground than background. Lilli, a typical Innovator, expresses a kind of ambivalence common to women in this group about where her dominant energies really lie.

QUESTION: What would you say your main energy goes to?
Lilli: "It goes back and forth. I would say that my marriage is the most important thing in my life, my work is crucial to my life and my energy and I probably have more energy around work than around almost anything else. I think right now it would be very hard for me to live without my work. It feeds me, it defines who I am, but not in the way that his work does."

So you would say that your marriage is the most important thing?

"Absolutely. They feed into each other, the work, especially since I have my own business now, is very much a part of my life, and my husband is a part of my work and my life and knows my clients, but I would say that if I were given the awful choice of choosing the one over the other, my husband is really my life, my love."

How does he feel about your work?

"He loves my work."

He's an artist, right?

"A painter."

He's been supportive?

"He's more than supportive, he's very much a part of it. He's a voice of reason, he's an anchor, he straightens me out about it, he reads with me, he's an amazing support."

Do you feel like you can do that with his painting?

"I think it's different in his painting, I think painting is a more solitary activity. I think he values my judgment in his painting. I have to be very conscious of giving him the time without him feeling like he has to grab it, because my work is so overwhelming and overpowering in the house, and I'm very selfish about what I need from him in support both in our daily life and in my work that sometimes I feel that I'm not supportive enough of him and his work. I think he would disagree with that, I think he thinks of me as being very supportive of his work and I am, but sometimes I feel selfish in that I take him away from it."

Then you don't think he feels that way? Do you talk about it?

"Yeah, and when he does feel that I am he's got to pull back and take the time for himself. But for the most part it works out fine. I think I'm also the most important thing in his life so we work it out and ... he doesn't finish a painting until I've seen it, he doesn't feel that a painting is finished until I've looked at it and talked to him about it. So in that way it doesn't mean he agrees with everything I say about the work but he thinks I'm vital to his work."

So, while Lilli and her husband have very different and demanding professional lives, the time they spend together is often mutually focused on one another's work. But togetherness *is* sometimes foreground, they often work at home together and Lilli says that what she most enjoys is simply spending most of her time with David. Because of their supportive styles, their separate work enhances an already devoted relationship.

The parallel form involves a relationship with two highly individualistic people who both pour the major share of their energy into their work or creative pursuits. While the energies of the two may be on parallel tracks, this does not preclude their being deeply attached to one another. It does mean that their individual focus is substantially more directed to work than to the relationship. Two people in a parallel relationship may be Creative Integrative or High Creative, or they may be some combination of High Creative and relational. What characterizes this relationship style is a high degree and frequency of separateness, a great deal of time spent alone, entirely different areas of concern and interest. It's a typical form of relatedness in demanding two-career partnerships, and a typical style in the kind of urban environment that Lilli Cohen works in.

The parallel structure does not suggest that two people are less dependent on relationship to meet deep emotional needs. It simply suggests that the couple prefer a high degree of autonomy and separateness and that their connection is more background, the work more foreground. Nevertheless the relationship may serve a supportive, stabilizing function—it may constitute its own form of passion.

Think back to Monica McGoldrick in chapter 7. Hers is a marriage that is a supportive/parallel blend. She and her husband are less involved with each other's work than Lilli and David. One of the deepest values to her in her relationship is that her husband "leaves her alone" to pursue her career. While to some, being "left alone" might not feel like support, Monica translates it that way. She equally gives Sophocles the space to pursue his own interests. Support can refer to "taking care of" details for the other, putting oneself aside at times to take on more child rearing or household tasks, or it can mean hiring someone else to take care of the details and providing unqualified emotional support, acceptance, and encouragement.

But Monica's relationship style shifts between supportive and parallel. While they cooperate and support one another, their visions aren't shared. The relationship is critical to both, but is more background than foreground as a broad base from which each organizes his or her creative life. When parallel couples have children, it's often the tasks of child rearing and family ritual that provide a point of connection and cooperation.

The disadvantage of the collaborative or supportive styles is a tendency for individuality to become blurred at times. Togetherness creates great potential for conflict and the need to distance emotionally to feel separate at all. The disadvantage of the parallel style is that two people function so autonomously that they may easily drift apart and fail to attend to the care of relationship. While couples in supportive or collaborative relationships may have to work to define areas of separateness more clearly, parallel couples need to attend more to being together.

The point in discussing these varied types of relationship is that women and men have been challenged more and more in their current lives to reconstitute their relationships in ways that make more sense for them and in ways that incorporate the generative as well as the relational aspects of love. The fit of a relationship is all-important to the well-being not only of the couple but of the family they may ultimately raise. Some couples resolve the need for relational contact by collaborating, some by adopting an involved, supportive stance, and some by creating space for more parallel work interests while cooperating and connecting around some point of mutual need and interest. The creation of a relational form that fits assumes a basic equality and mutual valuing of the needs and interests of both partners. The form of the relationship doesn't constitute a commentary on how passionately involved two people are—it simply comments on the ways that they've chosen to blend their separateness with relatedness.

Gertrude and Alice: The Complementary Couple

There is one other potential form of passionate relatedness.

It's a complex and difficult one because it intrinsically contains the seeds of its own destruction. It's the form most likely to fit for a Lover or the combination of a Lover and an Artist, a Lover and an Innovator. One of the most famous examples of it is the Gertrude Stein–Alice B. Toklas relationship. Alice herself described the nature of the relationship perfectly: "All Gertrude had to do was be a genius." Alice did everything else.[7]

A more modern version is the relationship where the one partner in a couple is either a busy professional, a businessperson, an artist, or a corporate employee. The other partner adopts a completely complementary stance in that his or her sole role is to complement and maintain the other's occupational and emotional life.

We call this the *complementary* type of relationship. It differs from the supportive form in that the one partner willingly agrees to make the other's work and interests central and the focus of his or her own creative energy. In the supportive pattern, each partner's work is central to himself and the larger context for the relationship is one of mutual support.

The danger in this pattern is that women in particular may adopt it because they haven't clearly defined their own needs and interests. The magnetism and energy of their partner becomes a compelling distraction from themselves. Or they may view their role as a way of conforming to the traditional "love story" of the culture. Often the relationship may become a statement of a woman's sense that she has no value herself. If one doesn't subordinate herself totally to the needs of a partner, she may do it with her children. All too often, the complementary form can become simply another name for what is really a traditional marriage.

But for some women, the complementary relationship becomes a choice that can be highly fulfilling and creative, so long as it is a clear choice. It may be a choice for a specific phase of a relationship. It suggests that two people have a joint vision or goal that can best be served by the one fully supporting the other because he or she has the skills to achieve it if freed from other constraints. The success of this type of relationship depends on the mutual acknowledgment by both of the sacrifices the more subordinate partner makes. It depends on an attitude of complete equality between the partners and an appreciation of the value of the accommodator's contributions by *both* the partner and the woman herself. Given these optimal conditions, this form of relatedness can be extremely powerful and alive as two people move toward a mutual goal with each playing the part they're most skilled at.

The complementary form of relationship can also serve the creative passions of women if the quid pro quo, or relational bargain, is an exchange of economic support for the freedom to create an emotional environment that serves as setting for the relationship. Many women have a passion for form and beauty, and they may express this passion in the creation of the home. Cooking, the arrangement of the foods on the plate, the setting of the table, the creation of an ambience, for some women are pleasurable creative activities, not tedious chores. The passion for aesthetic form may express itself in gardening, flower arranging, decorating, designing. Women have also been the keepers of rituals, the forms that ease life's transitions.

Often, historically, women used their homes as a setting for passionate connection of ideas, emotions, art, and people. What man in history has ever brought together the intellectual and literary salons of Mabel Dodge Luhan or Gertrude Stein?[8]

Creating an environment has often been a woman's artistic statement. If the complementary form allows her to do this, if her talents and energies are acknowledged and she takes on this role as a choice, she may be an artist creating a life, not just a Smiling Woman being an object. Some women manage both their home and their partner's businesses as well. The role is enjoyable and empowering. The question remains, however, to what degree a man would be likely to be a part of a complementary relationship in the role that is typically the woman's? When the concept of a "househusband" becomes more an acceptable form of the complementary relational style, this particular form will have achieved a real function in society that is free from the constraints of power imbalance and devaluation.

FAMOUS COUPLES

When we look for models of relational styles, we inevitably think of famous couples and the forms they choose. Much of our preoccupation with the famous has to do with our need to compare and contrast our own lives—to dream about forms we think we can't create for ourselves. The famed relationship between artist Georgia O'Keeffe and photographer Alfred Stieglitz, by our reckoning, might at different points have been collaborative, she the model and support for his photography, he the champion of her work—"at last a woman artist," he was to say.[9] Ultimately the form changed to become more parallel, she at Ghost Ranch in New Mexico or in Taos and Stieglitz at Lake George.

Margaret Mead and Gregory Bateson were collaborative, and ultimately, we think, competitive. The inability to devise a fluid form to accommodate their respective energies led to their divorce. Lillian

Hellman (*The Little Foxes* and *The Children's Hour*) and Dashiell Hammett (*The Thin Man*) were unconventional, unmarried lovers as were Katharine Hepburn and Spencer Tracy, who never divorced his wife. Hellman's relationship shifted back and forth between supportive and parallel. Hepburn and Tracy's was parallel. Elizabeth Taylor and Richard Burton tried to get the form right a number of times, a form to hold both their romantic passion and their passion for theater. Perhaps if their creativity had triumphed over their conventional adherence to marriage as a form they would have gotten it right after all.[10]

COUPLEHOOD, FRIENDSHIP, COMMUNITY

In terms of couples "getting it right" on both a personal and wider social level, we were fascinated by an interview we did on a fall evening in Cambridge, Massachusetts. Jeffrey MacIntyre had gathered his wife, Nancy Miriam Hawley, and four of his best friends, two other couples, to help us experiment with the idea of conducting a joint interview. These couples were not randomly gathered. It happened that each of the women, Paula, Judy, and Nancy, had been original members of the Boston Women's Health Collective and had been instrumental in the publication of the landmark book, *Our Bodies, Ourselves*, a text that had become almost a manifesto for the women's movement in the seventies.[11] Neither was their gathering random in the sense that, without our realizing it, the people we were about to interview constituted a kind of "couple collective."

As a result of their close associations and work on the book, the women in the group had formed a tight friendship network that the husbands ultimately became a part of. Now they spend time together in the summers in their adjoining properties in New Hampshire, and in general are one another's closest friends. After the interview, a pot-luck supper was planned, not an unusual event for this group.

Our interest was in knowing how these women, who had been so passionately involved in a social movement and in producing a major piece of the literature of that movement, had made their relationships work. And more significantly we wanted to know how their partners reacted to them and helped to create a relational fit that worked for themselves.

Of the three couples, Nancy Miriam Hawley and Jeff MacIntyre are perhaps the most collaborative. Both are therapists. They sometimes run therapy groups together and since they share very limited space in their Cambridge townhouse, the use of their one office space must be negotiated and planned. Jeff, in particular, seems to take a certain kind of pride in their capacity to cooperate. As they talk about it, it's clear that their collaboration is a skill that's developed over time in the relationship. That day they had been painting the office waiting room. "She was painting down there, I was painting over her shoulder, sort of a metaphor—just the ease with which we did it and we could keep chatting about other things, and just keep getting the job done, too. Ten years ago we would have bitten each other's heads off."

Nancy and Jeff's discussion comments on the development and flow of a relationship. The demand for flexibility was one of the first relational rules they established. Theirs is a second marriage for Nancy, and at the point when they met and began talking about marriage, Nancy was in the process of finishing work with the collective on *Our Bodies, Ourselves*. "Jeffrey wanted us to get married in the fall. It was really important to have a fall wedding. And I said, I'm involved with this book. I can't be involved in planning a wedding and doing this book and this book has got to be finished first. So we got married in May."

Jeffrey says, "Part of the reason our marriage got delayed is that I was really willing to subsume personal goals to a much greater good. That was very serious for me.

"I have always felt that I can support Nancy's passion because I always keep track of my own. But I go through stages with any issue that we have conflict about or differences about. We'll argue pretty vociferously about it ... but I have always had faith that even as disappointed as I get or as crazy as I get in the middle of conflict, that we can work out different things."

Of the three couples, the most parallel relationship is that between Paula Doress-Worters and Allen Worters, whose work interests are entirely separate. Paula is currently working on her doctorate in community and social psychology. She is a writer and women's health advocate. She has two children. Allen is an engineer. This is a second marriage for both. "Allen was very supportive of my work. It wasn't something that was in the way.... It kind of intrigued him that I had interesting work and that I had a life of my own. His biggest worry at the time was that I didn't need anybody—that I didn't need him for anything and I had all these friends and I had interesting work..."

Allen says, "Well, I agree that your work was intriguing and part of what helped the relationship to get started, but actually, as much as her work was the fact that I liked instantly every one of her friends— that drew me into the relationship and into the group. For the most part I don't share much in the way of values with the people I work with. I find it dull except in the work itself. So, without Paula I didn't have a whole segment of my life that I wanted to have there."

What Paula and Allen share is the need for relationship and connection with other people. Much of their time together involves contact with family and friends. But their passions for work are very much foreground and parallel. They are a couple who accommodate one another's differences well.

From Judy Norsigian, a partner of the third couple, we learn that Allen plays cello and piano with her on a purely amateur basis. One of Judy's passions is music and she shares it more with Allen than with her husband, Irv Zola. But most of the rest of Judy's creative life is shared with Irv—they have a supportive and often collaborative relationship. They don't share the same jobs but they share similar types of work. Irv is a professor of sociology and Judy still works with the Collective as a health activist and educator. They both write, speak, administer programs, travel together. They also share a unique living arrangement—they're part of a communal home that houses anywhere from twelve to fourteen family and friends at any given time.

Judy says of her relationship with Irv, "I don't think I'd be where I am right now if I didn't have the kind of support and pushing I've had from Irv over the last how many years. . . . He's been great in encouraging me to take time for music or put something else aside that might be an interesting distraction at the moment, but wouldn't serve me well if I looked at the larger picture . . . he's always helped me make time for things like that." Irv says, "We're both administrators and both writers so there are things we can exchange and help one another with." Judy agrees, "I think it's nice. It wouldn't be so terrible if we were in different fields, but there's something very nice about having common ground."

For Irv, as for Allen and Paula, one of the most satisfying parts of his relationship with Judy is the community of friends she brought into his life. "For me, being with Judy reconnected with the best part of my childhood, which was the large extended family and the importance of community. Our wedding was a pot-luck community wedding for four hundred people. And my sense is we've created the extended family community in a house."

The theme of support and collaboration is a dominant one for Judy and Irv. Their shared values involve the importance of close interaction with other people on both a personal and political level. This is a couple whose relationship is enhancing to the creative needs of both because the structure works in a deeply satisfying way.

One of the most notable qualities about these three couples is their interdependence on and intimacy with one another. They truly have formed a unique grouping that includes other couples not present that day, though these three seem to form the nucleus of the group. They share different kinds of time together and different kinds of activities and the relational aspects of their lives are valued and depended on by the men and the women equally. Their children relate to one another and child care is often a shared enterprise.

Allen reflects on the ways this community has been important to him: "Well, what it has done for me positively is that it has allowed me to have more male friends, something I never had before. I can be more emotional with these two guys than I could with anybody else."

Connection to this larger network of friends helps to support and nourish each of these couples. The community can tolerate difference and it can support varying forms of relatedness. There are no myths and stereotypes about how males and females must be. Because they so lovingly support one another's individuality, they gain connection as well. There may be a message for us all in the style of togetherness and community these couples have created.

NEW FORMS FOR THE FUTURE

Judy Lockard, a woman who is single by circumstance, builds an addition on her house so that her disabled mother can live with her. She buys a vacation home with a group of friends. Previously married and divorced, she would rather be partnered but won't compromise her individuality or her relational needs to the expectations of most of the men she has met.

Wilma Keppel, single by circumstance at age thirty, joins a co-housing group.

Extended families return to joint living as they used to in the early decades of the century because economics make it impossible for new couples or young adults to afford their own living space.

Lesbian couples bear or adopt children. Single women bear or adopt children—so do single men. Friends become surrogate fathers, uncles, aunts.

Families become racially and culturally mixed as couples adopt children, take in foster children, assume the care of disabled children.

In our survey, many women indicate that friendship is the most satisfying relational form for them, and even when married or in partnership, the relationship often most critical to their sense of well-being.

Two women who became friends through meetings at professional conferences make a mid-life career change, move together to a small New England town and open a business together. They are committed to sharing a life and a business, though they are not sexual partners. The one is the "surrogate aunt" of her friends' children. The other's closest love relationship is with a gay man.

For all that the "traditional family" form is touted by politicians and sometimes the media as the solution to the love problems of our society, what is clear is that it is a form that no longer fits for many people as it has been constructed in the past. When it isn't a fit, it doesn't serve the needs of children, who often suffer from a couple's misguided choices.

Critics of the retreat from family values point to the trend toward individualism in our society as the cause of the breakdown of family responsibility. Yet the larger trend may not involve individualism so much as the search for new forms of relatedness, a creative process of breaking down the old to replace it with something new. Critics of nontraditional relationship forms very rarely acknowledge the ways that imbalances of power and the structure of our assumptions about love made the family a very inhospitable arrangement, particularly for women, especially for children. Another question is, why shouldn't there be room for the individual in our culture? Being "single" or being focused on one's individual needs does not automatically mean one is either nonrelational, nonresponsible, and especially not unloving. It is only our outworn conceptions of the nature of "love" that leave the single, uncoupled, or differently coupled person in this society feeling like a pariah.

What we call the breakdown of the family in this society really represents the search for relational forms that make sense, that are a true fit for all concerned. As the love story in our culture changes, we need to find new ways to raise and support children and to support ourselves and one another. One form, the traditional heterosexual white middle-class marriage, can't work for all of us, particularly not as we become a more racially, culturally, and sexually diverse population.

FINAL NOTES ON PASSIONATE PATTERNS

The litmus test for any relationship is the aliveness and wholeness of its partners. It assumes not the absence of any conflict, change, disruption, but rather the ability to adapt to change flexibly, the assumption that the needs of both partners are equally important and must be addressed. The nonpassionate relationship becomes deadened by an absence of "fit." Which is to say that many of the multitude of problems experienced by modern couples could be circumvented by their making conscious choices about what *form* of relationship works best for them.

In order to do this, we need to know ourselves and we need to know we have creative choices. We need to assume that relatedness does not require us to be less subjects or to have less agency, but rather, in fact, that the success of relationship requires us to assume more power to define the shape of our relational lives.

CHAPTER FOURTEEN

The Courage to Be Alive

> *Renew your energy*
> *reclaim your fire*
> *And seize the power*
> *of your heart's desire*
> *Rebuild your vision, restore your soul*
> *Transform the part, and you'll transform the whole.*
> FROM *THE FAT OPERA*, LYRICS BY JO-ANN
> KRESTAN, MUSIC BY BETH ANDERSON

PASSION, LOVE, CREATIVE EXPRESSION—we've been making the case that these energies are the essence of our lives. It has been our premise that to live fully, meaningfully, we need to find better access to the power to create, to share our vision, to feel deeply. We need to overcome the cultural stories that imprison us, the divisions in our images of ourselves that lead us to believe falsely that we can love but we can't create. We need to reclaim our early loves, to find the continuity and through-line of our lives. We need to pick up the violin again and play, to find the chord that resonates in our hearts and sing.

The forms that we choose for our lives are critical. If the form is a good fit, whether in relationship, career, or artistic expression, passion will flow. If it's not, we need to find the courage to make alterations and adjustments. A small alteration can result in a very major change in the flow of energy in our lives.

As important as form is the language that we use to describe our experience. Language shapes our vision. Our view of ourselves has been blurred because in the past when we've thought of "love" our associations have been limited to words and phrases like "mother," self-sacrifice, lust, desire, giving up, selflessness, love "object," us or them. As we lift the cultural blinders from our language, we can see love as a broader, more complex energy with varying forms and expressions. A new language for love might include words like "lover," passion, empathy, attention, compassion, care, commitment, delight, us *and* them, connectedness.

This language is active, it suggests that we love as *subjects*, that we define the forms and varieties of our loving behavior. We have impact on the world around us that involves more than our biological role as bearers, nurturers, and caretakers. We know love as a mutual experience and we can expect others to support our dreams as much as we support theirs.

When we love as subjects, we are being creative. When we create as subjects, we're being loving. The old language for creativity confined us to ideas like artistic, poetic, talented, problem solver, insightful, driven to a goal. A new language for creativity includes words like generative, authentic, expressive, transcendent, transformational, in process, joyous, alive. Singer Susan Osborn says of creativity, "It's the thing that's moving from the inside that can't be denied." She says that when we have the tools to make creative choices, then that inner imperative has a place to move.[1] When we are creative, our inner imperatives can move ourselves and the world to change.

WHERE WE STAND NOW

We're left with a final question—where do women stand now, at this period in history? Are we coming into our own? Are we finding workable forms for our lives? Do we *believe* that it is critical to our own happiness and well-being to pursue our passions? Have we gained any standing in the world, or, like Lily Briscoe, do we struggle to articulate, "this is what I see, this is what I see,"[2] while we wait for somebody to notice? Are we waiting for a sense of our own value and energy to emerge only after love comes along, after the children leave home, after we go back to school, after it is validated and confirmed by someone else? Are we cutting off from love out of fear that we'll lose ourselves to the power of the old story?

The stories of the women in this book describe a transformation in progress. Whether Lovers, Leaders, Innovators, or Artists, we are beginning collectively and personally to give voice to our own stories, to experience the power of creative expression, the power of choosing the forms that fit our passions best. And in the larger cultural community there is beginning to be some small recognition and respect granted to women as creators with a valuable vision and undeniable power.

A case in point: On the front page of an August 1992 "Arts and Leisure" section in the Sunday *New York Times*, a headline reads, "Louise Bourgeois Comes into Her Own at Eighty." Bourgeois, an artist and sculptor mentioned earlier (chapter 2), has been chosen to represent the United States at the Venice Biennale. Her sculpture was recently featured in two major art surveys. The Guggenheim included her work in an exhibition alongside that of Brancusi, Kandinsky, and other male artists.[3]

At eighty, Bourgeois's success is a commentary on the increasing attention being paid to women artists. Recognition of her work is especially notable because that work has embraced as its themes all the issues that have so relegated women to the status of "women artists." Her work deals with the body, sexuality, gender, anxiety, death, loneliness, and has been described as expressing what is called an "unrestrained emotionalism." Bourgeois's whole artistic life has been involved with commenting on dichotomies and splits: "My goal is to find equilibrium between extremes, a sense of balance. . . . I feel the ambivalence in everything and it is frightening so I try to deal with it through my work . . . I try to visualize it and express the fragile center between extremes." Of the fact that recognition has come finally so late in her life she says, "It could have come earlier, but it's better than nothing at all."[4]

The context in which women are viewed and valued is certainly changing and our creativity is more in evidence and more valued than it ever has been. But we have to be ever vigilant—the split image and symptoms of "backlash" still influence our thinking about ourselves.

In earlier decades the exceptional women who made it in the mainstream acted as lightning rods for male ambivalence about women. They still do. It was 1939 when a male critic faulted Lillian Hellman for the "generic female inability" to master an "economy of emotion."[5] It was in 1946 when a male critic wrote of Louise Nevelson's first major exhibition in New York, "We learned the artist was a woman, in time to check our enthusiasm. Had it been otherwise, we might have hailed these sculptural expressions as by surely a great figure among the moderns." Nevelson did not exhibit in the galleries for ten years after this.[6] And it was in the 1970s that Holly Near, a couple of years before she performed for a sold-out audience at Carnegie Hall, was assured by record companies that she would never be a commercial success because her "voice had no element of *submission* (emphasis ours)."[7]

In the domain of love, women have been freed to lead larger lives, to be generative, to be workers. But politically, the conservative right tells us that what we need is a return to "Family Values"—which really means to return women to their traditional roles as caretakers, not creators. Women's roles remain burdened by the multiple responsibilities they're expected to assume. Our ideas about love are as confused as ever.

When we look at where we stand, the story is good and the story is bad, or at least complex and incomplete. It speaks again to a dialectical process and it points to the fact that whenever women set out to change, our personal adjustments always have larger political implications. When we set out to change the forms of our lives, we both struggle with and have impact on the larger world around us. We search for models to serve as guides to our change, but really we become the models, the answers we seek emerge in the form of our own process of change.

LOOKING TO THE FUTURE: PASSIONATE CONVICTION

Changing the forms of our lives is both a personal and a political statement. What moves us individually can't be separated from what moves us collectively. We are part of a larger whole. We know that forms of relatedness need to change on a more global level, because when we look around at the current state of the world we see the devastating impact of unworkable ways of living together in community and conducting the business of the world. We continue to be at war, with our environment, with other nations because they differ from us, with other classes and races. Men still devalue women. Human beings continue to experience violence and oppression, hunger, suffering that is unnecessary. The rich thrive, the poor become more disenfranchised. There is little justice, fairness, or equality even though we claim to believe in these ideals, take them for granted even, though they don't operate in reality.

Change grows from belief—the forms of our lives take shape in response to our sense of personal conviction. All of the women we spoke with, whether they were more relational or more creative in their basic energy, seemed to operate on some system of personal belief that directed their actions. Even in the *New York Times* article on Louise Bourgeois, belief emerged as a critical part of the ethos of her work. Some of her recent illustrations depict an image of a broken plant with a new stem growing out of the break. She says about it, "You destroy things or people and you feel sorry and you try to repair things. To me this repair becomes a source of great pleasure—to be able to heal."[8]

For Bourgeois, art is the form through which she expresses her deepest beliefs. For others of us, the choices by which we shape our lives become our most meaningful and creative expressions of conviction. We think of Frances Peabody who has championed so many causes throughout her life, who transcends any thought of difference, judgment, us versus them, by working passionately for the AIDS Coalition. We think of Paulette Hines who knew the pain of discrimination against herself but who now works for the well-being of all people who have to face adversity and pain.

Ann Ehringhaus, whose story opened this book, has passionate beliefs about healing and health. When we asked her where that conviction came from, she said, "It came from my whole life of working with people and wanting to make a difference . . . and that came from my parents. Both my father and mother are very committed to community and to other people. Our dinner time conversation centered around topics like, 'Ann, what are your feelings about personal good versus the public good?' This was when I was in the ninth and tenth grade and I thought to myself, I've been to my friend Leslie's house and they don't talk about this stuff. But my parents' message fell on fertile soil in me."

These stories point out the inaccuracy of what has become a pervasive indictment of women who embrace creative work as being too individualistic and self-oriented. Talk of "the New Familism" said to be emerging in our culture tells us "there is a shift away from an ethos of expressive individuality toward an ethos of family obligation and commitment."[9] The suggestion is that a woman's choice for individual expression automatically leads her to be more self-involved, less committed and loving. Our interviews don't substantiate this view. Women who thoughtfully make choices about their lives and seek to give expression to what is deepest in them tend to be stronger in their conviction that what is personal must take them into the larger world of involvement with others.

CRITICAL CONVICTION: "FINDING THE FRAGILE CENTER BETWEEN EXTREMES"

The synthesis of conviction and creativity leads to transformation. If the route to reclaiming passion for women begins with overcoming the sense of being split within themselves, then the route to changing forms on a more global level involves overcoming the splits that mar our beliefs, our thinking, our attitudes on all levels. Again, as Bourgeois says, "I feel the ambivalence in everything and it is frightening, and so I try to deal with it through my work, I try to visualize it and to express the fragile center between extremes."[10] Perhaps it is only the Artist, as we've said in chapter 6, who feels the pain of the world deeply enough to articulate it clearly, and who lives enough at the extremes of experience to overcome them.

We are a world awash in dichotomies, differences, splits and polarizations. We think in terms of male/female, adult/child, black/white, old/young, rich/poor, us/them, gay/straight, good/bad, right/wrong, weak/strong. We have to wonder whether these divisions are real, or whether, like the split in women's identities between creativity and love, the splits, the extremes, are created ones—created by the ways we are taught to think about our experience. Doesn't a real vision of wholeness contain and neutralize all extremes?

As we creatively evolve new forms for expressing our deepest convictions, we ultimately overcome and transcend these divisions.

To create means to transcend extremes, to take what seems separate and distinct and blend it into some new whole. The creative thrust of our current thinking needs to move toward seeing the likeness rather than the difference in all of us. We may be multicultural, multiracial, multisexual, multinational, but the larger context of our experience, our emotional responses to a life that is sometimes joyful, sometimes painful, always difficult and challenging, are more alike than different. If we acknowledge sameness, then we cannot elevate some groups of people at the expense of others. We cannot kill and we cannot hate because in hating the other, we will ultimately know that we hate ourselves.

If we acknowledge sameness, then one of the most polarized areas of our experience, the subject of the supposed "essential differences" of the sexes, will become less of an emotional and political battleground. Both men and women will be assumed to be responsible for care and creativity. Our political and economic structures will have to change to reflect this shift. And on a more broadly political level, we will stop devaluing feeling. When we can all own the capacity for love, passion, caring, emotionality, we will have less need for violence, and we will all have a greater stake in the protection of the vulnerable, the needy, ourselves. Just as the woman who overcomes her own sense of dividedness becomes more subject and more empowered to direct her own life, when we stop thinking in terms of differences and divisions, we can proceed with more wholeness toward a world view that respects both individuality and community, love for self and love for other.

When the San Francisco earthquake or Hurricane Andrew calls up our deepest empathy but the Colombian earthquake is a note on a newspaper page, when the homeless shiver under cardboard on our city streets while the summer houses of the rich are boarded up in winter, we must begin to notice, take these dichotomies into our hearts, feel the sameness of human suffering, recognize the total capriciousness of what we think of as national borders and know there are no national borders to pain, no real split, no real essential differences. We must be the man without work in Detroit, the woman in corporate management wondering if she is a real woman because she has no child, the father raising his son alone after a bitter divorce and questioning what story to tell his son of manhood, never having known his own father. We must know that we are the other and they are us. We must know that the planet we destroy is our own nest that we foul, and that when we hold our old cat in our arms as she gets the final shot that eases her passage from life, that we also hold that same life and death power over all the helpless of the earth. We must dissolve dichotomies and say with the Zen master: "I am the leaf, the cloud, the stone."[11]

CREATIVITY: IMAGINING ANGELS

Creativity, like love, allows us to rise above the constraints of the daily and the mundane, to see beyond the tragic and the defeating energies in our lives. It allows us to transcend and to make meaning of what might otherwise seem senseless. Ann Ehringhaus learned this early in her life. She says, "After four or five years of teaching, I realized that there are a lot of people who need help, so I started to do counseling. But then I realized through teaching photography to some of those people that having a creative outlet was more positive, and that I wasn't going to be able to solve their problems for them through counseling anyhow. I saw that, involved with creativity, people had a different understanding of themselves and their problems and they made something new happen. And the something new that happened was maybe more exciting in a way, just the fact that it was new, just the fact that they had made it. In terms of photography, it is a tangible product that we could put up on a wall at school and, you know, the most hard-core kid in the school has made this beautiful picture of a tree in bloom outside. I saw people get in touch with other parts of themselves that did not have a legitimate avenue of expression in their current lives. And their current lives, in a lot of cases, were dismal, really dismal. It seemed that through the art of photography they could change . . . if reality wasn't so hot, imagination was terrific, there was freedom in imagination and in creativity. . . . And I could give these kids access to another part of themselves where they could at least begin to have a vision. They could experience something different in them that could lead them somewhere else."

Passion, and the creative expression of it, can lead us many places, most notably to a deeper appreciation and awareness of ourselves. But staying alive to ourselves in the face of sometimes "dismal" life circumstances takes courage, commitment, conviction. We need to believe in our need for, and our right to, creative expression. And we need help to tap this energy, so we must provide it for one another by serving as models, guides, fellow singers in the chorus of change.

There is no denying that life is often inexplicably unfair and tragic. What we have is choice. We can choose to deaden ourselves to life in the present moment in our fear of physical death. Or, we can say with Ernest Becker, "The most that any one of us can seem to do is to fashion something—an object or ourselves—and drop it into the confusion, make an offering of it, so to speak, to the life force."[12]

Beth Anderson, a friend and composer who persistently pursues her musical career in spite of financial hardship and the relentless disappointments that are also part of creative work, has written a hauntingly beautiful operatic piece called "The Angel." The lyrics tell the story of the death of a child. In the program notes Anderson says, "The music is primarily tonal, and includes an old-time hymn, a little bit of fugue and a lot of angelic flying music. It's a story about the transformation of feelings and experience, no matter how brutal, into bliss. It's a story about the interconnectedness of all of our lives, the story within the story, about the simplicity of miracles and the complications of daily life, about the possibility of multiple realities and the reality of life after death, or rebirth and the rewards for a life bravely lived."[13]

Music is Beth's passion. Though it has not provided her with an easy life, pursuing that passion has made her alive. When her work is performed, when she makes her "offering to the life force," we all benefit from that aliveness and we know that someone else searches for meaning just as we do and we feel connected and moved. Passion moves within us all, and when we express that energy, when we raise our voices, sing at the top of our lungs, the world moves too.

Appendix: Questionnaire, Survey, and Data on Love and Creativity

QUESTIONNAIRE ON LOVE AND CREATIVITY

Name (optional): _____

Address: _____

Phone and best time to reach you: _____

Age: _____

Occupation: _____

Education: _____

Ethnic Background: _____

Relationship Status: _____

Children: _____

Please answer the questions quickly. In general, your first response is of the most interest to us. If there is more than one answer to a question please give us the answer that seems most generally true or feel free to elaborate. Say as much as you wish in response to any question that engages you—use the back or a blank sheet of paper for more space.

You are participating in a survey designed to help us understand the vital passions of women, their connections to themselves and to others, and the kindred themes of love and creativity.

1. Are you in love right now? _____

2. Have you ever been? _____

3. Can you describe how you experience yourself when you're in love?
   _____

4. How important is it to you to feel love for another person? _____

5. How important is it to you to feel loved? _____

6. What kind of love makes you feel most yourself, most alive? (e.g.,
   friendship, children, erotic, etc.) _____

7. Are you often aware of feeling love? _____

8. At what period in your life were your feelings of love most intense?
   young child   __
   adolescent   __
   young adult   __
   other (specify)   __

9. How have your ideas about love changed over time? _____

10. Do you feel more yourself or less yourself when you're in love? ____

11. Have you experienced the loss of a love, or the giving up of a love?
    Please tell us about it. _____

12. Do you often tell people that you love them? _____

13. Do you often talk about love as a subject? _____

14. Are you often aware of feeling love? _____

15. What is your first memory of feeling love? _____

16. Do you remember your first love? What happened? _____

17. What activity or situation makes you feel most alive, most involved,
    most engaged? _____

18. As a child, did you have a vision of something you would do or be?
    What was it? _____

19. How did the dream change over time? When did it change? What is it now? _____

20. What moments of your life do you remember as ones when you were most alive and committed? _____

21. How have you nourished or abandoned those moments, those activities, those relationships, those passions? _____
    a. If nourished, who supported you? _____
    b. If abandoned, what constraints got in the way? _____

22. What activity or experience makes you feel most focused in the present moment? _____

23. When do you feel you most express who you are? _____

24. Would you call that form of self-expression a passion? _____

25. Is that passion connected to a passion from your past? If so, how? If not, how is it different? _____

26. What gets in the way of your feeling connected to yourself? _____

27. What gets in the way of your feeling connected to the significant others in your life? _____

28. What helps you feel most connected to yourself? _____

29. What helps you to feel most connected to significant others? _____

30. Are there surefire shortcuts to those connections—e.g., music? Time alone? With self or others? Please explain. Do you make use of them often? If not, why not? _____

31. Did any practical concerns stop you from acting on a love? Or a creative dream? What were they? _____

32. What would you give up for love? _____

33. What would you sacrifice for a creative dream? _____

34. Do you consider that you suffered from any addictions? _____

35. Are you in recovery? Which? _____

36. Do you tell yourself a story about why you don't have the time for love? For self-expression? What is it? _____

37. What messages from others were most crucial in determining your choices and commitments about love? About creativity? Who were those others? _____

38. If we were to interview three other persons who have affected your choices the most, who would they be? _____

39. What do you value in life? _____

40. Do you consider that you have any kind of spiritual practice? _____

41. What choices have you made for love? _____

42. What choices have you made for "art"? _____

43. Do you think of yourself as a passionate person? _____

44. Were you more passionate at any other point in your life than you are now? When? What happened? _____

45. What convictions do you feel passionate about? Have they changed over time? _____

46. Have you retrieved/regained a lost connection to a passion of any sort? How and what? _____

47. What questions would you like us to ask other women above love or about self-expression? _____

DEMOGRAPHICS: QUESTIONNAIRE

Total Responses: 39

EDUCATION

H.S. Graduate	1
Some College	7
Coll. Degree	13
Some Graduate	1
Grad. Degree	15

RELIGION

Protestant	7
Catholic	5
Jewish	5
Buddhist	1
Unknown	21

ETHNIC

Russ/Amer	1
Amer/Ir/Germ	2
Anglo	20
Ir/Ital	2
Jewish	5
French	1
Polish	2
Hispanic	1
Unknown	5

GEOGRAPHIC DISTRIBUTION

N/NEast	17
S/SEast	6
Cen/MWest	2
N/NWest	1
W/SWest	4
Unknown	9
Urban	20
Rural	10

OCCUPATION

Counselor/Therapist	12
Teacher	5
Computer Specialist	2
Waitress	1
Photographer	1
Journalist	1
Realtor	1
Student	5
Dog Breeder	1
Housewife	1
Admin. Asst.	1
Production Mgr.	1
Nurse	2
EPA Professional	1
Clinical Asst.	1
Consultant	1
Political Exec.	1
Carpenter	1

RELATIONSHIP STATUS/CHILDREN

	Married	Have Kids	Single	Divorced	Separated	Lesbian
Artists (8 of 39)	1	1	6			1
Leaders & Innovators (24 of 39)	9	12	8	3	1	3
Lovers (6 of 39)	5	4	1			

AGE BREAKDOWN

	10–19	20–29	30–39	40–49	50–59	60–69	70–79	80–89	Total
Artists		1	3	4					
Leaders & Innovators	1	6	3	10	3	1			
Lovers		1	2	1	2				

SURVEY ON LOVE AND CREATIVITY

Age: _____

Occupation: _____

Education: _____

Ethnic origin: _____

Relationship status: **S   M   D   W   OTHER** _____

Religious affiliation: _____

Birthplace: _____

Current geographical area: _____

Urban _____ or Rural _____

How many: brothers _____ sisters _____

Position in family (i.e., youngest girl, middle, between two brothers, etc.):

_____

Are you currently in a twelve-step program? **Y N** Which? _____

Are you currently in therapy? _____

Do you have children? **Y N**

You are participating in a survey designed to explore the interplay between love and creativity in women's lives. By love we refer to caring feeling for the significant people and interests in your life. By creativity we refer to many different forms of self-expression that can emerge as hobbies, artistic work, career. Creativity suggests an individual statement that uniquely expresses you and your approach to life.

Please circle the response that *most* reflects your feelings. Some questions permit but do not require more than one response. Feel free to add comments. Thank you.

1. How would you characterize the current story of love in your life?

    a. Love lost

    b. Love hoped for but not attained

    c. Love that you were afraid to risk for

    d. Love destroyed by others

    e. Love conflicted

    f. Love fulfilled

    g. Other _____

2. How would you characterize the story of the love that has most affected you in your life?

    a. Love lost

    b. Love hoped for but not attained

    c. Love that you were afraid to risk for

    d. Love destroyed by others

    e. Love conflicted

    f. Love fulfilled

    g. Other _____

3. Which feelings *most* characterize your experience when you feel love for someone? Choose up to three.

    a. Vulnerability/openness

    b. Knowing and being known

    c. Intense physical attraction

    d. Excitement/sense of possibility

    e. Aliveness

    f. Protectiveness

    g. Deep empathy

h. Acceptance

i. Giving/self-sacrificing

j. Other _____

4. How do you know it when you are loved?

a. I feel accepted and understood

b. I have a sense of safety/security

c. I know it when someone tells me often/expresses affection

d. I know it when someone does a lot for me

e. I have a basic sense of being valued

f. Other _____

5. How do you feel when you are deprived of love?

a. Alone and isolated

b. Like something's wrong with me

c. Empty

d. Incomplete

e. Not connected to myself

f. Fine—I feel love for myself

g. Other _____

6. In what relationship do or did you experience the most love *from* someone?

a. Spouse or romantic partner

b. A love from the past

c. Children

d. Parents

e. Friends

f. Siblings

g. Pet

h. Other _____

7. In what situation have you experienced or do you experience the greatest love *for* someone? Choose up to three answers and please number them in order of importance.

    a.   Love of a romantic partner/spouse

    b.   Love of a child

    c.   Love of parents

    d.   Love of siblings

    e.   Love of friends

    f.   Love of an activity or interest

    g.   Love of your home

    h.   Love of animals

    i.   Love of work

    j.   Other _____

8. What experience do you think of first when you think of "love"?

    a.   Passionate feeling

    b.   Passionate sex

    c.   Parenting

    d.   Service to others

    e.   Spirituality

    f.   Love of certain experiences or activities

    g.   Aesthetic pleasure

    h.   Friendship

    i.   Other _____

9. In your family how often did people express love verbally or physically?

    a.   Frequently

    b.   Sometimes

    c.   Almost never

    d.   Other _____

10. Which loves have been most fulfilling/satisfying?

    a.   Partner/spouse

    b.   Child

    c.   Parents

    d.   Siblings

    e.   Friends

f. Activity or interest

g. Home

h. Pet

i. Work

j. Religion

k. Other _____

11. Which loves have been most disappointing?

a. Partner/spouse

b. Child

c. Parents

d. Siblings

e. Friends

f. Activity or interest

g. Home

h. Pet

i. Work

j. Religion

k. Other _____

12. How often do you talk about or express love for others?

a. Frequently

b. Sometimes

c. Never

d. Other _____

13. What factor is most important in a marriage/intimate partnership? (choose two)

a. Passionate feeling

b. Sexual compatibility

c. Sense of security (choose one)

(1) emotional

(2) financial

(3) loyalty

d. Friendship

e. Trust/sense of acceptance

f. Willingness to have children

g. Nurturing

h. Common interests

i. Common values

j. Other _____

14. At what period in your life were your feelings of love most intense?

a. Young child

b. Adolescent

c. Young adult (up to 30)

d. Mid-life (30–60)

e. Beyond 60

Comment? _____

15. Can you describe in a phrase or a sentence how your feelings of love have changed over time _____

_____

_____

16. Did any practical concerns ever stop you from pursuing a love relationship?

a. Yes (why?) _____

b. No (why?) _____

17. As a child, what dreams or fantasies did you have about what you would do with your life?

a. Dreamed I would be a _____

b. Dreamed of being happily married with children

c. Dreamed of doing good for others

d. Dreamed of being rich and/or famous

e. Dreamed of having a passionate love relationship

f. Dreamed of a life of travel and excitement

g. Dreamed of being successful/accomplished in the workplace

h. Other _____

18. Did any practical concerns stop you from acting on this dream?

    a. Wasn't practical (time, money, etc.)

    b. Women didn't do this kind of thing

    c. Family discouraged me

    d. Feared I didn't have talent

    e. Relationships became more important

    f. I pursued my dream

    g. Other _____

19. As a child, did you have a talent or a creative outlet that you later gave up?

    a. Yes (what?) _____

        _____

    b. No

    If Yes: What factors caused you to give it up?

    a. Not enough talent

    b. Not enough money to pursue it

    c. Fear of not being good enough

    d. Lack of support

    e. Didn't take it seriously

    f. Was actively discouraged

    g. Other things demanded my time—it became less important

    h. Other _____

20. What experience makes life most meaningful for you? You may rank these. Choose two.

    a. Being loving or giving to others

    b. Earning money

    c. Being deeply involved with a cause

    d. Work (what?) _____

    e. Creative activity

    f. Appreciating nature

    g. Spirituality

    h. Other _____

21. What is your preferred form of creative activity?

    a. Craft work (knitting, quilting, needlework, potting, etc.)

    b. Writing

    c. Painting

    d. Performing (music, drama)

    e. Photography

    f. Teaching, counseling

    g. Scientific/academic study

    h. Other _____

22. What factors most block you from pursuing this activity more than you do?

    a. Time

    b. Money
        (1) need to make a living
        (2) not enough money to buy equipment or take lessons

    c. Fear of being inadequate at it

    d. Fear of being selfish—taking too much time from relationships

    e. Lack of support from spouse

    f. Lack of my own "space"

    g. Lack of discipline

    h. Fear of being too obsessed with it

    i. Other _____

23. What do you consider to be the elements of "creative or self-expressive" activity?

    a. It takes me "out of myself"

    b. Self-expression—I express who I am and what I feel

    c. It feels like a loving act . . . something I give to others

    d. A sense of freedom

    e. Pleasure

    f. Other _____

24. Choose the phrase that most describes your feelings about "time"

    a. I have enough of it—I don't think much about it

    b. I don't have enough of it for myself *because* of

        (1) Work

        (2) Focus on family's needs

        (3) Don't set priorities

        (4) Feel guilty if I take it for myself

        (5) Demands of friends

        (6) Volunteer activities

        (7) Other _____

    c. I'm not good at organizing it

    d. If I had more of it, I'd be more creative

    e. I'd like more time to give my partner and children

       Comment _____

25. Some choices we make in life become turning points. They tend to make us feel more whole and in touch with parts of ourselves. Others alienate us from ourselves. Which choices in your life have:

    a. Made you feel most whole?

        (1) Career

        (2) Choices regarding relationships: marriage or romantic partnerships, divorce, remaining single, changing to alternate life-style

        (3) Having children

        (4) Not having children

        (5) Choices regarding extended family

        (6) Choice of community of friends

        (7) Geographical location

        (8) Pursuit of a creative activity

        (9) Giving up of a creative activity

        (10) Spiritual choices

        (11) Other _____

    b.   Made you feel most alienated and conflicted within yourself?

        (1)   Career

        (2)   Choices regarding relationships: marriage or romantic partnerships, divorce, remaining single, changing to alternate life-style

        (3)   Having children

        (4)   Not having children

        (5)   Choices regarding extended family

        (6)   Choice of community of friends

        (7)   Geographical location

        (8)   Pursuit of a creative activity

        (9)   Giving up of a creative activity

      (10)   Spiritual choices

      (11)   Other

26.   Choose the phrase that most describes the role of money in your life

    a.   I think that if I had more of it I would do more of what I wanted with my life

    b.   Having it has trapped me into continuing the status quo

    c.   It is of less importance to me than time

    d.   I feel conflicted about having it

    e.   It's not my money; my partner earns it and I don't feel that it belongs to me

    f.   Having to earn it blocks me from being more creative

    g.   Other _____

27.   I would describe my relationship with my family of origin (biological family) as primarily

    a.   Totally estranged

    b.   Emotionally cut off (superficial ritual contact but no real personal relationships)

    c.   Close

    d.   Close but with conflict

    e.   Other _____

28. Does the energy you put into relationship

   a. Block creativity/self-expression?

   b. Interrupt creativity/self-expression?

   c. Enhance creativity/self-expression?

   d. Have no impact on creativity/self-expression?

   e: Other _____

29. Does the energy you put into creative work

   a. Make you less available for involvement in important relation-ships?

   b. Cause conflict in your relationships?

   c. Enhance relationships?

   d. Have no impact?

   e. Become something to share in relationships?

   f. Other _____

30. As you envisioned your life growing up, what seemed *most* important?

   a. Marriage or other form of primary relationship

   b. Parenting

   c. Career

   d. Creative work outside of career

   e. All of the above

   f. Other _____

31. Has this idea changed over time?

   a. Yes

   b. No

   c. Comment _____

32. If yes, what seems *most* important now?

   a. Marriage or other form of primary relationship

   b. Parenting

   c. Career

   d. Creative work outside of career

e.   All of the above

f.   Other _____

33.   In general, what moments of your life do you experience as ones when
      you are most alive and engaged?

a.   Creative activity, engaged with a hobby (writing, painting, sculpt-
     ing, etc.)

b.   Physical activity (jogging, hiking, swimming, etc.)

c.   Group discussions (talking with friends, debating political issues,
     etc.)

d.   Performing (acting, singing, dancing, etc.)

e.   Working
     at: _____

f.   Spiritual practice

g.   Parenting

h.   Serving others
     by: _____

i.   Other _____

34.   Do you think of yourself as a passionate person?

a.   Yes

b.   No

c.   Sometimes

35.   What would you name as the passions of your life?

a.   Creative activity/hobbies

b.   Physical activity

c.   Work at: _____

d.   Relationships (friends, family, lovers, etc.)

e.   Performing

f.   Group discussions

g.   Spiritual practice

h.   Parenting

i.   Social service (_____)

j.   Other _____

36. How have you nourished those passions?

    a. Doing them

    b. Reading about them

    c. Teaching them

    d. Thinking about them

    e. Making or saving money to do them

    f. Learning from others

    g. Other _____

37. Who supported you in nourishing these passions?

    a. Spouse

    b. Family

    c. Friends

    d. Lovers

    e. Teachers

    f. Self

    g. Other _____

38. If you have abandoned a passion, what constraints got in the way?

    a. Discouraging messages from those close to me

    b. Too much focus on others' needs

    c. Self-denial

    d. Practical constraints (time, money, space, etc.)

    e. Institutional constraints (discrimination, etc.)

    f. Other _____

39. In what ways do you feel you most express who you are?

    a. Work: _____

    b. Creative activity

    c. Physical activity

    d. In relationships

    e. Group discussions

    f. Performing

g. Spiritual practice

h. Social service

i. Parenting

j. Other _____

40. What connections can you make between the things you feel passionately about?

a. Intuitive connections (you sense a similarity in yourself while doing each thing)

b. Physical connections (each activity uses the same skills)

c. Emotional/mental connections (each activity makes you feel the same: successful, loved, creative, useful, etc.)

d. Other _____

41. Are your current passions connected in any way to things that were important to you earlier in your life? Are they connected to childhood wishes at all?

a. Yes: wishes for success/accomplishment

b. Yes: wishes for acceptance

c. Yes: wishes for love

d. Yes: wishes for self-understanding

e. Yes: other _____

f. No

42. What tends to block you from feeling connected to yourself?

a. Self-doubt/self-judgment

b. Overburdened/overscheduled

c. Guilt

d. Focusing too much on needs of others

e. Poor body image

f. Pressure

g. Lack of solitude

h. Other _____

43. What gets in the way of your feeling connected to the significant others in your life?

  a.   Body image (good/bad)

  b.   Fear (of commitment, abandonment, pain, love, etc.)

  c.   Impatience

  d.   Lack of physical contact (touching, sex, hugging, etc.)

  e.   Lack of communication

  f.   Personal expression (of love, need, etc.) difficulty because of self-doubt

  g.   Lack of trust

  h.   Conflict/competition

  i.   Hurts from the past

  j.   Other _____

44. What helps you feel most connected to yourself?

  a.   Love from others

  b.   Solitude

  c.   Creative activity

  d.   Physical activity

  e.   Sensual activity (sex, masturbation, hot baths, etc.)

  f.   Meditation

  g.   Attending to your own needs

  h.   Other _____

45. What do you feel you need more of in your life?

  a.   More loving connections with others

  b.   More time to pursue creative interests

  c.   More money

  d.   Better connection with myself

  e.   More commitment to social causes

  f.   Other _____

46. What helps you feel most connected to significant others?

  a.   Ritual celebrations

  b.   Talking (both listening and being listened to)

    c.   Honesty

    d.   Touching (sex, hugging, hand-holding, etc.)

    e.   Performing tasks together (work, housekeeping, exercise)

    f.   Playing together

    g.   Other _____

47. Are there surefire shortcuts to feeling reconnected to yourself?

    a.   Yes: music

    b.   Yes: physical activity

    c.   Yes: solitude

    d.   Yes: creative activity

    e.   Yes: time to think

    f.   Yes: time with others

    g.   Yes: other _____

    h.   No

48. Did any practical concerns stop you from acting on a love?

    a.   Yes

    b.   No

    Why? _____

    _____

49. On a creative dream?

    a.   Yes

    b.   No

    Why? _____

    _____

DEMOGRAPHICS: SURVEY

Total Responses: 222

GEOGRAPHIC DISTRIBUTION

Urban =	121
Rural =	85
None =	15
North/Northeast =	116
South/Southeast =	35
Central/Midwest =	20
Northwest =	12
Southwest =	20
Unknown =	19

EDUCATIONAL BACKGROUND

Less than high school	2
High school graduate	44
Some college	45
College	80
Some graduate school	6
Graduate degree	31

RELIGION

Protestant	113
Catholic	42
Jewish	8
Feminist Spiritual	2
None	39
Other	12

ETHNIC

Caucasian	173
Not specified	26
Jewish	6
Italian	6
Hispanic	4
African American	3
Native American	3
Asian	1

AGE BREAKDOWN

	10–19	20–29	30–39	40–49	50–59	60–69	70–79	80–89	Total
Innovators	3	5	3	3	5	2	0	0	21
Artists	0	8	7	9	5	1	0	0	30
Leaders	7	17	21	14	15	6	3	1	84
Lovers	2	25	22	24	8	5	1	0	87
Totals	12	55	53	50	33	14	4	1	222

HAVING CHILDREN

# in Field	Whole Field	Have Kids	Oldest	Middle	Youngest
51 Creative	Innovators & Artists	30 (58%)	12	11	15
171 Relational	Leaders & Lovers	116 (68%)	60	0	47
117 Divergent	Artists & Lovers	78 (66%)	42	18	28
105 Integrative	Leaders & Innovators	68 (65%)	30	19	34
222	Survey	146 (66%)	72	37	62

RELATIONSHIP STATUS*

	Creative Innovators & Artists	% of Total (51 in field)	Relational Lovers & Leaders	% of Total (171 in field)
Married	25	49%	94	55%
Single	16	31%	37	22%
Widowed	2	.04%	6	.035%
Lesbian	2	.04%	0	—
Divorced	2	.04%	25	15%
Separated	1	.02%	5	.03%

* Note these figures are for survey data only and do not include status of women who participated in long interviews.

BREAKDOWN BY OCCUPATION

Traditional Professional:

Teacher	10
Desktop publisher	1
Dietician	1
Software support engineer	1
Systems analyst	1
Computer programmer	2
Child program admin.	1
Retail store owner/mgr.	2
Public relations	1
Business analyst	1
Asst. manager	1
Librarian	3
Accountant	2
Historian	1
Attorney	1
Restaurant owner	1
Buyer	1
Technical app. specialist	1
Newspaper editor	1
Manager pharm. research	1
Banking/finance	5
Social worker	3
Counselor	2
Clin. psychol./therapist	3
Speech/lang. pathologist	2
Pharmacist	1
Pharm/med. info specialist	1
Med. tech. advisor	1
Product safety specialist	1
Dir. arts/culture prog.	1
Nurse manager	1

Total = 55

Traditional Nonprofessional:

Secretary/admin. asst.	18
Nurse	13
Library assistant	1
Salesperson/cashier	9
Dental hygienist	1
Vet. technician	1
Teacher asst./aide	2
Hairdresser	2
Bookkeeper	4
Physical/massage therapist	2
Computer operator	1
Bank teller/processor	2
Medical asst./coordinator	4
Food service	1
Daycare/caregiver	3
Cook	1
Production worker	1
Horticulturist	1
Office clerk	2

Total = 69

Nontraditional Professional:

Minister	5
Innkeeper	1
Writer	2
Floral designer	1
Artist	3
Actor	1
Musician	3
Physician	1
Display designer	1
Interior designer	4
Graphic artist	1
Sculptor	1
Designer/craftsman	1
Dancer/teacher	2
Theater/talent producer	3

Total = 30

Nontraditional Nonprofessional:

Head custodian	1
Auto repair	1

Total = 2

None/not specific:	9
Homemaker/mother:	23
Student:	26
Retired:	6
Unemployed:	2

Notes

A PASSION OF HER OWN

1. Ann Ehringhaus, *Ocracoke Portrait* (Winston-Salem, N.C.: John F. Blair, 1988), ix, xi.
2. Eleanor Munro, *Originals: American Women Artists* (New York: Simon & Schuster, 1979), 26.
3. We particularly recommend the following books by Lucy Lippard: *From the Center: Feminist Essays on Women's Art* (New York: E. P. Dutton, 1976) and *Overlay: Contemporary Art and the Art of Prehistory* (New York: Pantheon Books, 1983). A sense of Lucy's city life was derived in part from her novel, *I See/You Mean* (Los Angeles: Chrysalis Books, 1979).
4. Susan Watrous and Bob Blanchard, "An Interview with Holly Near," *The Progressive*, March 1990.

THE OBJECT OF HIS AFFECTION

1. Virginia Woolf, *To the Lighthouse* (New York: Harcourt, Brace & World, Inc., 1927).
2. Ibid., 77.
3. Ibid., 22.
4. Ibid., 75.
5. For a discussion of this point, see Susan Gubar, "The Blank Page," and Issues of Female Creativity in *The New Feminist Criticism: Essays on Women, Literature and Theory*, Elaine Showalter, ed. (New York: Pantheon Books, 1985).

6. Robert Fritz, *Creating* (New York: Fawcett Columbine, 1991), 15.

7. Ibid., 15–17, 19.

8. Mary Catherine Bateson, *Composing a Life* (New York: The Atlantic Monthly Press, 1989).

9. Bill Moyers, *Creativity with Bill Moyers* [Video recording, 28 min.] (Washington, D.C.: Corporation for Entertainment & Learning, PBS Video, 1989). Originally shown on public television, written, produced, and directed by Janet Roach. "Host Bill Moyers examines how creative, artistic women handle their lives." Interview with Judy Chicago, Benjie Lasso, and Mary Gordon.

10. Ravenna Helson, "Creativity in Women: Outer and Inner Views Over Time," in *Theories of Creativity*, M. A. Runco and R. S. Albert, eds. (Newbury Park: Sage Publications, 1990), 46–47.

11. Jill Kerr Conway, *The Road from Coorain* (New York: Alfred A. Knopf, 1990), 187.

12. Kathy Weingarten, "Consultations to Myself on a Work/Family Dilemma: A Postmodern, Feminist Reflection," *Journal of Feminist Family Therapy* (Binghamton, N.Y.: The Haworth Press, Inc., 1992), vol. 4:1, 3–4.

13. For a more in-depth discussion of aspects of the subject/object split in psychoanalytic and linguistic theory see Rosemary R. Reuther, *New Woman, New Earth: Sexist Ideologies and Human Liberation* (New York: Seabury Press, 1975); Teresa De Lauretis, *Alice Doesn't: Feminism, Semiotics, Cinema* (Bloomington, Ind.: Indiana University Press, 1984); Jessica Benjamin, *The Bonds of Love: Psychoanalysis, Feminism, and the Problem of Domination* (New York: Pantheon Books, 1988); Juliet Mitchell, *Women: The Longest Revolution* (New York: Pantheon Books, 1984); Nancy J. Chodorow, *Feminism and Psychoanalytic Theory* (New Haven: Yale University Press, 1989).

14. This idea is discussed by Deborah Tannen in *You Just Don't Understand: Women and Men in Conversation*, 1st ed. (New York: Morrow, 1990).

15. Nancy J. Chodorow, *Feminism and Psychoanalytic Theory* (New Haven: Yale University Press, 1989), 188.

16. See Carol Gilligan and Eve Stern, "The Riddle of Femininity and the Psychology of Love," in *Passionate Attachments: Thinking about Love*, Willard Gaylin and Ethel Person, eds. (New York: The Free Press, 1988).

17. See the interpretations of Freudian Theory offered by Reuther, Mitchell, Chodorow, Benjamin (cited above) and Juanita Williams in, *Psychology of Women: Behavior in a Biosocial Context* (New York: W. W. Norton & Co., Inc., 1977). See also an excellent review of feminist thinking about Freudian Theory by Phyllis Grosskurth in "The New Psychology of Women," *New York Review of Books*, October 24, 1991.

18. Rosemary R. Reuther, *New Woman, New Earth: Sexist Ideologies and Human Liberation* (New York: Seabury Press, 1975), 145.

19. Juanita Williams, *Psychology of Women: Behavior in a Biosocial Context* (New York: W. W. Norton & Co., Inc., 1977), 10.

20. See Francesca M. Cancian, "The Feminization of Love" in *Signs: Journal of Women in Culture and Society*, vol. 11:4, 1986.

21. For a brief overview of the Object Relations School of Psychoanalytic thought, see Drew Westen, "Psychoanalytic Approaches to Personality" in L. Pervin, ed., *Handbook of Personality Theory and Research* (New York: The Guilford Press, 1990). See also Jane Loevinger, *Paradigms of Personality* (New York: W. H. Freeman and Co., 1987).

22. Jean Baker Miller, *Toward a New Psychology of Women* (Boston: Beacon Press, 1976).

23. Hazel Markus and Susan Cross, "The Interpersonal Self" in L. Pervin, ed., *Handbook of Personality: Theory and Research* (New York: The Guilford Press, 1990).

24. Carol Gilligan, *In a Different Voice, Psychological Theory and Women's Development* (Cambridge: Harvard University Press, 1982).

25. See Jane Loevinger's discussion of Gilligan in *Paradigms of Personality* (New York: W. H. Freeman & Co., 1987).

26. Rachel Hare-Mustin and Jean Marecek, eds., *Making a Difference: Psychology and the Construction of Gender* (New Haven: Yale University Press, 1990), 17.

27. Jessica Benjamin, *The Bonds of Love: Psychoanalysis, Feminism, and the Problem of Domination* (New York: Pantheon Books, 1988).

28. For an overview of family systems theories we recommend Ann Hartman and Joan Laird, *Family Centered Social Work Practice* (New York: The Free Press, 1983); also *Handbook of Family Therapy*, Alan S. Gurman and David P. Kniskern, eds. (New York: Brunner/Mazel, 1981).

29. For an overview of Feminism and Family Therapy see Marianne Ault-Riche, ed., *Women and Family Therapy* (Rockville, Md.: Aspen Systems, 1986); Lois Braverman, ed., *Women, Feminism and Family Therapy* (New York: Haworth Press, 1988); and McGoldrick, Anderson, and Walsh, *Women in Families; a Framework for Family Therapy* (New York: W. W. Norton & Co., Inc., 1989).

30. See Rachel Hare-Mustin and Jean Marecek, eds., *Making a Difference: Psychology and the Construction of Gender* (New Haven: Yale University Press, 1990) for a more detailed discussion of "essential difference."

31. See Carol Tavris, *The Mismeasure of Woman* (New York: Simon & Schuster, 1992).

32. See Codependency movement literature such as Melody Beattie's *Codependent No More* (New York: Harper & Row, 1987), and Anne Wilson Schaef's *Codependence: Misunderstood—Mistreated* (San Francisco: Harper & Row, 1986).

33. Robin Norwood, *Women Who Love Too Much* (New York: St. Martin's Press, 1985).

34. Mary Kay Blakely, "The Tender Trap: Is the Price of Love Total Surrender?" *Ms. Magazine*, June 1988, 18–19.

35. For a discussion of some exceptions to this statement, see Riane Eisler's *The Chalice and the Blade* (San Francisco: Harper & Row, 1987).

36. Ruth Sidel, *On Her Own: Growing Up in the Shadow of the American Dream* (New York: Viking Penguin, 1990).

37. Tillie Olsen, *Silences* (New York: Delacorte Press/Seymour Lawrence, 1965).

38. Patricia Reiss, *Through the Goddess: A Woman's Way of Healing* (New York: Continuum, 1991).

39. Jean Shinoda Bolen, *Goddesses in Every Woman* (New York: Harper & Row, 1984).

40. See Rosemary R. Reuther's discussion of Jung in *New Woman, New Earth: Sexist Ideologies and Human Liberation* (New York: Seabury Press, 1975).

41. Toni Grant, *Being a Woman* (New York: Avon Books, 1988), 6.

42. See Kenneth Gergen, *The Saturated Self* (New York: Basic Books, 1991).

43. James Hillman, as quoted in *The Goddess Within* by Jennifer Barker Woolger and Roger J. Woolger (New York: Fawcett Columbine, 1987), 10.

44. Willard Gaylin, *Rediscovering Love* (New York: Penguin Books, 1986).

THE SHADOW OF HER SMILE

1. Arlene Raven, "Arts: The Archaic Smile," *Ms. Magazine* (New York: Lang Communications, Inc.), July/August, 1992, vol. 3:1, 68.

2. Ibid., 72.

3. Ravenna Helson, "Creativity in Women: Outer and Inner Views Over Time," in *Theories of Creativity*, M. A. Runco and R. S. Albert, eds. (Newbury Park: SAGE Publications, 1990), 46–47.

4. Germaine Greer, *The Obstacle Race: The Fortunes of Women Painters and Their Work* (New York: Farrar, Straus & Giroux, 1979), 108.

5. Ibid., 14.

6. Ibid., 52.

7. Ibid., 14.

8. Ibid.

9. "Did Einstein's Wife Contribute to His Theories?" *New York Times*, Tuesday, March 27, 1990.

10. Germaine Greer, *The Obstacle Race: The Fortunes of Women Painters and Their Work* (New York: Farrar, Straus & Giroux, 1979), 52.

11. Tillie Olsen, *Silences* (New York: Delacorte Press/Seymour Lawrence, 1965).

12. See Germaine Greer, *The Obstacle Race;* Whitney Chadwick, *Women, Art and Society;* Tillie Olsen, *Silences;* and Eleanor Munro, *Originals: American Women Artists.*

13. Christine Ammer, *Unsung: A History of Women in American Music* (Westport, Conn.: Greenwood Press, 1980).

14. Jennifer Barker Woolger and Roger J. Woolger, *The Goddess Within* (New York: Fawcett Columbine, 1987).

15. Bella Abzug, quoted in the article "1949–1992 Fire and Storm: The Years in Question," *Performing Arts Magazine* (Los Angeles: Performing Arts Network, Inc.), Sept. 1992, vol. 26:9, 13.

16. Judy Mann, "Limiting Expectation," *Washington Post*, September 18, 1991, sec. C, p. 3.

17. Susan Schroeder, *The Quiltmaker's Art*, Joanne Mattera, ed. (Ashville, N.C.: Lark Books, 1981).

18. With the vote came a trend toward the involvement of women in the work force and in professional ranks and a corresponding image of independence. By the late 1920s this trend appears to have plateaued as women, disillusioned with their new roles, turned away from politics and reform back to what has been called the "New Victorianism," a popular emphasis on sexual happiness for women in marriage. Women themselves would no longer sacrifice marriage and family for "independence." Frank Stricker, "Cookbooks and Law Books," in *A Heritage of Her Own*, Nancy F. Cott and Elizabeth H. Pleck, eds. (New York: Simon & Schuster, 1979), 477–79.

19. Joan Ellis, *Voices from the Silent Generation* (unpublished manuscript).

20. Sherna Berger Gluck, *Rosie the Riveter Revisited: Women, The War, and Social Change* (New York: NAL Penguin Inc., 1987). Also see Deborah Luepnitz, *The Family Interpreted: Feminist Theory in Clinical Practice* (New York: Basic Books, 1988).

21. Sherna Berger Gluck, *Rosie the Riveter Revisited: Women, The War, and Social Change* (New York: NAL Penguin Inc., 1987).

22. Before the war there were only 12 million employed women—25 percent of the labor force in 1941. Two thirds were unmarried, with many immigrant, minority, and working class. With the war the number of working wives doubled, and female union membership tripled, standing at over three million by 1945. See Andrea S. Walsh, *Women's Film and Female Experience: 1940–1950* (New York: Praeger Publishers, 1984), 53.

23. William Henry Chafe, *The American Woman: Her Changing Social, Economic and Political Roles, 1920–1970* (New York: Oxford University Press, 1972), 190.

24. Marjorie Rosen, *Popcorn Venus: Women, Movies and the American Dream* (New York: Coward, McCann & Geoghegan, 1973).

25. Sherna Berger Gluck, *Rosie the Riveter Revisited: Women, The War, and Social Change* (New York: NAL Penguin Inc., 1987), 26.

26. Joan Ellis, *Voices from the Silent Generation* (unpublished manuscript).

27. ASCAP, *The Hit Songs* (New York: American Society of Composers,

Authors and Publishers, 1979). You can probably identify most of the songs by their ideas. Remember "Cherry Pink and Apple Blossom White?" This was our imported vision of heterosexual bliss from the French in the fifties. It was a hit in 1955 in America.

28. Whitney Chadwick, *Women, Art, and Society* (London: Thames and Hudson Ltd., 1990).

29. Ibid., 297–98.

30. Ibid., 300.

31. Ibid., 302.

32. Ibid., 306.

33. Ibid., 303–4.

34. Marjorie Rosen, *Popcorn Venus: Women, Movies and the American Dream* (New York: Coward, McCann & Geoghegan, 1973). Also see Andrea S. Walsh, *Women's Film and Female Experience: 1940–1950* (New York: Praeger Publishers, 1984).

35. Joan Ellis, *Voices from the Silent Generation* (unpublished manuscript).

36. Ibid.

37. Mayumi Oda, in *The Japan Times Weekly*, "Mayumi's Liberation" by Frederick Shaw Myers, Jan. 18, 1992, vol. 32:3.

38. See Whitney Chadwick, *Women, Art and Society* (London, England: Thames and Hudson, Ltd., 1990).

39. Interview with Lucy Lippard.

40. Susan McClary, *Feminine Endings: Music, Gender and Sexuality* (Minneapolis: Univ. of Minnesota Press, 1991).

41. Elizabeth Wood, "Settling Old Scores" in *The Women's Review of Books*, September 1991, vol. 8:12, 11.

42. Regina Barreca, *They Used To Call Me Snow White . . . But I Drifted: Women's Strategic Use Of Humor* (New York: Viking Press, 1991).

43. Susan Faludi, *Backlash: The Undeclared War Against American Women* (New York: Crown Publishers, Inc., 1991).

THE SUBJECT IS HERSELF

1. For a discussion of women and narrative theory, see Joan Laird, "Women & Stories: Restorying Women's Self Constructions" in McGoldrick, Anderson, and Walsh, *Women in Families; a Framework for Family Therapy* (New York: W. W. Norton & Co., Inc., 1989).

2. Carolyn G. Heilbrun, *Writing a Woman's Life* (New York: W. W. Norton & Co., Inc., 1988).

3. According to Heilbrun, accomplishment and achievement do not dominate the narratives of women. Even May Sarton, the famed journalist, published one journal in 1968 and in 1973 published a second journal that integrated all the anger and despair she had left out the first time. Both books deal with the same period of her life. *Writing a Woman's Life*, 12, 13.

4. The research of Kathryn Miller Krogh, "Women's Motives to Achieve and to Nurture in Different Stages," *Sex Roles*, vol. 12:1/2, 1985, 75–89, supports this finding.

LOVERS: THE HIGH RELATIONAL PATTERN

1. Annie Dillard, *The Writing Life* (New York: Harper & Row, 1989).
2. Joan Ellis, *Voices from the Silent Generation* (unpublished manuscript).
3. Anonymous, *Rehab* (unpublished manuscript).
4. Advertising jingle.
5. Anonymous, *Rehab* (unpublished manuscript).
6. Edna St. Vincent Millay, *Collected Sonnets of Edna St. Vincent Millay* [*Fatal Interview*] (New York: Harper & Row, 1941), 99.
7. Sara Ruddick, *Maternal Thinking: Toward a Politics of Peace* (New York: Ballantine Books, 1989).
8. Ibid.
9. Arlie Hochschild, *The Second Shift* (New York: Viking Press, 1989) and Ruth Sidel, *On Her Own: Growing Up in the Shadow of the American Dream* (New York: Viking Press, 1990).

ARTISTS: THE HIGH CREATIVE PATTERN

1. Katherine Bradford, *Personal Correspondence*, April 15, 1992, and Nov. 1992.
2. Claudia Bepko and Jo-Ann Krestan, *Too Good for Her Own Good* (New York: Harper & Row, 1990).
3. Kristin Field, "Painter Whittles Away at Chaos," *Daily Vidette* (Normal, Ill.: Illinois State University, 1991).
4. Quoted in the brochure of the Victoria Munroe Gallery for the show 1991 Exhibition of Paintings: Katherine Bradford.
5. Mihaly Csikszentmihalyi, *Flow: The Psychology of Optimal Experience* (New York: Harper & Row, 1990).
6. Kenneth J. Gergen, *The Saturated Self* (New York: Basic Books, 1991), 150.
7. Ibid.
8. Otto Rank, *Art and the Artist: Creative Urge and Personality Development* (New York: Agathon Press, 1932).
9. Ibid., 385.
10. Norma Marder, Stan Lindberg, eds., "Deceptive Cadences" in *The Georgia Review*, Spring/Summer, 1990, 174. Norma gave us the following description of herself recently. "In 1980 I gave up singing for writing. I spent the next twelve years teaching myself to write by writing the same book over and over and over again. My first novel,

An Eye for Dark Places, will be published by Little, Brown in June 1993. I sold it over the transom with no agent, and if that isn't singing at the top of our lungs I don't know what is. [The writing not the selling.]"

11. Beth Anderson as described in the *New Groves Dictionary of American Operatic Composers.*

12. Writer Katherine Ann Porter, as quoted in Tillie Olsen, *Silences* (New York: Delacorte Press/Seymour Lawrence, 1965), 165.

13. From Beth Anderson's interview for the notes on the Richmond Symphony's recording of her "Revel."

14. Tillie Olsen, *Silences* (New York: Delacorte Press/Seymour Lawrence, 1965), 256.

15. Carrie A. Hall and Rose G. Keetsinger, *Romance of the Patchwork Quilt in America* (New York: Bonanza Books, 1935).

16. L. Beck, "Mentorships: Benefits and Effects on Career Development," *Gifted Child Quarterly*, vol. 33:1, 22–28.

17. [Jo-Ann]: "I was always told that I couldn't sing, thus singing was a source of shame for me. Forty years after that first grade experience, I participated in an all day singing workshop with Susan Osborn, former lead singer for the Paul Winter Consort. Singing is Susan's spiritual 'practice.' First, each of the ninety men and women in the room, under her direction, took a deep in breath then sighed an exhalation, letting a hum escape. The group did this several times until the hums became sustained notes, and the notes swelled into a musical 'om' that resonated. In breath, out breath, with music becoming louder and more harmonic until after some minutes the group spontaneously exhaled musically and stopped. Everyone seemed to know the breath was winding down. Next, the group sang old spirituals, like 'Swing Low, Sweet Chariot,' everyone by now singing and hearing their own voice. This went on for an hour or so. Then, warmed up and feeling joyous, each individual in the group introduced themselves by singing their first name. Some were shaking; having been shamed for singing in public earlier in life; they sang quickly, one syllable per note; others developed entire arias for one syllable names. . . . Ne, ne, ne ne, ne, ne, ne, ne, ne e, e, e, ned. After each name was sung the entire group imitated and sang the name back exactly as they heard it. When it was my turn I quietly spoke 'Oh, shit.' Susan turned and sang along 'Oh, shiiiiiiitttttt' to me. I then had to sing Jo-Ann. I had been aware as the process went on that those who put more out . . . sang their names louder and longer . . . got more back from the group, so I managed three syllables for Jo-Ann. As individuals were witnessed by the sung response of the group, many wept."

18. Stanley Scott, ed., *Northern Lights: Studies In Creativity.* Presque Isle: University of Maine, Summer and Winter 1986.

19. Mary Daly, *Beyond God the Father: Toward a Philosophy of Women's Liberation* (Boston: Beacon Press, 1985).

20. Paraphrase of Thich Nhat Hanh in *The Heart of Understanding* (Berkeley: Parallax Press, 1988), 28.
21. Holly Near, as quoted in an interview by Susan Watrous and Bob Blanchard, in *The Progressive*, March 1990.
22. Matthew Fox, *Compassion* (Minneapolis: Winston Press, Inc., 1979), 127, 137.
23. Roxana Robinson, *Georgia O'Keeffe: A Life* (New York: Harper & Row, 1989), 166.

LEADERS: THE RELATIONAL INTEGRATIVE PATTERN

1. Betty Carter, in the Foreword to *Women in Families: A Framework for Family Therapy*, Monica McGoldrick, Carol Anderson, Froma Walsh, eds. (New York: W. W. Norton & Co., Inc., 1989), vii.
2. Some of Monica's publications include, Monica McGoldrick and Randy Gerson, *Genograms in Family Assessment*; *The Changing Family Life Cycle*, with Betty Carter, ed.; *Ethnicity and Family Therapy*, with John Pearce and Joseph Giordano, eds.; and *Women in Families: A Framework for Family Therapy*, with Carol Anderson and Froma Walsh, eds.
3. See D. H. DeMuth, "Some Implications of the Nuclear Threat for Families and Family Therapists," in *Political and Social Contexts of Family Therapy*, M. P. Mirkin, ed. (Boston: Allyn and Bacon, 1991), and B. Berger-Gould and Donna Hilleboe DeMuth in *The Global Family Therapist: Integrating the Political, Personal, and Professional* (Boston: Allyn and Bacon in press).

INNOVATORS: THE CREATIVE INTEGRATIVE PATTERN

1. Norma Marder, "Deceptive Cadences," *Georgia Review* (Women in the Arts, Summer, 1990), 171.
2. Richard B. Woodward, "The Disturbing Photography of Sally Mann," *New York Times Magazine*, September 27, 1992, sec. 6, 29–36.
3. Mary Catherine Bateson, *Composing a Life* (New York: The Atlantic Monthly Press, 1989), 9.
4. Norma Marder, "Deceptive Cadences," *Georgia Review* (Women in the Arts, Summer, 1990), 166.
5. Ibid., 171.
6. Ibid., 180.
7. Ibid., 169.

VISIONARIES: THE WOMAN OF PASSIONATE CONVICTION

1. Barbara Peabody, *The Screaming Room* (New York: Avon Books, 1986).
2. See for instance, Paulette Hines and Nancy Boyd Franklin, "Black Families" in *Ethnicity and Family Therapy*, John Pearce and Joseph Giordano, Monica McGoldrick, Carol Anderson, Froma Walsh, eds. (New York: W. W. Norton & Co., Inc., 1989), and Paulette Moore Hines, "The Family Life Cycle of Poor Black Families," in Betty Carter and Monica McGoldrick, eds., *The Changing Family Life Cycle* (New York: Gardner Press, 1988).
3. *Ellsworth American* (Ellsworth, Me.: March 5, 1992).
4. Marian Sandmaier, *The Invisible Alcoholics: Women and Alcohol Abuse in America* (New York: McGraw-Hill, 1980), 41–42.
5. *Brunswick Times-Record* (Brunswick, Me.: July 1992).

THE EARLY DEATH OF LOVE, OR, I USED TO PLAY THE VIOLIN

1. Otto Harbach and Jerome Kern, "Smoke Gets in Your Eyes," ASCAP: American Society of Composers, Authors and Publishers (Los Angeles: Polygram International Publishing).
2. Mihaly Csikszentmihalyi, *Flow: The Psychology of Optimal Experience* (New York: Harper & Row, 1990).
3. Adrienne Rich, in Paula Bennett's, *My Life a Loaded Gun: Dickinson, Plath, Rich, and Female Creativity* (Urbana and Chicago: University of Illinois Press, 1986).
4. Paula Bennett, *My Life a Loaded Gun: Dickinson, Plath, Rich, and Female Creativity*.
5. Linda Schierse Leonard, *Witness to the Fire: Creativity and the Veil of Addiction* (Boston: Shambhala Publications, Inc., 1989), xv–xvi.

CHOICE POINTS AND TRANSFORMATIONS

1. Rollo May, *The Courage to Create* (New York: Bantam Books, W. W. Norton & Co., Inc., 1975), 4.
2. The Michell Cassou quotation was tacked to the wall of the metal studio at Haystack Mountain School of Arts and Crafts, Sunset, Maine. We first saw it in July 1992 during a visit to a friend at Haystack. For a brief discussion of artist Cassou's work, see Ann Cushman, "Are You Creative?" First printed in *Yoga Journal*, reprinted in *UTNE Reader*, March/April, 1992.
3. Barbara Garrison, quoted in the "Sunbeams" Section, *The Sun, A Magazine of Ideas*. Chapel Hill, N.C., August, 1992.

4. Willard Gaylin, *Rediscovering Love* (New York: Penguin Books, 1986).

IN HER OWN GOOD TIME

1. Quoted in Christina Tree and Mimi Steadman, *Maine: An Explorer's Guide* (Woodstock, Vermont: The Countryman Press, 1989), 180.
2. Anne Morrow Lindbergh, *Gift From The Sea* (Vintage Edition) (New York: Random House, 1955), 40.
3. One of Lucy Lippard's many interests is archaeology. In 1983 she published *Overlay: Contemporary Art and the Art of Prehistory* (New York: Pantheon Books, 1983), 102. Much of the following material on time is cited in that book in the chapter called "The Forms of Time: Earth and Sky, Words and Numbers."
4. Ibid., 97–98.
5. Ibid., *Overlay*, 97–98.
6. Ibid., 105.
7. Immanuel Kant, *Critique of Pure Reason*, trans. Norman Kemp Smith (New York: St. Martin's Press, 1958).
8. Martin Heidegger, *An Introduction to Metaphysics*, trans. Ralph Manheim, originally published in German by Max Verlag in 1953 (New Haven: Yale University Press edition, 1959).
9. *Encyclopaedia Britannica* 15th ed., vol. 15 (Chicago: University of Chicago), 582.
10. A review of these ideas can be found in Stephen Hawking's *A Brief History of Time: From the Big Bang to Black Holes* (New York: Bantam Books, April 1988; trade paper edition, June 1990), 33. Numerous experiments demonstrated that "true time" could not be experimentally demonstrated, thus forcing a paradoxical distinction between true time and apparent time. In 1905 Einstein (or now some think his wife) demonstrated the theory of relativity. That is, that if each observer applied the same method of analysis to his own data, then events that appeared simultaneous to one would appear to have taken place at different times to observers in different states of motion.

    Stephen Hawking writes, "Before 1915, space and time were thought of as a fixed arena in which events took place, but which was not affected by what happened in it ... space and time are now dynamic quantities: when a body moves or a force acts, it affects the curvature of space and time—and in turn the structure of space-time affects the way in which bodies move and forces act. Space and time not only affect but also are affected by everything that happens in the universe."
11. John Hanson Mitchell, *Ceremonial Time* (New York: Warner Books, Doubleday, 1984), 1–2.
12. The romantic period of a concern with beauty yielded to the mod-

ernist emphasis on functionality, and now, in the postmodern era, we live with an uneasy melange of styles and competing values. The telecommunication revolution and its byproducts like fax machines, and satellite transmissions of events create a thorough bombardment of our psyches with too much data that Kenneth Gergen refers to as "The Saturated Self." From Kenneth Gergen, *The Saturated Self* (New York: Basic Books, 1991).

We ask, what is right, what is beautiful, what will last? As Jeremy Rifkin pointed out, even our contemporary architecture is not meant to look as if designed for eternity unlike the granite monuments of turn of the century Paris. We heard Jeremy Rifkin address these ideas during the Family Therapy Networker Symposium in 1990.

13. Rollo May who wrote extensively on love and creativity knew this well. In *Love and Will* (New York: W. W. Norton & Co., Inc., 1969), 282–83, he wrote, "This brings us to the problem of time. In cases of impotence we recognize an all too familiar pattern: the impression of being compulsively hurried: 'we undressed immediately,' the patient says. May says, 'we fly to sex in order to avoid eros . . .' "

14. Amy Saltzman, *Downshifting* (New York: HarperCollins, 1991), 76.

15. John Robinson, "Time on Your Hands? You May Have More than You Know," *New York Times*, July 3, 1991. He analyzes several reasons for the feeling of pressure we experience, including the large number of baby boomers who are now in their thirties and forties when demands on time are greatest. Witold Rybczynski, in *Waiting for the Weekend*, discusses the "nagging feeling that our free time should be used for some purpose [translate goal] higher than having fun." He states that with tighter economic times and two-paycheck families, "we've lost '9.6' hours of leisure time in the past 15 years alone." Even pursuits like reading take too much time. Researchers are not in total agreement on the objectivity of time won or lost.

See also, book review, Cheryl Merser, "Feeling the Weight of the Weekend" in *USA Today*, Friday, Aug. 30, 1991.

16. Krishnamurti, in discussing the concept of psychological time, discusses the psychological recording of an event that becomes memory and questions whether time would exist in the sense of memory if it were possible to give tremendous and total attention to the moment. See J. Krishnamurti, "The Flame of Attention," *Freedom from the Known* (New York: Harper & Row, 1969), 72–73, 111–112.

The Dalai Lama speaks in "The Experience of Change: Interview with H.H. the Dalai Lama," *Parabola*, Spring, 1990: "If there is no process of change, then one cannot conceive of time in the first place." The notions of space and time as taught by the Eastern mystics have now been confirmed by modern physics. See Fritjof Capra, *The Tao of Physics* (New York: Bantam Books, 1975).

17. The Tibetan Buddhist Master, in writing about the ability to know the situation in the very moment of nowness, without being influenced by memory of the past or expectation of the future, talks about

the present moment as having no barriers at all. From Chogyam Trungpa, *Meditation in Action* (London, England: Shambhala Publications, 1969).

18. Sonia Johnson, a radical feminist, says of living in the present, "In fact we ignore the evidence of our perceptions, or deny how we feel or give up even a bit of what we want for some 'good' in a nonexistent future. We are cutting ourselves off from the moment, off from life, out of creativity and power. This is so because . . . our lives are not means to some end. Since time is not linear and past and future do not therefore actually exist. . . . In our atomic universe, *now* is what time *is*. In *The Ship that Sailed into the Living Room* (Estancia, N. Mex.: Wildfire Books, 1991), 128, 147–150.

19. See Matthew Fox, *A Spirituality Named Compassion* (Minneapolis: Winston Press, Inc., 1979), 117. Also Carol Ochs, *Women and Spirituality* (Totowa, N.J.: Rowman and Allanheld, 1983), 85. "Creating—as opposed to creation—focuses on the process rather than the product. Overriding concern with a product, an outcome, or a goal results from a linear view of time. Implicit in such a view is a means-ends relationship in which the value of any action is measured by its contribution to the outcome or goal. The linear view of time plays a central role in Western theological systems, which emphasize an end of days, a final judgment and an afterlife. Contrasting with the linear view of time is the cyclical view, which is rooted in women's tradition both historically and, more important, ideologically. The cyclical view of time emphasizes not the goal of life but the processes of life—the processes of creating, mothering, and letting go. Women giving birth to a child create not an end product but a process—an infant that immediately partakes of the process of change. Mothering and letting go are processes that similarly foster another process—life."

20. "The race car driver is fearless. He speeds past death. In his speed is endless virility. As a lover he amazes flesh. Women fall. He is like lightning in his gestures. His will pervades all matter. He sees no boundaries. He tolerates no entanglements. Nothing must slow him down. Slowness is his enemy. He does not stay in one place. He never spends time. Time is his executor." See further paragraphs in a section on Speed in *Woman and Nature*, by Susan Griffin (New York: Harper & Row, 1978), 122.

21. Abraham Joshua Heschel in his classic, *The Sabbath: Its Meaning for Modern Man* (New York: Straus & Co., expanded edition, 1952), 5, 76. "The Sabbath is spirit in the form of time. We usually think that the earth is our mother, that time is money and profit our mate. The seventh day is a reminder that God is our father, that time is life and the spirit our mate."

22. Anne Morrow Lindbergh, *Gift From The Sea* (New York: Random House, Vintage Book Edition, 1978), 120.

23. Hanne Haavind and Agnes Andenes, from University of Oslo, Nor-

way. *Care and the Responsibility for Children: Creating the Life of Women Creating Themselves*, a paper presented at the Fourth International Interdisciplinary Congress on Women at CCNY, Hunter College, June 1990. "Everything that is not explicitly defined and accepted as something the male partner has consented to consider and eventually participate in rests with her . . . her participation is never specified. It is always taken for granted as the unspoken and unlimited totality of what carrying out the care and domestic work may make you realize."

24. Ibid.
25. Ibid.
26. Caroline Bird, *The Two Paycheck Marriage* [UNESCO Study] (New York: Rawson, Wade Publishers, 1979).
27. *New York Times*, July 3, 1991.
28. Lillian Rubin, *Intimate Strangers: Men and Women Together* (New York: Harper & Row, 1983).
29. Barry Stevens, *Don't Push the River (It Flows by Itself)* (Lafayette, Calif.: Real People Press, 1970).
30. Brenda Euland, *If You Want to Write* (St. Paul: Graywolf Press, 1987).

THE PASSIONATE RELATIONSHIP: CREATING NEW FORMS

1. Anne-Marie Dunatov, "Childless by Choice," *American Health*, June 1992, vol. XI: 5, 87.
2. Katherine Mansfield as quoted in Tillie Olsen's *Silences* (New York: Delacorte Press/Seymour Lawrence, 1965), 215.
3. Ravenna Helson, "Creativity in Women: Outer and Inner Views Over Time," in *Theories of Creativity*, Runco and Albert, eds. (Newbury Park: Sage Publications, Inc., 1990), 32.
4. Ibid., 34.
5. Tillie Olsen, *Silences* (New York: Delacorte Press/Seymour Lawrence, 1978), 219. For instance, as Tillie Olsen says, "I am haunted by the writer-wives (or long-time wives) of notable literary men: Eleanor Clark, Janet Lewis, Caroline Gordon, Jane Bowles, Elizabeth Hardwick, Mary Ellmann, Diana Trilling, Hope Hale Davis, Ann Birstein, Helen Yglesias . . . the husbands: Robert Penn Warren, Yvor Winters, Allen Tate, Paul Bowles, Robert Lowell, Richard Ellmann, Lionel Trilling, Robert Gorham Davis, Alfred Kazin, Jose Yglesias." It is the husbands whose names we are apt to know.
6. Sylvia Plath quoted in Tillie Olsen, *Silences* (New York: Delacorte Press/Seymour Lawrence, 1978), 36.
7. Alice B. Toklas, of her services to Gertrude Stein, quoted in *Silences*.
8. Luhan started in Greenwich Village as a "patroness of the avantgarde," *The Desert is No Lady*, p. 15 and then shifted from muse to subject after her move to New Mexico in 1917.

9. "At last a woman artist," he was to say. Benita Eisler, *O'Keeffe and Stieglitz: An American Romance* (New York: Penguin Books, 1991).

10. Mabel Dodge Luhan was central in promoting the Southwest to painters, photographers and writers. Among them were Georgia O'Keeffe, Paul and Beck Strand, D. H. and Frieda Lawrence, John Marin and Ansel Adams. See Roxana Robinson, *Georgia O'Keeffe: A Life* (New York: Harper & Row, 1989). Also see Mabel Dodge Luhan's four volumes of memoirs, particularly *Edge of the Taos Desert: An Escape to Reality* (Albuquerque, N. Mex.: University of New Mexico Press edition, reprint 1988) and *Winter in Taos* (Taos, N.Mex.: Las Palomas de Taos, 1982) for an extraordinary account of a woman reshaping the form of her life to totally express her passions.

11. The Boston Women's Health Book Collective, *The New Our Bodies, Ourselves* (New York: Simon & Schuster, Inc., 1984).

THE COURAGE TO BE ALIVE

1. From Jo-Ann's memory of a Susan Osborn workshop at the Common Boundary Conference in Washington, D.C., Nov. 1991.

2. Virginia Woolf, *To the Lighthouse* (New York: Harcourt, Brace & World, Inc., 1927).

3. Michael Kimmelman, "After Many a Summer, a Sculptor Comes of Age," *New York Times:* Arts and Leisure, sec. 2, p. 1, Aug. 30, 1992.

4. Ibid.

5. Lillian Hellman quote from "Where are the Women Playwrights?" by Helen Krich Chinoy in Helen Krich Chinoy and Linda Walsh Jenkins, *Women in American Theatre* (New York: Crown Publishers, Inc.), 129.

6. From Whitney Chadwick, *Women, Art and Society* (London, England: Thames and Hudson, Ltd., 1990), 308. The critical response to Louise Nevelson's first major exhibition in New York in 1946, after which she did not exhibit in the galleries for ten years, was ... "We learned the artist was a woman, in time to check our enthusiasm" wrote one critic. "Had it been otherwise, we might have hailed these sculptural expressions as by surely a great figure among the moderns."

7. Holly Near, as quoted in an interview by Susan Watrous and Bob Blanchard, in *The Progressive*, March 1990.

8. Michael Kimmelman, "After Many a Summer, a Sculptor Comes of Age," *New York Times:* Arts and Leisure, sec. 2, 1, Aug. 30, 1992.

9. See Barbara Dafoe Whitehead, "A New Familism?" in *Family Affairs* (Newsletter of the Institute for American Values), Summer, 1992, vol. 5:1/2.

10. Michael Kimmelman, "After Many a Summer, a Sculptor Comes of Age," *New York Times:* Arts and Leisure, sec. 2, 1, Aug. 30, 1992.

11. Paraphrase of Thich Nhat Hanh in *The Heart of Understanding* (Berkeley: Parallax Press, 1988), 28.

12. Ernest Becker, *The Denial of Death* (New York: The Free Press, 1973).

13. Beth Anderson, *The Angel*, musical composition with lyrics by Anthony Calabrese. Premiered at the Shore Festival of Classics, Ocean Grove, New Jersey, 1988.

Bibliography

Amabile, Teresa M. *The Social Psychology of Creativity*. New York: Springer-Verlag, 1983.

American Society of Composers and Publishers. *The Hit Songs*. New York: 1979.

Ammer, Christine. *Unsung: A History of Women in American Music*. Westport, Conn.: Greenwood Press, 1980.

"Are You Creative?," *UTNE Reader*, March/April 1992, No. 50. Minneapolis: Lens Publishing Co.

Armstrong, Louise. "The Message and the Media," *Women's Review of Books*, January 1988, vol. V:4.

Ault-Riche, Marianne, ed. *Women and Family Therapy*. Rockville, Md.: Aspen Systems, 1986.

Bachtold, Louise M., and Emmy E. Werner. "Personality Characteristics of Creative Women," *Perceptual and Motor Skills*, 1978, vol. 36, 311–19.

Bailey, William C., Clyde Hendrick, and Susan S. Hendrick. "Relation of Sex and Gender Role to Love, Sexual Attitudes and Self-esteem," *Sex Roles*, 1987, vol. 16:11/12.

Barnette, Edmund L. "A Program to Meet the Emotional and Social Needs of Gifted and Talented Adolescents," *Journal of Counseling and Development*, May 1989, vol. 67:9, 525–28.

Barreca, Regina. *They Used To Call Me Snow White . . . But I Drifted: Women's Strategic Use Of Humor*. New York: Viking Press, 1991.

Barzun, Jacques. "The Paradoxes of Creativity," *American Scholar*, vol. 8, No. 7, Summer 1989, pp. 337–51

Bateson, Mary Catherine. *Composing a Life*. New York: The Atlantic Monthly Press, 1989.

Beattie, Melody. *Codependent No More*. New York: Harper & Row, 1987.

Beck, L. "Mentorships: Benefits and Effects on Career Development," *Gifted Child Quarterly*, vol. 33:1.

Becker, Audrey. "New Lyrics by Women: A Feminist Alternative," *Journal of Popular Culture*, Summer 1990, vol. 24:1, pp. 1–22.

Becker, Ernest. *The Denial of Death*. New York: The Free Press, 1973.

Benjamin, Jessica. *The Bonds of Love: Psychoanalysis, Feminism, and the Problem of Domination*. New York: Pantheon Books, 1988.

Bennett, Paula. *My Life a Loaded Gun: Dickinson, Plath, Rich, and Female Creativity*. Urbana and Chicago: University of Illinois Press, 1986.

Bepko, Claudia, and Jo-Ann Krestan. *Too Good for Her Own Good*. New York: Harper & Row, 1990.

Berger-Gould, B., and Donna Hilleboe DeMuth. *The Global Family Therapist: Integrating the Political, Personal, and Professional*. Boston: Allyn and Bacon, in press.

Bergmann, Martin S. *The Anatomy of Loving*. New York: Columbia University Press, 1987.

Bird, Caroline. *The Two Paycheck Marriage*. New York: Rawson, Wade Publishers, Inc., 1979.

Blakely, Mary Kay. "The Tender Trap: Is the Price of Love Total Surrender?" *Ms. Magazine*, June 1988.

Boden, Margaret A. *The Creative Mind: Myths and Mechanisms*. New York: Basic Books, 1990.

Boyle, Sarah-Patton. *The Desert Blooms: A Personal Adventure in Growing Old Creatively*. Nashville: Abingdon Press, 1983.

Bradford, Katherine, *Personal Correspondence*, April 15, 1992, and November, 1992.

Braff, Phyllis. "In the Choices of Albee, Imagination Prevails." *The New York Times*, February 11, 1990.

Braverman, Lois, ed. *Women, Feminism and Family Therapy*. New York: Haworth Press, 1982.

Brecher, Edward. *Love, Sex and Aging: A Consumer's Union Report*. Mount Vernon, New York: Consumer's Union, 1984.

Brodkey, Harold. "Love Speeches," *Ms.*, Sept. 1986, p. 48.

Brunswick Times-Record. Brunswick, Me: July 1992.

Cancian, Francesca M. "The Feminization of Love," *Signs: Journal of Women in Culture and Society*, 1986, vol. 11:4.

Capra, Fritjof. *The Tao of Physics*. New York: Bantam Books, 1975.

Carter, Betty, and Monica McGoldrick. *The Changing Family Life Cycle: A Framework for Family Therapy*. New York: Gardner Press, 1988.

Chadwick, Whitney. *Women, Art, and Society*. New York: Thames and Hudson Inc., 1990.

Chafe, William Henry. *The American Woman: Her Changing Social, Economic and Political Roles, 1920–1970*. New York: Oxford University Press, 1972.

Chinoy, Helen Krich, and Linda Walsh Jenkins. *Women in American Theatre*. New York: Crown Publishers, Inc., 1981.

Chodorow, Nancy J. *Feminism and Psychoanalytic Theory*. New Haven, Conn.: Yale University Press, 1989.

Christ, Carol P. *Laughter of Aphrodite*. San Francisco: Harper & Row, 1987.

Conway, Jill Kerr. *Road From Coorain*. New York: Alfred A. Knopf, 1990.

Cott, Nancy F., and Elizabeth H. Pleck, eds. *A Heritage of Her Own: Toward a New Social History of American Women*. New York: Simon & Schuster, 1979.

Csikszentmihalyi, Mihaly. *Flow: The Psychology of Optimal Experience*. New York: Harper & Row, 1990.

Cushman, Ann. "Are You Creative?" *Yoga Journal*, reprinted in *UTNE Reader*, March/April, 1992.

Daly, Mary. *Beyond God the Father: Toward a Philosophy of Women's Liberation*. Boston, Mass.: Beacon Press, 1985.

De Lauretis, Teresa. *Alice Doesn't: Feminism, Semiotics, Cinema*. Bloomington, Indiana: Indiana University Press, 1984.

DeMuth, D. H. "Some Implications of the Nuclear Threat for Families and Family Therapists," in Mirkin, M. P., ed., *Political and Social Contexts of Family Therapy*. Boston: Allyn and Bacon, 1991.

"Did Einstein's Wife Contribute to His Theories?" *New York Times*, Tuesday, March 27, 1990.

Dillard, Annie. *The Writing Life*. New York: Harper & Row, 1989.

Dinesen, Isak. *Last Tales*. New York: First Vintage Books, 1975.

Doubiago, Sharon. *Psyche Drives the Coast: Poems 1975–1987*. Port Townsend, Wash.: Empty Bowl Press, 1990.

Dowling, Colette. *The Cinderella Complex: Women's Hidden Fear of Independence*. New York: Summit Books, 1981.

Durham, C. A. "The Subversive Stitch," *Women's Studies*, Jan 1990, vol. 17:3/4, 344–47.

Edmondson, Brad. "For Love or Money: Making a Living Versus Making a Life," *UTNE Reader*, July/August 1991, No. 46.

Edwards, Betty. *Drawing on the Artist Within*. New York: Simon & Schuster, 1986.

Ehrenreich, Barbara, Elizabeth Hess, and Gloria Jacobs. "Re-Making Love: The Real Sexual Revolution," *Ms.*, July 1986, 40–43, 82.

Ehringhaus, Ann. *Ocracoke Portrait*. Winston-Salem, North Carolina: John F. Blair, 1988.

Eisler, Riane. *The Chalice and the Blade*. San Francisco: Harper & Row, 1987.

Ellis, Joan. *Voices from the Silent Generation* (unpublished manuscript).

Ellsworth American. Ellsworth, Me.: March 5, 1992.

Euland, Brenda. *If You Want to Write*. St. Paul: Graywolf Press, 1987.

"Faces of the Goddess," *Woman of Power: A Magazine of Feminism, Spirituality, and Politics*, Fall/Winter, 1990, vol. 15.

Faderman, Lillian. *Surpassing the Love of Men: Romantic Friendship and Love Between Women from the Renaissance to the Present*. New York: William Morrow and Company, Inc., 1981.

Faludi, Susan. *Backlash: The Undeclared War Against American Women*. New York: Crown Publishers, Inc., 1991.

Farley, Frank H. "Note on Creativity and Scholastic Achievement of Women as a Function of Birth Order and Family Size," *Perceptual and Motor Skills*, 1978, vol. 47, 13–14.

Field, Kristin. "Painter Whittles Away at Chaos," *Daily Vidette*. Normal, Ill.: Illinois State University, 1991.

Foa, Uriel G., Barbara Anderson, John Converse, Jr., William A. Urbansky, Michael J. Cawley III, Solveig M. Muhlhausen, and Kjell Y. Tornblom. "Gender-Related Sexual Attitudes: Some Crosscultural Similarities and Differences," *Sex Roles*, 1987, vol. 16:9/10, 511–19.

Fox, Matthew. *A Spirituality Named Compassion*. Minneapolis: Winston Press, Inc., 1979.

Friedman, Jean E., and William G. Shade. *Our American Sisters: Women in American Life and Thought*. Lexington, Mass.: D. C. Heath and Company, 1982.

Fritz, Robert. *Creating*. New York: Fawcett Columbine, 1991.

Fromm, Erich. *The Art of Loving*. World Perspectives, Ruth Anshen, ed. New York: Harper & Row, 1956.

Galerstein, Carolyn L. *Working Women on the Hollywood Screen: A Filmography*. New York: Garland Publishing, Inc., 1989.

Garrison, Barbara. Quoted in *The Sun: A Magazine of Ideas*. Chapel Hill, N.C.: August, 1992.

Gaylin, Willard. *Rediscovering Love*. New York: Penguin Books, 1986.

Gaylin, Willard, and Ethel Person, eds. *Passionate Attachments: Thinking About Love*. New York: The Free Press, 1988.

Gergen, Kenneth. *The Saturated Self*. New York: Basic Books, 1991.

Gilbert, Sandra M., and Susan Gubar. *The Norton Anthology of Literature by Women*. New York: W. W. Norton & Co., 1985.

Gill, Diane L. "Competitiveness Among Females and Males in Physical Activity Classes," *Sex Roles*, 1986, vol. 15:5/6, 233–47.

Gilligan, Carol. *In a Different Voice: Psychological Theory and Women's Development*. Cambridge, Mass.: Harvard University Press, 1982.

Gilligan, Carol, and Eve Stern. "The Riddle of Femininity and the Psychology of Love," in *Passionate Attachments: Thinking about Love*, Willard Gaylin and Ethel Person, eds. New York: The Free Press, 1988.

Gilligan, Carol, Nona P. Lyons, and Trudy J. Hanmer, eds. *Making Connections: The Relational Worlds of Adolescent Girls at Emma Willard School*. Cambridge: Harvard University Press, 1990.

Gluck, Sherna Berger. *Rosie the Riveter Revisited: Women, The War, and Social Change*. New York: New American Library, Penguin Inc., 1987.

Grainger, Ruth Dailey. "Ways to Nurture Your Creativity," *American Journal of Nursing*, Jan. 1991, vol. 91:1, 14–17.

Grant, Toni. *Being a Woman*. New York: Avon Books, 1988.

Greer, Germaine. *The Obstacle Race: The Fortunes of Women Painters and Their Work*. New York: Farrar, Straus & Giroux, 1979.

Griffin, Susan. *Woman and Nature*. New York: Harper & Row, 1978.

Grosskurth, Phyllis. "The New Psychology of Women," *New York Review of Books*, October 24, 1991.

Gruber, Howard, and Doris B. Wallace. *Creative People at Work*. New York: Oxford University Press, 1989.

Gryskiewicz, Stanley S., ed. *Creativity Week II*. North Carolina: Center for Creative Leadership, 1980.

Gubar, Susan. "The Blank Page and Issues of Female Creativity," Elaine Showalter, ed., in *The New Feminist Criticism: Essays on Women, Literature and Theory*. New York: Pantheon Books, 1985.

Guilford, J. P. *Creative Talents: Their Nature, Uses and Development*. Buffalo, N.Y.: Bearly Limited, 1986.

Gurman, Alan S., and David P. Kniskern, eds. *Handbook of Family Therapy*. New York: Brunner/Mazel, 1981.

Halas, Celia. *Why Can't a Woman be More Like a Man?* New York: Harper & Row, 1956.

Hall, Carrie, and Rose G. Kretsinger. *The Romance of the Patchwork Quilt in America*. New York: Bonanza Books, 1935.

Hanh, Nhat Thich. *The Heart of Understanding*. Berkeley: Parallax Press, 1988.

Harbach, Otto, and Jerome Kern. "Smoke Gets in Your Eyes," ASCAP (American Society of Composers, Authors and Publishers). Los Angeles: Polygram International Publishing.

Hare, A. Paul. *Creativity in Small Groups*. London, England: Sage Publications, 1982.

Hare-Mustin, Rachel, and Jean Marecek, eds. *Making a Difference: Psychology and the Construction of Gender*. New Haven: Yale University Press, 1990.

Hartman, Ann, and Joan Laird. *Family Centered Social Work Practice*. New York: The Free Press, 1983.

Hawking, Stephen. *A Brief History of Time*. New York: Bantam Books, 1988, 33.

Heilbrun, Carolyn G. *Writing a Woman's Life*. New York: W. W. Norton & Co., Inc., 1988.

Helson, Ravenna. "Women Mathematicians and the Creative Personality," *Journal of Counseling and Clinical Psychology*, 1971, vol. 36:2, 210–20.

———. "Creativity in Women: Outer and Inner Views Over Time," in *Theories of Creativity*, M. A. Runco and R. S. Albert, eds. Newbury Park: Sage Publications, 1990.

Heschel, Abraham Joshua. *The Sabbath: Its Meaning for Modern Man*. New York: Straus & Co., expanded edition, 1952.

Hite, Shere. *Women and Love*. New York: St. Martin's Press, 1987.

Hochschild, Arlie. *The Second Shift*. New York: Viking Press, 1989.

Horvath, Hal. "Children and Creativity," *Humanist*, Jan. 1989, vol. 49:1.

Johnson-Laird, Phillip N., and Robert J. Sternberg, eds. "Freedom and Constraint in Creativity," *The Nature of Creativity*. New York: Cambridge University Press, 1988.

Jong, Erica. "The Artist as Housewife, The Housewife as Artist," *Ms.*, April, 1972, 64–66, 100, 104–5.

Jordan, Judith V., Alexandra G. Kapla, Jean Baker Miller, Irene P. Stiver, and Janet L. Surrey. *Women's Growth in Connection: Writings from the Stone Center*. New York: The Guilford Press, 1991.

Kant, Immanuel. Trans. Norman Kemp Smith. *Critique of Pure Reason*. New York: St. Martin's Press, 1958.

Kemp, John R. "Overcoming Difficulties Through Art," *American Artist*, Feb. 1991, vol. 44:583, 48–55.

Kneller, George F. *The Art and Science of Creativity*. New York: Holt, Rinehart & Winston, Inc., 1965.

Kreps, Bonnie. *Subversive Thoughts, Authentic Passions: Finding Love Without Losing Your Self*. San Francisco: Harper & Row, 1990.

Krishnamurti, J. "The Flame of Attention," *Freedom from the Known*. New York: Harper & Row, 1969.

Krogh, Kathryn Miller. "Women's Motives to Achieve and to Nurture in Different Stages," *Sex Roles*, 1985, vol. 12:1/2.

Kuhn, Annette. *Women's Pictures: Feminism and Cinema*. London, Eng., and Winchester, Mass.: Pandora Press, Unwin Hyman Ltd., 1983, 1990.

Laird, Joan. "Women & Stories: Restorying Women's Self Constructions," in McGoldrick, Anderson, and Walsh, *Women in Families; A Framework for Family Therapy*. New York: W. W. Norton & Co., Inc., 1989.

Leonard, Linda Schierse. *Witness to the Fire: Creativity and the Veil of Addiction*. Boston: Shambhala Publications, Inc., 1989.

Lerner, Harriet G., *The Dance of Deception: Pretending and Truth-Telling in Women's Lives*. New York: HarperCollins, 1993.

Levine, Suzanne, and Harriet Lyons, eds. *The Decade of Women: A Ms. History of the Seventies in Words and Pictures*. New York: Paragon Books, 1980.

Lindbergh, Anne Morrow. *Gift From The Sea*. New York: Random House, 1955.

Lippard, Lucy. *I See/You Mean*. Los Angeles: Chrysalis Books, 1979.

———. *From the Center: Feminist Essays on Women's Art*. New York: E. P. Dutton, 1976.

———. *Overlay: Contemporary Art and the Art of Prehistory*. New York: Pantheon Books, 1983.

Loevinger, Jane. *Paradigms of Personality*. New York: W. H. Freeman & Company, 1987.

Luepnitz, Deborah Anne. *The Family Interpreted: Feminist Theory in Clinical Practice*. New York: Basic Books, 1988.

Luhan, Mabel Dodge. *Winter in Taos*. Taos, N.Mex.: Las Palomas de Taos, 1982.

———. *Edge of the Taos Desert: An Escape to Reality*. Albuquerque, N.Mex.: University of New Mexico Press, reprint 1988.

MacKinnon, Catharine A. *Toward a Feminist Theory of the State*. Cambridge, Mass.: Harvard University Press, 1989.

Mann, Judy. "Limiting Expectation," *The Washington Post*, September 18, 1991, sec. C.

Marder, Norma. "Deceptive Cadences" in *The Georgia Review*, Spring/Summer, 1990.

Mason, Mary G. and James Olney, eds., "The Other Voice: Autobiographies of Women Writers." *Autobiography: Essays Theoretical and Critical*. Princeton, N.J.: Princeton University Press, 1980, 207–35.

Mattera, Joanne, ed. *The Quiltmaker's Art: Contemporary Quilts and their Makers*. Asheville, N.C.: Lark Books, 1981.

May, Rollo. *Love and Will*. New York: W. W. Norton & Co., Inc., 1969.

————. *The Courage to Create*. New York: W. W. Norton & Co., Inc., 1975.

Maynard, Fredelle. *Guiding Your Child to a More Creative Life*. New York: Doubleday & Company, Inc.

Mayne, Judith. *The Woman at the Keyhole*. Bloomington, Ind.: Indiana University Press, 1990.

McClary, Susan. *Feminine Endings: Music, Gender and Sexuality*. Minneapolis: Univ. of Minnesota Press, 1991.

McGoldrick, Monica, and Randy Gerson. *Genograms in Family Assessment*. New York: W. W. Norton & Co., Inc., 1985.

McGoldrick, Monica, Carol Anderson, and Froma Walsh, eds., *Women in Families: A Framework for Family Therapy*. New York: W. W. Norton and Co., Inc., 1989.

McGoldrick, Monica, John Pearce, and Joseph Giordano. *Ethnicity and Family Therapy*. New York: Guilford Press, 1982.

Merriam, Sharon B., and M. Carolyn Clark. *Lifelines: Patterns of Work, Love, and Learning in Adulthood*. San Francisco: Jossey-Bass Publishers, 1991.

Merser, Cheryl. "Feeling the Weight of the Weekend," *USA Today*, Fri., Aug. 30, 1991.

Millay, Edna St. Vincent. *Collected Sonnets of Edna St. Vincent Millay* (Fatal Interview). New York: Harper & Row, 1941.

Miller, Jean Baker. *Toward a New Psychology of Women*. Boston: Beacon Press, 1976.

Mirkin, M. P., ed. *Political and Social Contexts of Family Therapy*. Boston: Allyn and Bacon, 1991.

Mitchell, John Hanson. *Ceremonial Time*. New York: Warner Books, 1984.

Mitchell, Juliet. *Women: The Longest Revolution*. New York: Pantheon Books, 1984.

Moustakas, Clark E. *Creativity and Conformity*. New York: D. Van Nostrand Company, 1967.

Moyers, Bill. *Creativity with Bill Moyers*. 28 min. Video recording, Washington, D.C.: Corporation for Entertainment & Learning, PBS Video, 1989.

Munro, Eleanor. *Wedding Readings: Centuries of Writing and Rituals on Love and Marriage*. New York: Viking, 1989.

————. *Originals: American Women Artists*. New York: Simon & Schuster, 1979.

Myers, Frederick Shaw. "Mayumi's Liberation," *The Japan Times Weekly*, Jan. 18, 1992, vol. 32:3.

Near, Holly. *Fire in the Rain . . . Singer in the Storm: An Autobiography*. New York: William Morrow and Co., Inc., 1990.

Nebel, Cecile. *The Dark Side of Creativity: Blocks, Unfinished Works and the Urge to Destroy*. Troy, New York: Whitson Publishing Company, 1988.

Nicholson, Linda J., ed. *Feminism/Postmodernism*. New York: Routledge, 1990.

Norwood, Robin. *Women Who Love Too Much*. New York: St. Martin's Press, 1985.

Norwood, Vera, and Janice Monk, eds. *The Desert is No Lady: Southwestern Landscapes in Women's Writing and Art*. New Haven: Yale University Press, 1987.

Ochs, Carol. *Women and Spirituality*. Totowa, N.J.: Rowman & Allanheld, 1983.

Olsen, Tillie. *Silences*. New York: Delacorte Press/Seymour Lawrence, 1978.

Palmer, William J. *The Films of the Seventies: A Social History*. Metuchen, N.J.: The Scarecrow Press, Inc., 1987.

Parabola. The Magazine of Myth and Tradition, 1988.

Partnow, Elaine. *The Quotable Woman: Volume Two 1900–The Present*. Los Angeles: Pinnacle Books, 1977.

Peabody, Barbara. *The Screaming Room*. New York: Avon Books, 1986.

Pervin, L., ed. *Handbook of Personality Theory and Research*. New York: The Guilford Press, 1990.

Porter, Sylvia. *Love and Money*. New York: William Morrow and Company, Inc., 1985.

Rank, Otto. *Art and the Artist: Creative Urge and Personality Development*. New York: Agathon Press, 1932.

Rappaport, Herbert. *Marking Time*. New York: Simon & Schuster, 1990.

Raven, Arlene. "Arts: The Archaic Smile," *Ms. Magazine*. New York: Lang Communications, Inc. July/August, 1992, vol. 3:1.

Reiss, Patricia. *Through the Goddess: A Woman's Way of Healing*. New York: Continuum, 1991.

Reuther, Rosemary R. *New Woman, New Earth: Sexist Ideologies and Human Liberation*. New York: Seabury Press, 1975.

Rieber, R. W., and Kurt Salzinger, eds. *Psychology: Theoretical-Historical Perspectives*. New York: Academic Press, 1980.

"Ritual and Magic," *Woman of Power: A Magazine of Feminism, Spirituality, and Politics*, Winter, 1991, vol. 19.

Robinson, Roxana. *Georgia O'Keeffe: A Life*. New York: Harper & Row, 1989.

Rohrbaugh, Joanna Bunker. *Women: Psychology's Puzzle*. New York: Basic Books, Inc., 1979.

Rosen, Marjorie. *Popcorn Venus: Women, Movies and the American Dream*. New York: Coward, McCann and Geoghegan, 1973.

Ruddick, Sara. *Maternal Thinking: Toward a Politics of Peace*. New York: Ballantine Books, 1989.

Ruddick, Sara, and Pamela Daniels, eds. *Working It Out: 23 Women Writers, Artists, Scientists, and Scholars Talk About Their Lives and Work*. New York: Pantheon Books, 1977.

Runco, Mark A., and Robert S. Albert, eds. *Theories of Creativity*. Newbury Park: Sage Publications, 1990.

Saltzman, Amy. *Down-Shifting: Reinventing Success on a Slower Track*. New York: HarperCollins, 1991.

Sandmeir, Marian. *The Invisible Alcoholics: Women and Alcohol Abuse in America*. New York: McGraw-Hill, 1980.

Sarason, Seymour B. *The Challenge of Art to Psychology*. New Haven, Conn.: Yale University Press, 1990.

Scarf, Maggie. *Intimate Partners: Patterns in Love and Marriage*. New York: Random House, 1987.

Schaef, Anne Wilson. *Codependence: Misunderstood—Mistreated*. San Francisco: Harper & Row, 1986.

Scott, Stanley, ed. *Northern Lights: Studies in Creativity*. Presque Isle: University of Maine, Summer and Winter, 1986.

Sidel, Ruth. *On Her Own: Growing Up in the Shadow of the American Dream*. New York: Viking Penguin, 1990.

Simmel, George. *On Women, Sexuality and Love*. London, England: Yale University Press, 1984.

Simonton, Dean Keith. "Creativity in the Later Years," *Gerontologist*, Oct. 1990, vol. 30:5.

Singer, Irving. *The Nature of Love*. Chicago: University of Chicago Press, 1987.

Solomon, Robert C. *Love: Emotion, Myth and Metaphor*. New York: Anchor Press, 1981.

Souhami, Diana. *Gertrude and Alice*. London, England: Pandora Press, 1991.

Steil, Janice M., and Karen Weltman. "Marital Inequality: The Importance of Personal Attributes, and Social Norms on Career Valuing and the Allocation of Domestic Responsibilities," *Sex Roles*, 1991, vol. 24:3/4, 161–77.

Stern, Karl. *The Flight from Woman*. New York: Farrar, Straus and Giroux, 1965.

Stevens, Barry. *Don't Push the River (It Flows by Itself)*. Lafayette, Calif.: Real People Press, 1970.

Stone, Carole. "The Female Artist in Kate Chopin's The Awakening: Birth and Creativity," *Women's Studies*, 1989, vol. 13:1/2.

Stricker, Frank, Nancy F. Cott, and Elizabeth H. Pleck, eds. "Cookbooks and Law Books," *A Heritage of Her Own*. New York: Simon & Schuster, 1979.

Stronach-Buschel, Bettina. "Trauma, Children and Art," *The American Journal of Art Therapy*, Nov. 1990, vol. 29, 48–52.

Tannen, Deborah. *You Just Don't Understand: Women and Men in Conversation*, 1st ed. New York: Morrow, 1990.

Tavris, Carol. *The Mismeasure of Woman*. New York: Simon & Schuster, 1992.

Torrance, E. Paul, Jack H. Presbury, and A. Jerry Benson. "Children and Creativity," *Children's Needs: Psychological Perspectives*, 1986.

Torrance, E. Paul. *The Search for Satori and Creativity*. Buffalo, New York: The Creative Education Foundation, Inc. and Creative Synergetic Associates, Ltd., 1979.

Ueland, Brenda. *If You Want to Write*. St. Paul, Minn.: Graywolf Press, 1987.

Walsh, Andrea S. *Women's Film and Female Experience: 1940–1950*. New York: Praeger Publishers, 1984.

Waterman, Melissa. "By Form or Chance? The Search for Pattern in Nature," *Habitat: Journal of the Maine Audubon Society*, vol. 8:6, December 1991.

Watrous, Susan, and Bob Blanchard. "An Interview with Holly Near," *The Progressive*, March, 1990.

Weingarten, Kathy. "Consultations to Myself on a Work/Family Dilemma: A Postmodern, Feminist Reflection," *Journal of Feminist Family Therapy*. Binghamton, N.Y.: The Haworth Press, Inc., 1992.

Weisberg, Robert. *Creativity and Other Myths*. New York: W. H. Freeman and Co., 1986.

Wells, Debbie. *Backporch Restaurant Cookbook*. Ocracoke, N.C.: The Backporch Restaurant, May, 1992.

Williams, Juanita. *Psychology of Women: Behavior in a Biosocial Context*. New York: W. W. Norton, 1977.

Woodward, Richard B. "The Disturbing Photography of Sally Mann," *New York Times Magazine*, September 27, 1992.

Woolf, Virginia. *To the Lighthouse*. New York: Harcourt, Brace & World, Inc., 1927.

Woolger, Jennifer Barker, and Roger J. Woolger. *The Goddess Within*. New York: Fawcett Columbine, 1987.

Index